FOOD
The Growing Challenge for Human Survival

About the Author

Bimalendu Bhattacharya, educated at Calcutta University and at the London School of Economics and Political Science (as a Commonwealth Scholar), has consistently pursued a career of teaching and research, having taught in many institutes, including Gauhati University (Assam), Indian Institute of Technology (Kharagpur IIT, West Bengal), Presidency College (now University), Kolkata, and the University of North Bengal (West Bengal), at the last of which he had been a Senior Professor, Head of the Department as well as the Dean of the Faculty of Science. His research in Geography spans a large area with publications in India and abroad, and a number of books including *'Samaj Bignaniya Bhugol'* (Social Geography in Bengali) jointly with Professor Anima Bhatthacharya, published by the West Bengal Government, *'Urban Development in India: Since Pre-Historic Times'* (New Delhi), *'Sikkim: Land and People'* (New Delhi), *'Geography of a Himalayan Kingdom: Bhutan'* in joint authorship with A. Bhattacharya and Neil Fraser (New Delhi), *'Urbanization, Urban Sustainability and the Future of Cities'* (New Delhi), *'Geography of Deprivation: An Unfair World'* (New Delhi) and *'Global Urban Process: Growth of Towns and Cities'* (New Delhi).

FOOD

The Growing Challenge for Human Survival

Bimalendu Bhattacharya

CONCEPT PUBLISHING COMPANY PVT. LTD.
NEW DELHI-110059

ISBN-13: 978-93-88937-50-4

First Published 2020

Published and Printed by :

Concept Since 1974

Concept Publishing Company Pvt. Ltd.
A/15-16, Commercial Block, Mohan Garden,
New Delhi-110059 (INDIA)
T: 011 25351460, 011 25351794
E : publishing@conceptpub.com, *W* : www.conceptpub.com

Cataloging in Publication Data--Courtesy: D.K. Agencies (P) Ltd. <docinfo@dkagencies.com>

Bhattacharya, Bimalendu, 1931- **author.**
Food : the growing challenge for human survival / by Bimalendu Bhattacharya.
pages cm
Includes bibliographical references and index.
ISBN 9789388937504

1. Food supply. 2. Agriculture. 3. Food sovereignty. 4. Food security. I. Title.

LCC HD9000.5.B43 2020 | DDC 363.8 23

Dedicated to
All the Hungry and Malnourished
People of our time

Preface

Perhaps, my earliest personal experience of the issue in this book was witnessing the happenings of the Great Bengal Famine of 1943, watching people dropping dead in front of my eyes, quite often with highly emaciated children in their arms, left an indelible impression on my mind with a big question, like—Why people have to die so helplessly when, as I believed, there were over two thousand sacks of rice, each carrying a little over two 'maunds' (1 maund = 82.3 lbs.) in them lying stacked in piles in the central hall of our school, under lock and key, for the use of the army involved in the Second World War (1939-45). Incidentally, our place having been very close to the 'Burma Front', at that time under Japanese occupation, the British army, consisting of various regiments representing American to African, was stationed in and around our small township but what was very painful is that people arriving from surrounding rural areas for a mouthful of food died in hundreds (taking a toll of 1.5 million in the entire province of Bengal) in front of our eyes when rice stored in our school hall went off, giving out bad smell, polluting the air. I can still remember the smell of putrefying rice which had remained for a long time and the entire stock had to be buried in the open field in front of our school ground later. The army remained an inactive spectator of this human tragedy unfolding in front of their eyes.

It was undoubtedly a man-made famine, as Nobel Laureate Amartya Sen claims in his book entitled, '*Poverty and Famines*', OUP, 12th Impression, 2008, and this crushing distress was not due to any normal scarcity of food. The truth is that the grinding poverty was the result of the enforced task of protection for meeting war-supplies without any care for the common people's requirements. Poverty is still there in the developing countries where, even now, a little less than one-quarter of the total global population (2015) goes hungry and malnourished, incapable of buying enough food to feed the family, due to poverty. This entrapment of such a huge section of the humanity dislodged from the basic human right to 'entitlement to food', as Sen calls it (2008), is, perhaps, the greatest puzzle of the modern time, reflecting the most callous attitude of the affluent countries when perfect food wasted by retailers and consumers amount every year to an incredible 1.6 billion tons globally, worth at least $1 trillion, coming from different sources. For example, rich households reject food as excess or, in the US, sometimes crops are not harvested at all as they fail to reach cosmetic standards. As a result, food is not available 'at all times at all places' and thus one of the basic human rights has been denied to many people, thus denying human freedom.

Such an uncompromising situation urged one to carry out a careful investigation of the problem, making an evaluation of the present global status of food availability, which remains under stress, giving rise to disparities and imbalances when consumption of food is the major consideration. Factors like population stabilization, lack of education and healthcare facilities dwarfing the possibilities of creative activities as well as fruitful utilization of 'human capital', outlandish trading policies forcibly imposed by affluent countries on the economically handicapped ones, highly objectionable agricultural incentives in the form of stalling agricultural production by the farmers in affluent countries. The base of poorer countries has been shaken and, above all, the overall control of the corporate economy in deciding agricultural production policies and thus converting many of the countries in the developing world, turning their former self-sufficiency in food into importing ones, have shaken the economic base of these countries. At the same time, the corporate industrial economy has been doubly responsible for continuing environmental degradation, destroy biodiversity, which poses one of the greatest threats to human survival, and, lastly, land clearance for agricultural expansion, mostly done under the pressure of corporate houses for the production of crops used either for the production of biofuel, to feed cars but not humans, or as animal-feed, needed to supplement animal-protein food. This is enforced increasingly by the affluent section of the world.

Undoubtedly, humanity today is facing the worst time since the beginning of increasing carbon foot-print, which is very likely to increase faster in the absence of checking emissions, as decided by 'Kyoto Protocol'. With the world's largest emitter having withdrawn from the 'pact/understanding' jointly taken by all countries to satisfy the coal lobby, is going to be ultimately fatal, sparing no country in the world.

The grim reality is that there is no escape from foodlessness if it cannot be produced in sufficient amount as it is affected now by climate change. The irony is that this consciousness is being ignored by those who are still under the impression that money can buy food, however high the price is. But, what is very much regrettable is that if food is lacking in the broader sense, as it is going to happen unless mankind is fast enough to realise that any further delay in checking as well as decreasing the rate of emission effectively, the associated climate change will react faster in upsetting the food production system beyond repair, jeopardizing human life whether in the south or in the north without distinction by the end of this century, as asserted by concerned scientists. A situation like this is inevitable, making both food and water the rarest commodities for the human (as well as animal) world, considered as the darkest period of human history, where man makes himself the victim of his own thoughtless actions.

Acknowledgements

In writing this book I felt very largely indebted to my predecessors working for a long time on this issue, bringing out its most critical role in human life in particular, endangering its sustainability in not very distant future, resulting from man's extremely careless action jeopardising natural balance. My probe into this highly critical situation has immeasurably been enriched by the works of many experts to whom my debt remains unbound for borrowing their views in constructing my own conclusion. In this connection I have greatly been influenced by the works of authors like David Tilman, Michael Clark, Vaclav Smil, Paul R. Ehrlich, John Kerbs, Lester R. Brown, Jeffrey D. Sachs, Mike Davis, Tim Dyson, Amartya Sen, Jonathan A. Foley, Eric Holt-Giménez, Fred Magdoff, Brian Tokar, Donella Meadows etc., to name a few, acknowledged at proper places, for my enlightenment in grasping the situation.

At the same time I am highly indebted to Neil Fraser, with his background of Oxford-grooming followed by a long teaching and research experience in Edinburgh University, for his help in collecting materials from research journals not available for outsiders and, finally, with a critical editing of the manuscript I have written.

Similarly, my indebtedness knows no bounds to Dr. (Professor) Bashabi Fraser, my daughter, as well as Dr. Rupsha Fraser (a scientist by profession and my grand-daughter) for their unfailing encouragement and timely criticism, contributing immensely to bring this book to its present form.

I am equally grateful to Dr. Ballari Bagchi for assisting me as a geographer during the process of writing. At the same time I have greatly benefited for the cartographic assistance rendered by Mrs. Jyotsna Baidya for this book.

I also take this opportunity to offer my gratitude to Mrs. Anna Shepherd in Edinburgh for very kindly typing the manuscript as a very benevolent gesture in her retired status.

However, all my efforts would have been futile had it not been for the help of M/s Concept Publishing Company Pvt. Ltd., New Delhi, who, with the greatness of their mind, came forward to print this book for publication, for which I remain immensely indebted to them.

Bimalendu Bhattacharya

Contents

List of Tables and Figures

LIST OF TABLES

LIST OF FIGURES

1
Food: The Major Challenge

Introduction

Food happens to be the greatest challenge today, almost threatening human survival in the face of growing environmental challenges unfavourable for sustaining the productive process. Food is closely linked to the productivity of the agro eco-systems directly depending on their continued viability, providing the overwhelming majority of crops, livestock feed, and livestock on which human nutrition depends. In 1994, global agriculture provided 95 per cent of all animal and plant protein and 99 per cent of calories humans consumed.[1]

As such agricultural land plays a vital role in agro eco-systems, and altogether covers about 36 mha or 28 per cent of the Earth's land area, excluding Greenland and Antarctica and this increased worldwide in the previous three decades in spite of decrease in many industrialized countries. Globally, about 31 per cent of the agro eco-systems are croplands and 69 per cent are pastures with wide variations in their proportions among different regions.[2] However, it is quite alarming to note that providing so long food for the mankind they are slowly changing their character, shifting more to meet industrial requirements than human requirements for food. Before making further elaboration of this point one needs to consider the fact that the sources supplying food have gone through incredible changes. For example, food required by *Homo sapiens*, or modern man, appearing between 200,000 and 250,000 years ago[3] were directly supplied by nature or environment where they lived, waiting to be collected by a process known today as hunting or gathering, and eaten 'raw', or in its original form involving no process of altering their character through cooking. The 'wear' on the grinding surface of fossil teeth tells the story about their diet, consisting of meat and vegetable matter, using stone tools for cutting flesh off bones, use of which goes back to 2.5 million years with Homo Habilis, know as *Handy Man* by its discoverer Louis Leakey. They made stone tools, living in East Africa though it is possible that the use of tool goes further back, almost 3.3 million years as discovered in Ethiopia.[4]

Undoubtedly, drastic changes in the nature of food took place with the discovery of cooking, most likely first introduced about 1.9 million years back though archaeological evidences indicate that the

> ".....use of controlled fire dates back to only about 250,000 years.... (However) in Israel, archaeologists have discovered an 800,000-year-old hominin site with signs of fire and a hearth, around which various activities were carried out, such as making flint tools, roasting seeds, and eating fish, crabs, and a variety of mammals. There may be as yet undiscovered remains of controlled fire from even earlier times, such as the 1.0-1.5 million-year-old charred bones discovered at Swart Krans in South Africa."[5]

Quite evidently, cooked food more easily digestible, contributed to great changes to the anatomy and the physiology of our ancestors instead of having wild raw foods "too tough, too toxic and too bitter". The situation went through a revolutionary change, though long after this, with the introduction of agriculture, taking place around 10,500 years ago.

> "Although there is some doubt about whether it had five, seven, or more independent origins, agriculture appeared over a period of a few thousand years, probably independently in South-west Asia (present day Iraq), China, New Guinea, North, Central and South

> America. Different crops and livestock were domesticated in different places. In South-west Asia, for instance, people farmed olives, wheat, peas, goats, and sheep while in Central America they farmed maize, beans, squash, and turkeys. It seems plausible that in each area hunter-gatherers chose the crops and animals from the foods they were already eating that were suitable for domestication. Perhaps crops were originally planted by accident, when seeds and fruit that had been gathered in the wild were dropped and grew around small human settlements.... Once agriculture started, it spread around the world rapidly, presumably because agricultural populations reproduced more rapidly than hunter-gatherers."[6]

Interestingly, the early farmers, though unconsciously, became geneticists, through thousands of generative processes selecting seeds for edible plants, or the breed of animals and out of many thousands of plants or animal species only very few have come to dominate world agriculture. For example,

> "...in the high valley of Andes, hunter-gatherers may have unearthed and consumed one such plant, the potato, by 8000 B.C., but millennia passed before Andeans first cultivated that tuber.... Growers cultivated thousands of different strains, each with its own hereditary material or germ plasm. These traditional varieties are today known as 'land races'. Some growers continue to raise many of the old varieties—such as potatoes being sold by a woman in Cuzco (the capital of Inca Empire), Peru—in the regions where they originated. Their (plant breeders') vigour and genetic diversity help provide insurance for the future of our food supply ... clear cutting across virgin lands destroys valuable natural vegetation, and in tropical rain forests—home to half of Earth's plant and animal species—some 60 acres a minute are denuded ... The resulting loss of naturally diverse germ plasm—much of it not yet studied—is called genetic erosion. It is estimated that by the middle of this century (21st) one-

> quarter of the world's 250,000 plant species may vanish, victims of deforestation, the shift to monoculture, overgrazing, water control projects and urbanization."[7]

In fact, out of thousands of plant species domesticated through thousands of years since the beginning of agriculture, very few today dominate world agriculture, such as just three major crops—maize, rice and wheat among cereals which, according to FAO, together account for almost 87 per cent of grain production worldwide and 43 per cent of all calories consumed, while six other crops—barley, sorghum, oats, millet, rye and triticale (a hybrid of wheat and rye)—comprise the rest, which include leguminous crops like beans, peas and lentils. Similarly, out of about 148 large herbivorous mammals domesticated, a very small number of species, only fourteen were chosen, such as sheep, goats, cattle and pigs dominate the world food chain today, along with chickens, turkeys, ducks and geese constituting the great majority of the farmed birds.[8]

On the other hand, the development of "miracle" seeds through crossbreeding plants aimed at increasing food production, involving mainly rice and wheat in poor countries proved to be a revolutionary step (Green Revolution) towards meeting food crisis, particularly making India and Indonesia self-sufficient. Indeed, as a result of 'Green Revolution' the world population almost doubled between 1960 and 2000 but the amount of food produced increased only by 25 per cent and it was not spread uniformly around the world, having greater effect in Asia and South America. It had been by two-and-a-half-fold increase in yield per hectare though the land under production increased by less than 20 per cent. At the same time, better scientific handling of livestock and dairy agriculture resulted in a four-fold increase in the number of chickens, a doubling in the number of pigs, but recording more modest increases in sheep and cows, and all these huge benefits saved lives of many billions of people in the developing world. However, undeniably, the benefits of 'Green Revolution' came at a cost, such as it uses up world's one of the most scarce as well as fast dwindling resources, like water, accounting for almost two-thirds of the fresh water used by man worldwide. Besides, it involves the use of large amounts of energy in the production of fertilizers, pumping water for irrigation and farm machinery. Further, it caused serious decline in biodiversity, crucial to future food production, by way of taking away 'food for the rest of nature' along with decline in 'abundance of wild species of plants and animals in intensely farmed landscapes. In the UK, for instance, formerly common farmland birds such as the skylark declined by almost 70 per cent in the period between 1960 and 2000. Hence, the euphoria did not last long as the miracle seeds ultimately proved to be less resistant to local insects and viruses. Though this hurdle has finally been overcome through further research, the miracle seeds meanwhile have caused an irreparable damage to agriculture, accelerating the loss of genetic diversity. Sri Lanka provides and irrefutable instance in this regard, where 2000 traditional varieties of rice grown by farmers as recently as 1959, has gone down to five principal varieties grown today. India provides another very striking example of large scale extinction of local land races, where 30,000 varieties of rice once grown by local farmers have come down barely to 10 varieties representing over 75 per cent of total production now. It has been noted that extinction of 'land races' at this rate with improved varieties is likely to remove as much as 60,000 plant species, or one-fourth of the world's total within the space of the following decades, as predicted by Rhoades (1991)*, thereby exposing the entire productive system to an almost defenceless position[9] in the absence of a greater variety of local seeds developed over generations of acclimatised local conditions.

Role of Agroecosystems in Human Life

> "Since the dawn of settled agriculture, humans have been altering the landscape to secure food, create settlements and pursue commerce and industry.... These transformations of the landscape are the defining mark of humans on ecosystems, yielding most of the food, energy, water and wealth we enjoy."[10]

---

* Robert Rhoades, The World's Food Supply at Risk, *National Geographic*, Washington, Vol. 179, No. 4. 1991.

It may be noted that expansion of agriculture into forests, grasslands and wetlands, a process still in extant in many parts of the world, has been the greatest source of natural eco-system conversion.

Worldwide human activities in the form of agriculture as well as urban or built-up areas have converted approximately 29 per cent or almost 3.8 billion hectares of the land area of which conversion to croplands and managed pastures cover about 3.3 billion hectares or roughly 26 per cent of the land area. In effect, agriculture has displaced one-third of temperate and tropical forests and one-quarter of natural grassland[11] and, according to the predictions of the United Nations, an additional one-third of the existing global land could be converted over the next hundred years. (Note A)

Table 1.1: Land Conversion of Natural Ecosystems for Agriculture and Urbanization

Region	*Percentage of Land Converted*
Asia (excl. Middle East)	44
Central America and Caribbean	28
Europe and Russia	35
Middle East and North Africa	12
North America	27
Oceania	9
South America	33
Sub-Saharan Africa	25

Source: World Resources 2000-2001, People and Ecosystems: The Fraying Web of Life, United Nations Development Programme, United Nations Environment Programme, World Bank, World Resources Institute.

Alongside comes human consumption which directly impacts ecosystems through overharvesting of plants, animals along with other forms of biological depletion. It may be observed that increasing consumption resulting from population growth as well as simultaneous improvement in the economic status of people, especially in the developing world, involving a higher rate of food consumption, consisting of grains, meat, fish and wood has a worsening effect on ecosystems as reflected in the supply and demand of the major food consumables.

According to reports available, 'cereal consumption has more than doubled in the three decades since 1961 and about 34 per cent of the world's grain crop was fed to livestock raised for meat.

Interestingly, there has been a four-fold increase in fertilizer use since 1961 and by 2020, the demand for cereals is expected to increase nearly 40 per cent with a demand for meat increasing by nearly 60 per cent. Similarly, the consumption of fish has multiplied by over six times since 1950, to 122 million metric tons by 1997. It may be noted in this context that there is wide variation in the volume of consumption, becoming much larger in the developed countries consuming "twice as much grain, twice as much fish, three times as much meat (and) nine times as much paper and eleven times as much gasoline as someone living in a developing nation (Table 1.2). The highly contrasting nature of consumption is highlighted by the fact that the high-income countries representing about 16 per cent of the world's

Table 1.2: Annual Per Capita Consumption of Food and Other Consumables in Different Countries (Selected High-, Medium-, and Low-income Countries)

Country	*Total Vol. of Private Consumption (1997)*	*Fish (Kg.) (1997)*	*Meat (Kg.) (1998)*	*Cereals (Kg.) (1997)*	*Paper (Kg.) (1998)*	*Fossil Fuels (Kg. of Oil Equitable)*
United States	$21,680	21.0	122.0	975.0	293.0	6,902
Singapore	$16,340	34.0	77.0	159.0	168.0	7,825
Japan	$15,554	66.0	42.0	334.0	239.0	3,277
Germany	$15,229	13.0	87.0	496.0	205.0	3,625
Poland	$5,087	12.0	73.0	696.0	54.0	2,585
Trinidad & Tobago	$4,864	12.0	28.0	237.0	41.0	6,394
Turkey	$4,377	7.2	19.0	502.0	32.0	952
Indonesia	$1,808	18.0	9.0	311.0	17.0	450
China	$1,410	26.0	47.0	360.0	30.0	700
India	$1,166	4.7	4.3	234.0	3.7	268
Bangladesh	$780	11.0	3.4	250.0	1.3	67
Nigeria	$692	5.8	12.0	228.0	1.9	186
Zambia	$625	8.2	12.0	144.0	1.6	77

Source: World Resources 2000-2001, People and Ecosystems: The Fraying Web of Life, United Nations Development Programme, United Nations Environment Programme, World Bank, World Resources Institute.

population, accounted for 80 per cent of the money spent on private consumption in 1997, representing $ 14.9 trillion of the total of $ 18 trillion in sharp contrast to the poorest 35 per cent of the world's population, consumers in low-income countries represented less than 2 per cent of all private consumption of $ 257 million.[12]

In consideration of these facts, agriculture appears to be the only option, or the fundamental instrument for sustaining development and poverty reduction. It has to be taken into account that three out of every four poor people in developing countries live in rural areas, of whom 2.1 billion live on less than $2 a day and 880 million on less than $ a day, and most of them depend on agriculture as their livelihood. Agriculture, as such, could be used as a unique instrument for economic growth in the agriculture-based countries, implementing a 'productivity revolution' in small-holder farming. One cannot deny its contribution to,

> "development as an economic activity, as a livelihood and as a provider of environmental services.... Agriculture can be a source of growth for the national economy, a provider of investment opportunities for the private sector, and a prime driver of agriculture-related industries and the rural non-farm economy. Two-thirds of the world's agricultural value added is created in developing countries. In agriculture-based countries it generates on average 29 per cent of the gross domestic product (GDP) and employs 65 per cent of the labour force. The industries and services linked to agriculture in value chains often account for more than 30 per cent of GDP in transforming and urbanized countries."[13]

However, the major concern of agriculture in providing food security in countries such as those of Sub-Saharan Africa, South Asia etc. exposed to recurrent food emergencies, is dependence on the vagaries of uncertain climate remains unpredictable. It is the source of livelihood for about 80 per cent of rural people, providing jobs for 1.3 billion small landholders and landless workers. Of the 5.5 billion people in the developing world, 3 billion live in rural areas, meaning nearly half of the global population, of whom about 2.5 billion depend on agriculture and 1.5 billion are small-holders. On the other hand, agriculture plays a very important role as a spoiler as well as promoter of environmental services. For instance, as the largest user of water, it contributes to water scarcity, depletion of underground water, agrochemical pollution, soil exhaustion, global climate change, and accounts for up to 25/30 per cent of greenhouse gas. In contrast, which go almost unrecognized, are the services promoting environmental welfare, such as sequestering carbon, managing watersheds and preserving biodiversity.[14]

Nonetheless, the fact cannot be ignored that "food security has already been severely undermined in the poorest countries of the world, many located in Sub-Saharan Africa owing to their export thrust to Northern consumers",[15] resulting primarily from a drastic change in the nature of products traded to Northern countries. This was the result of sharp change in the dietary habits of the people living in Northern countries, in spite of health concern consumption of red meat keeps going up, and to combat obesity, heart diseases and digestive tract disorders caused primarily for the consumption of products like high-fat dairy and meat as their own agricultural products which needed to be replaced by more fish and white meat, more fibrous vegetables, and fruit into the diet along with using vegetable oils low in polysaturates as cooking medium sourcing from dozens of tropical countries. The limited capacity of Northern agriculture to satisfy the growing requirement of the healthy food led to large pressure on the tropical countries, giving rise to an unsatisfactory trade flow threatening food scarcity coupled with price-rise in the latter. But,

> "this is only possible because massive annual subsidies are doled by the State to the farmers and agro-business in North America and Europe, paying farmers often to restrict acreage, and reach a target price which is higher than the market price.... Clearly it is the interest of advanced countries to export their artificially maintained surpluses of cereals and dairy products to the rest of the world. The main players in the world wheat export market are the U.S., Canada and the

> European Union ... (As a result) the developing countries concerned must lose their self-sufficiency in food grains production and become net food importers."[16]

As a matter of hard truth, there has been a visible reduction in the production of food crops in the developing countries resulting from the diversion of the best irrigated land and increasing investment to non-food crops in these countries for export to Northern countries, going side by side with decline in staples consumed by local people. The stark reality of major shift in agricultural production with greater emphasis on import-oriented non-food crops did not help much in using exchange earnings in importing food required by people in the developing countries since such earnings did not increase in spite of increase in the volume of exports because the prices fell. In fact, the export promotion policy in these countries is undermining food security for the people in Asia. Already there has been a 'one-third drop' in cereals output per head for 60 per cent population in Sub-Saharan Africa, bringing them to "the brink of starvation and actual famine" in some areas.[17]

> "India has opened up the agricultural sector to virtually unprotected trade and launched agro-export promotion less than five years ago, and already the area under food grains has fallen by 5.4 million hectares while per capita food output has been on a declining trend with crop and resource diversion to exportables like cotton, prawns, fruits, vegetables and flowers ... . Can such a basic necessity as good grains, whose availability at an affordable price affects the very life of millions of our people, be left to the operation of 'market forces', that is set on a declining trend because the rich abroad and at home demand products out of our limited tropical lands. It is monstrous that in order that Europeans and North Americans can eat prawns, cheap low fat meat cooked in healthy vegetable oils, fruits and vegetables their own lands cannot produce in winter, and give flowers to each other, that Asians must see their food security destroyed and that our poor cannot get enough

> food to keep body and soul together. Yet it is precisely this scenario—a replication of the Sub-Saharan experience—which awaits us in Asia under the present policies."[18]

One of the highly diversified tropical countries producing a large variety of fruits and vegetables is the Philippines, presenting a very disheartening picture in this regard following since early 1980s policies of opening up further to trade with greater thrust on exports, leading to a sharp decline in areas under food grains amounting to 170,000 hectares in just two regions between 1989 to 1993, along with cutting down all support to its farmers and going in for "even larger imports of subsidized cheaper wheat replacing rice as it is already doing". We have to remember that the subsidized wheat (the subsidy on wheat was 46 per cent of the price for the U.S. and 80 per cent for the EU) does not benefit the consumers as the peasants and labourers dependent on agricultural employment in the Philippines, whose livelihoods get destroyed as a result of decline in the productive activities they were engaged in.[19]

Agriculture and its Transformation

On the whole, agriculture's performance has been quite impressive, the gross domestic product (GDP) having expanded globally by an average 2 per cent a year between 1980 and 2004, more than the growth of population by 1.6 per cent a year, and it brought down the real price of grain in world markets by about 1.8 per cent a year over this period.[20]

Interestingly, agricultural growth achieved by the developing countries during this period was much faster, 2.6 per cent a year, than in industrial countries with 0.9 per cent a year, accounting for an overall agricultural growth of 79 per cent during this period with their share of world agricultural GDP rising from 56 per cent in 1980 to 65 per cent in 2004. In fact, gains in productivity because of improved inputs in Asia and other developing countries was the major propelling factor of growth than expansion of land devoted to agriculture. For instance, crop yields in East Asia increased by 2.8 per cent a year in 1961-2004 in contrast to 1.8 per cent annually in industrial countries. As a result of rising productivity, the prices of cereals, especially for rice as the major staple food in the developing world, have been declining as well as for the major export products, such as cotton and coffee.

Widespread use of irrigation water, improved seeds and application of fertilizers has been instrumental in raising yield of cereals while the benefits of improvement even extended to rain fed agriculture. The practice of irrigation continuing for millennia in Asian agriculture expanded further through the 1990s and 2000s covering today 39 per cent of the crop in South Asia, 29 per cent in East Asia and the Pacific, but only 4 per cent in Sub-Saharan Africa.

The use of improved seeds was adopted widely in the 1960s and areas devoted to improved varieties expanded to about 80 per cent of the area under cereal crops in South and East Asia by 2000 from less than 10 per cent in 1970, but covered only 22 per cent of the cereal crops in Sub-Saharan Africa in 2000, starting late. Similarly, among other ingredients taking a decisive role in raising crop-yield are chemical fertilizers and the global share of their use in the developing countries having increased from 10 per cent in 1960 to over 60 per cent today. Higher fertilizer use in the developing countries accounts for at least 20 per cent of growth over the past three decades.[21]

Diversification in the higher-value crops already initiated in developing countries' agriculture opened up great opportunities for further expansion of the export market. Higher income and dietary changing patterns of people, particularly in the urban areas of the world, 'shifting away' from cereals, roots, tubers and pulses to livestock products, vegetable oils, fruits and vegetables are pushing agricultural practices into new grounds of production as a result of which "horticulture, oil seeds and livestock are expanding the fastest, with new markets also emerging for feed grains, livestock and biofuels"[22] (Fig. 1.1) leading to the **horticultural revolution**, making fruits and vegetables as the fastest growing agricultural markets in developing countries with 'production increasing by 3.6 per cent a year for fruits and 5.5 per cent for vegetables' during the period 1980-2004. The most impressive contribution in this

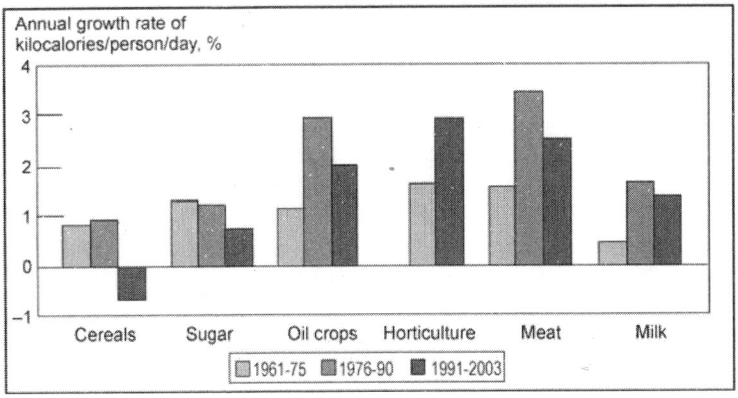

Fig. 1.1: Per Capita Shift to Fruits, Vegetables meat and Vegetable Oils in Food Consumption in Developing Countries

Source: FAO 2006, A World Development Report 2008.

regard has been made by China, providing 58 per cent of the increase in global horticultural products, 38 per cent from all other developing countries leaving 4 per cent for the developed world, while in India fruits and vegetables represented the most important growth sector for crop production. In comparison to cereal production, returns from land in horticulture—is 10 times that of cereals per hectare in addition to off-farm jobs engaged in processing, packaging, and marketing with greater employment opportunities for women. On the other hand, and like the Green Revolution, horticulture is largely handled by the private sector with greater shares of specialized agribusinesses and supermarkets in its management while the interest of small-holders, as in the developing countries are ignored. (Note B)

Along with horticultural revolution changing the character of world agriculture, there has been another revolution playing a crucial role in agricultural transformation worldwide, a revolution in livestock and aquaculture in the urbanized areas of Asia and Latin America. The growing demand of poultry, pork, fish and eggs along with beef and milk products was at its root. The consumption of milk in India, for example, nearly doubled between the early 1980s and the late 1990s. The characteristic switch of livestock production from extensive (grazing) to intensive (stall-fed) along with poultry, pig and dairy cows has increased the demand for feed grains, including oil seeds when 28 per cent of grain consumption was already being used as animal feed in developing countries (See Note C.). In addition, aquaculture, turning out to be the fastest growing food-production sector, with an average annual growth rate of 10 per cent since the mid-1980s, represents today over 30 per cent of the total food fish production, and 90 per cent of this is taking place in developing countries, China alone accounting for 67 per cent of global production. Providing employment opportunities in fish production and services for aquaculture became an important source of generating income such as 12 million people in Asia are employed in aquaculture and more than 50 per cent of the workers employed in fish depots and processing plants in Bangladesh and Vietnam are women, earning wages though low, but higher than in other agricultural activities (The World Bank, 2008).*

The significance of these developments in the agricultural sector of the developing countries is highlighted by two important contributions, such as greater intake of protein and larger volume of trade in high-value exports (Fig. 1.2). The diversified diets may be a source of waste pollution and incidence of diseases requiring proper environmental planning. But, on the other hand, the economic gain derived from expanding trade of high-value agricultural products taking an outstanding place in exports of the developing countries has a significant role in the economy of the relevant countries. Such as,

> "exports of horticulture, livestock, fish, cut flowers and organic products now make up 47 per cent of all developing-country exports. Far more than the 21 per cent for traditional tropical products, such as coffee, tea and cotton .... Developing countries have been gaining global market share, in 2004 they held 43 per cent of the world trade in fruit and vegetables (excluding bananas and citrus)."[23]

---

* The World Bank, *The World Development Report 2008, Agriculture For Development.*

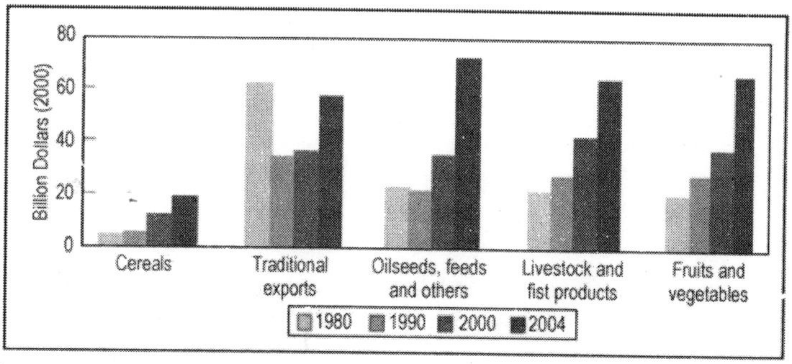

Fig. 1.2: Rapid Expansion in High Value Exports in Developing Countries

Source: United Nations Commonly Trade Statistics Database. World Bank: World Development Report, 2008.

Export markets in non-traditional agricultural products are dominated by Brazil, Chile, China and Mexico beside the Sub-Saharan countries, such as Kenya, are gradually taking growing shares.

Another revolution started in recent years in the agricultural production based on maize, sugar, cassava, oil palm and other crops related to the production of biofuel as a challenge to increasing prices of fossil fuels, another threat to food production. However, the major question posing a greater threat to human society is whether the existing agricultural system can meet the growing further demand for feeding the people. According to estimates made by experts in the field, the growth in cereal production is going to change from 0.9 per cent annually in 1969 to 1999, to 1.3 per cent per year between 2000 and 2030. Similarly, meat consumption is going to fall from 2.9 per cent per year to 1.7 per cent annually, primarily resulting from slowing rate of population growth (1 per cent a year).

One of the major handicaps of agricultural production in meeting the food demand in future is that there is no scope of increasing the cropland area. As observed by Dyson (1996),

> "About 45 per cent of the world's present cropland lies in Europe/F.S.U. (For Soviet Union) and North American/Oceania—a fact which helps explain the high levels of per capita food production of these regions. In

> the Middle East and South Asia virtually all of the estimated potential arable land is already being cropped. And the same is true throughout most of the Far East, where the major reserves of unexploited land are chiefly found in sparsely populated parts of Indonesia and Cambodia. The circumstances of Sub-Saharan Africa and Latin America are somewhat different. In these regions—under one-fifth of potential arable land is currently cropped."[24]

However, according to some sources, there is further scope for agricultural expansion in Latin America, though this is often at the expense of forests and woodlands. This is also happening in Sub-Saharan Africa, driving agricultural expansion into forest or grazing lands obviously requiring large investments in infrastructure and '"human and animal disease control to convert these lands to productive agriculture".'

Land available worldwide for agricultural expansion suffers from various constraints at many locations, significantly undermining the productive process. The major impediments in this respect are pollution, salinization and soil degradation. According to an estimate, globally 5 to 10 million hectares of agricultural land are annually lost to severe soil degradation. This is

> "most severe in such hotspots as the foothills of the Himalayas; sloping areas in Andes; Southern China and Southeast Asia; rangelands in Africa, and Central and West Asia; and the arid lands of Sahel. Most land degradation is the result of wind and water erosion... overgrazing and degradation of pastoral areas are widespread in much of the steppe of North Africa, the Middle East and Central Asia and the Sahel,"[25]

most of it resulting from wind and water erosion, besides overgrazing and degradation of pastoral areas.

Acute water scarcity is another very important limiting factor affecting agricultural production. Already agriculture in developing countries uses up 85 per cent of the available fresh water and irrigation accounts for 40 per cent of the value of agricultural production in these countries. The existing situation is, however, very much threatened largely by growing competition between two sectors—agriculture on one hand and industry and urbanization on the other—putting pressure on available water, virtually negating any future expansion of agricultural operations. In this regard, it needs to be considered in view that 'approximately 1.2 billion people live with absolute water scarcity' (Fig. 1.3), another 478 million live with water scarcity, while 1.5 billion having inadequate access due to the absence of proper infrastructure for tapping available resources. The present irrigated food production is maintained in large areas of China, South Asia and the Middle East through 'unsustainable' extraction of water from surface or groundwater resources. The rate of excess withdrawal of groundwater is over 25 per cent in China and 56 per cent in some parts of Northwest India[26] (See Note D).

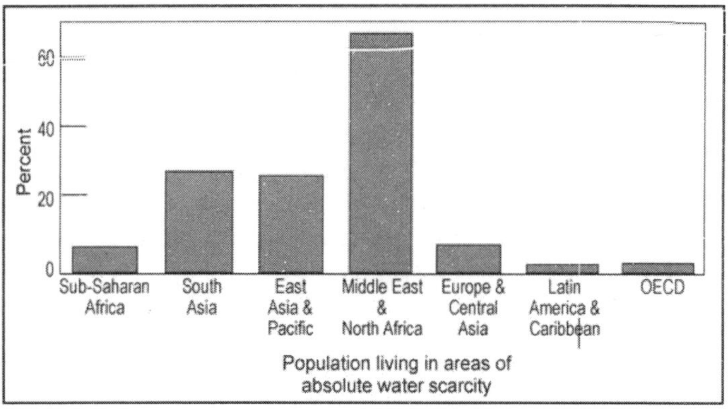

Fig. 1.3: Water Scarcity Affects millions of People in Asia, the Middle East and North Africa

Source: International Water Management Institute World Bank: World Development Report 2008.

India's plight in this regard can be assessed from the fact that, even being one of the wettest countries in the world, with enough water, about 20,000 villages here face an acute shortage of water and the output of food grain has declined by 8.5 million tons in 2014-15. According to Natarajan, ex-member of the now-defunct Planning Commission of India, the 'percapita annual rainwater harvesting in India is 200m^3 while in the US it is 5,961m^3, in Australia 4,717m^3, Brazil 3,388m^3 and in China it is 2,486m^3, which means that in India only 12.07 per cent of the surface water is effectively utilized, leaving 87.93 per cent discharged into the sea. In order to arrest this loss, the presently defunct Planning Commission suggested harvesting of about 450km^3 to meet the demand of the population, likely to grow to 1.69 billion in 2050 (UN, 2014 Revision),

> "For the healthy life of every citizen, it is necessary to harvest 1,700m^3 water per annum, as per the Water Resources Standards... According to the 'International Journal of Research in Engineering and Technology (2014)', by harvesting and harnessing the unutilized rainwater and adopting site-specific recharge strategies like check-dams, percolation ponds, recharge wells etc. India could garner the advantages—additional irrigation potential to 35 million tons of food grain; hydropower generation of 34,000 to 40,000 MW, protection to 85 million people from drought and 40 million hectares of land from floods. The annual financial benefit accrual is Rs. 12,000 core and an estimated 86 million people will benefit. There will also be an increase in employment potential. These measures will prevent groundwater depletion and check seawater intrusion in coastal aquifers."[27] (See Note E).

Climate Change and Agricultural Scenario

At the same time, among the factors affecting severely the future of world agriculture as the source of food for humanity, global warming is of the greatest concern, and if emissions continue at today's rate, the global average temperature is likely to rise by 2°C-3°C over the period of a few decades. It is highly frightening to note that the dramatic melting of Arctic ice is driving to extreme weather conditions that affect hundreds of millions of people across North America, Europe and Asia, scientists at the cutting edge of climate research believe. Severe winters are now strongly linked to soaring polar temperatures say researchers, with deadly summer heat waves and floods probably linked to it. Scientists now fear the Arctic meltdown has kick-started abrupt changes in the planet's atmosphere, bringing extreme weather to heavily populated areas. The northern ice cap has been shrinking since the 1970s with global warming, driving the loss of about three-quarters of its volume so far. But the recent heat of the Arctic has shocked scientists, with temperatures 33°C above average in parts of Russian Arctic and 20°C higher elsewhere (See Note F).

> "Arctic Sea ice extent slumped to a record low (2016), winnowed by warming air and seas and by unhelpful wind patterns. The region's 2016 temperature has been 3.5°C (6.3°f) warmer than it was a century ago.... In November (2016) the sprawl of sea ice across the Arctic covered 888,000 sq. miles (2.3m sq. km)—an area 10 times larger than the UK but smaller than the long-term average."[28]

However, the effects of climate change have not been uniform, as many regions have already become wetter, such as in the UK where, according to a report, major flooding is 'now likely to happen every year'. Though,

> "the effects of climate change in the UK have so far been mainly related to flooding, the CCC (the Committee on Climate Change) has also said that the nation is poorly prepared for deadly heat waves, water shortages and difficulties in producing food.... The CCC ... has ... warned the government that there are no plans to deliver half of the cuts in carbon emission needed in the 2020s."[29]

In this regard, India presents a case where the impacts of climate change are already visible, particularly in rural India. For instance, 2009 and 2010 have been the warmest years ever recorded since 1900 and even the coolest year (2008) in 2007-2012 had been the 13th warmest in last 110 years. The increasingly erratic weather is already having its toll on farming.[30] As a matter of fact, nine states in India are reeling under drought while the monsoon rainfall has been decreasing since 1960.

> "Between 1900 and 2000, there used to be one drought per decade on an average, while between 2000 and 2015 there have already been five. Climate change has a severe effect on Indian agriculture, so much so, that it is undoing a lot of the achievements of the Green Revolutions ... (It) may be pointed out that an increase in temperature by 2°C decreases grain yield by 15 to 17 per cent. ... Short season vegetables and fruits are the worst effected by changes (in temperature), particularly during the critical periods of their growth." [31]

As a matter of fact, Sahel, the Mediterranean, Southern Africa and parts of Southern Asia are becoming drier, and this trend is going to continue.

Interestingly, in the opinion of experts, crop yields are expected to increase particularly in temperate areas but decline in the tropical region with moderate warming and is likely to be an overall impact on global crop production in areas with slight to medium warming of less than 3°C.

> "But the continued effects of higher average temperatures, greater variability of temperature and precipitation, more frequent and intense droughts and floods, and reduced availability of water for irrigation can be devastating for agriculture in many tropical regions. One-third of the population at risk of hunger is in Africa, one quarter in Western Asia, and about one-sixth in Latin America."[32]

The close link between rising temperature and other debilitating factors like droughts, floods, availability as well as necessity of irrigation water etc. makes it essential for taking effective measures for controlling temperature rise. Scientists suggest cutting,

> "soot deposit as the easiest and fastest way to check global warming. Deposits of soot, or unburned carbon particles blackening the Arctic have changed ice from 'a

> reflection of sunlight to an absorber of heat, accelerating melting of ice and snow', which started to change global weather patterns. Reducing concentration of soot particles and other 'short-lived climate pollutants' is the only way to control rise in temperature. The work of some scientists has finally 'established that reducing soot emissions could lower Arctic temperatures by 0.2°C within a few decades ... coal-fired power stations are a leading source of soot, as are dirty vehicles' engines and industrial chimneys, but even in developing countries where people have little access to electricity and powered transport, soot is produced by indoor fires used for cooking .... Reducing the domestic burning of wood in Asia, cutting the flaring of gas in Russia, and emissions from diesel vehicles globally"[33] will have great impact on reducing the rate of global warming.

Price of food is an important denominator determining its availability for all sections of population in a society. Energy used for agricultural production is going to be more expensive, adding to the production cost of agriculture and put greater pressure on food prices. Recent studies indicate that greater emphasis on the production of biofuel in response to rising price of crude oil particularly among the rich nations, making greater demand on food crops like maize etc., will raise its price as much as 40 per cent by 2020, which will have a spillover effect on substitute grains like wheat, making it increasingly more expensive, hitting hard on the purchasing capacity of people, mainly in the lower rung of the society.

> "Econometric analysis suggest that US grain prices (which determine world prices) would rise by 18-20 per cent of any increase in crude oil prices not including the effects on the demand side through biofuels."[34]

This, undoubtedly, has a very serious repercussion, stifling human freedom for food and, as observed by the FAO, higher food prices, as a consequence of spiralling demand for food crops consumed in biofuel production, have triggered an increase in hunger worldwide, the number of chronically hungry people in 2007 having increased by 75 million from 848 million in 2003-2005, bringing the total number of undernourished people worldwide to 923 million in 2007 (Figs. 1.4 and 1.5). In regional analysis, the largest in the number of undernourished people occurred in Asia and the Pacific and in Sub-Saharan Africa, the rising prices plunging an additional 41 million in Asia and the Pacific, and 24 million in Sub-Saharan Africa.[35]

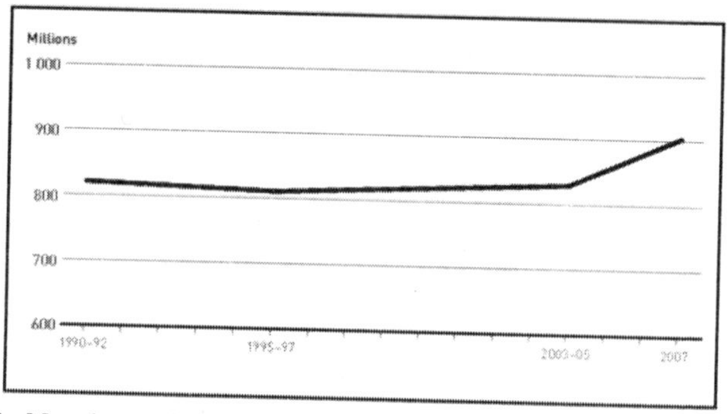

Fig. 1.4: Numbers of Undernourished People in the Developing World, 1990-92 to 2007

Source: FAO, The State of Food Insecurity in the World.

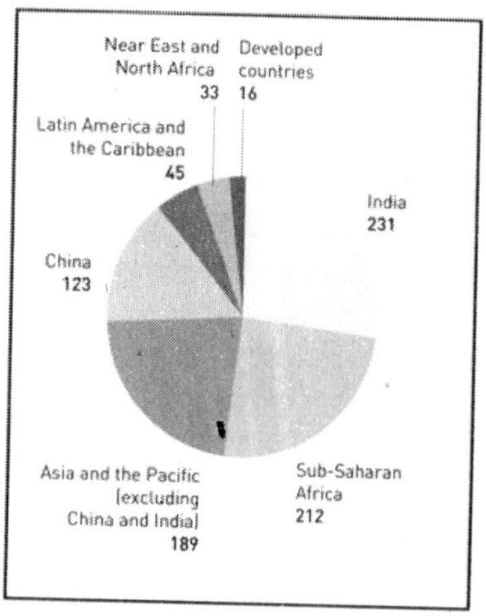

Fig. 1.5: Proportion of Undernourished People in the Developing World, 1990-1992 and 2003-05 (millions)

Source: FAO, The State of Food Insecurity in the World, 2008.

It is estimated by the FAO (2008), there were 47 countries in 2007 facing food crisis with 27 of them in Africa, 10 in Asia with another 10 in other parts of the world. Natural disasters like droughts or prolonged dry spell, slow onset or sudden onset of floods, cyclones, hurricanes etc. disrupting agricultural productive system were at the back of food crisis, particularly floods among them having increased in intensity as well as occurrence from 14 per cent of all natural disasters in the 1980s to 20 per cent in the 1990s and 27 since 2000, with the occurrence of about 50 floods per year in the mid-1980s to 200 today worldwide have played a very strong role as an indicator of climate change having serious impact on the production of food.[36]

Hence, climate change in its various forms has a determining role in the prevalence of food insecurity. For having a good grasp of the whole situation it is necessary to realise that, in the dry regions, the frequency of droughts is likely to increase further by the end of the 21st century in contrast to scarcity of water resources as projected to increase at high latitudes. The resulting interaction of—

> "increased temperature; increased sediment, nutrient, and pollutant loadings from heavy rainfall; increased concentrations of pollutants during droughts; and disruption of treatment facilities during floods will reduce raw water quality and pose risks to drinking water quality. (As such, all aspects of food security are potentially affected by climate change, including food production, access, use and price stability) .... For wheat, rice and maize in tropical and temperate regions, climate change without adaptation is projected to negatively impact production at local temperature increases of 2°C or more above late 20th century levels, although individual locations may benefit .... Projected impacts vary across crops and regions and adaptation scenarios, with about 10 per cent of projections for the 2030-2049 period showing yield gains of more than 10 per cent and about 10 per cent of projections showing yield losses of more than 25 per cent compared with the late 20th century. Global temperature increases ... combined with

increasing food demand, would pose large risks to food security, both globally and regionally."[37]

The huge impact of sustained global warming greater than the threshold would lead to the complete loss of the Greenland ice sheets over a millennium or more, causing a sea-level rise of up to 7m. We have to remember that a key aspect of climate change is the rise of sea level, the Fourth IPCC Report projects a range of 18-59 cm over the next century (See Note G). According to this report (IPCC) greenhouse gases in the atmosphere have increased substantially since 1750, far exceeding the levels before the Industrial Revolution, resulting from the use of fossil fuels and changes in land use as the main drivers. The increases as recorded have been from the pre-industrial level of 280 parts per million (ppm) to 379 ppm in 2005—far exceeding the natural range of the last 650,000 years.

The extremely frightening situation cannot be visualized without referring to the fact that a sea-level rise of just one metre would result in a chaos of irredeemable measure, making Asia with the longest exposed coastline the most affected area, putting about 50 million people and $ 1 trillion of economic assets in a highly threatening position. By 2070, coastal cities, such as Kolkata, Mumbai and Dhaka located on low plains will be exposed though economic damage will be higher in places like Guangzhoe in China, New York and Miami. Many parts of the world will face severe dislocation with a rise in temperature of 2°-3°. The Himalayan region and the areas fed by its waters are likely to experience unprecedented flooding from melting of its glaciers and swelling of glacial lakes. More than 8 million cubic metres of water is supplied by the Himalayan glaciers every year to Asiatic rivers like Yangtze and Yellow in China, the Ganga, Brahmaputra and Yamuna in India and Bangladesh and the Indus in Pakistan. The loss of glacier-melt water, even for one river like the Ganga alone would reduce flow by two-thirds in July-September, causing severe water shortages for 500 million people and 37 per cent of India's irrigated land.*

---

* Nicholas Stern, *A Blueprint for a Safer Planet: How to Manage Climate Change and Create a New Era of Progress and Prosperity*, Boley Head, London. 2009.

> "In terms of human disaster, the poorest countries will be suffering most, given their limited capacity to respond to the challenges. More than 300 million people are currently exposed to tropical cyclones which are expected to become more intense. Hundreds of millions of people might additionally be infected by malaria and similar figure holds for those suffering from undernourishment caused by droughts and rural poverty in addition to current levels. Bangladesh, a country with 150 million people and an average income of $ 1,300 (measured in purchasing power parity) is already experiencing regular flood."[38]

Agricultural production and food security quite evidently are threatened by climate change with effect on rainfall, temperature and availability of water. First, the drought-affected areas in Sub-Saharan Africa are likely to expand 60-90 million hectares more, making dry land areas suffering a loss of US $ 26 billion by 2060 (2030 prices). Similarly, Latin America and South Asia will go through same experience of losses of agricultural production, adding an additional number of 600 million affected by malnutrition. The sufferance of people is going to multiply further with growing water supply reaching from changes in run-off patterns and glacial melt, as mentioned above, comprising flows of water for irrigation, making an additional 1.8 billion people living in water-scarce environments by 2020. The regions affected most comprise Central Asia, Northern China and the northern part of South Asia facing a threatening prospect associated with retreat of glaciers—at a rate of 10-15 metres a year in the Himalayas resulting in increase in flow of seven of Asia's great rivers followed by a decline in glaciers' melt completely jeopardising the irrigational facilities. The collapse of tropical glaciers will hit hard on water security in the Andean regions as well, while several already highly water-stressed regions like the Middle East will experience further great loss in water availability.

As a matter of fact,

> "glacial melting poses threats to more than 40 per cent of the world's population ... (with) thousands of glaciers

located across the 2400 kilometres of the Himalayan range are at the epicentre of the emerging crisis. These glaciers form vast water banks. They store water and snow in the form of ice, building up stores during the winter and releasing them during the summer. ...The Gangotri glacier, one of the main water reservoirs for the 500 million people living in the Ganga basin, is shrinking by 23 metres a year. One recent study by the Indian Space Research Organization, using satellite images and covering 466 glaciers, found a 20 per cent reduction in size."[39]

Looking from another angle, one may realize with greater conviction the role of agriculture in providing and sustaining food security for mankind. Agriculture having made a firm niche in the global ecosystems as represented by forests, grasslands, rivers, coastlands, deep sea waters, islands and mountains and even cities, making itself the productive engine of the planet,[40] appears as an independent entity, converting other ecosystems into areas for providing the bulk of human food supply. The ability of the agroecosystems, as they are called, in keeping pace with 'food, feed and fibre' demands, and in increasing per capita food production consistently over the decades face today an enormous challenge in meeting the food requirements for another 2 billion people over the next three decades, between 2015 and 2045 makes a threatening prospect. This is largely because the land suitable for further agricultural expansion is limited, as mentioned earlier, unexploited land still available for further expansion is largely confined to locations like the Congo and the Amazon Basins lying quite far from regional population concentrations, makes them almost unapproachable because of poor communications. Besides, soils in such tropical forests may not turn out to be very productive and, as has been found in many instances, may prove to be of much lower agricultural potential.

Further, conversion of land suitable for agricultural expansion is ruled out in the face of stiff competition from the fast rate of urbanization accompanied by industrialization, along with the growth of infrastructural facilities in favour of them. At present, it is only in Sub-Saharan Africa that such possibilities exist, where a significant fraction of increasing demand for food will be met by expanding the area of cropland. Elsewhere, the overwhelming bulk of future food demands have to be met through more productive use of existing cropland.

As a matter of fact, in densely populated parts of India, China, Indonesia, Egypt and Western Europe, limits to further expansion were reached long ago. Hence, increase in yield-rates from the same available land under cultivation becomes essential. In some areas of Asia production has already been successfully intensified by 'raising multiple crops a year through irrigation and use of new crop varieties with shorter growth cycles, while on high-quality non-irrigated lands production has been intensified mainly by giving up or shortening fallow-periods and making continuous cultivation using modern technologies. Production of high value perishables, such as vegetables and dairy products, around major cities, or even within cities (urban agriculture) destined for urban markets have made intensification a highly successful process.

Areas where at least 30 per cent of the land is used for producing crop or covered by highly managed pasture are defined as agricultural areas, and using this definition, agrosystems, based on satellite imagery cover about 28 per cent of the total land area which including some overlap with forest and grassland ecosystem (excluding Greenland and Antarctica) cover 37 per cent as estimated by the FAO. According to this source, 69 per cent of agroecosystems consist of permanent pastures while the remaining area is under crops. Pasture land dominates in some of the agro-ecosystems, such as 89 per cent in Oceania, 83 per cent in Sub-Saharan Africa, 82 per cent in South America and 80 per cent in East Asia. In contrast, croplands constitute the large portion of the area of the of the agrosystems, like 92 per cent in South Asia, 84 per cent in Southeast Asia and 94 per cent in India. On the other hand, annual crops such as wheat, rice, maize and soybeans dominate the croplands occupying 91 per cent of the total area while the remaining area is devoted to the production of permanent crops, such as tea, coffee, sugarcane and most fruits.[41]

However, serious concerns have been expressed by experts about the productive capacity of the agroecosystems in regard to withstanding further stress imposed by intensification. Such stresses include increased erosion, depletion of soil nutrient, salinization and waterlogging, and reduction of genetic diversity among major crops.

While dairy and perishable vegetables are generally raised in agroecosystems close to densely populated areas, intensively managed croplands operate mostly away from the major concentrations of populations. Interestingly, the growth of urban and peri-urban agriculture has increased since 1980s especially in developing countries, though developed countries are no exception to their development, and by the early 1990s almost 800 million people were directly engaged in urban agriculture. In June 2005, the FAO reported that urban and peri-urban agriculture carried on in both developing and developed countries, supplying food to some 700 million urban residents worldwide practised on mostly small plots, vacant lots, yards, even rooftops, containers, parks, airports and hospitals, involving an estimated 200 million people in the production of food for sale.[42]

However, according to the FAO, total area used for agriculture 'expanded slowly' between 1966 and 1996, from 4.55 billion hectares to 4.92 billion hectares, about 8 per cent increase and slowing down later in conversion of land to agriculture resulting from competition from other, non-agricultural uses of land, giving rise to decrease in the use of land for agriculture in many industrial countries and later in some of the growing economies of East Asia, including China. During this period a total of 49 million hectares of land has been removed from agricultural production in three regions—United States, Western Europe and Oceania taking place—in the preceding 20-30 years. In Eastern Europe as well agricultural land has decreased significantly. In contrast, total agricultural land, approximately 223 million hectares, has remained constant. Nevertheless, expansion of agricultural land is yet quite significant in some regions, nearly by 0.8 per cent per year in China and Brazil during 1986-1996 and by 1.38 per cent in West Asia.

Intensification has been rapid in the agroecosystems in spite of expansion of global agriculture having been modest. With population growing alongside and land available for agriculture becoming scarcer, inputs like improved varieties of seeds, water, fertilizers and pesticides have been applied more intensively to keep pace with growing demand for increasing population along with change in food habits propelled by economic growth of the developing countries. Pressure of population growth is the highest where nearly all of the cropland is harvested each year, sometimes two to three times a year made possible with greater inputs: irrigation, new varieties of quick-growing seeds and proper dose of fertilizer replacing the traditional practice of 'leaving land fallow for restoring fertility'. Continuous evidence of the use of even marginal lands for food production is available in Africa to meet growing demands for food. However, undeniably the pressure of this high degree of intensification may lead to environmental depredation and farmers who are very much aware of this take necessary steps, such as,

> "planting trees to control erosion, regulating cultivation around local water sources, restricting pesticides and other pollutants, rehabilitating degraded soils, and adopting new technologies."[43]

Increasing the use of fertilizers over the years for having higher yield is mirrored in the fact that the total global consumption amounts to about 137 million tons a year (1997).

The economic importance of the produce of the agrosystems providing food, animal feed and fibre is worth approximately $ 1.3 trillion a year and agriculture makes itself the most important activity in the economies of the low-income countries accounting for 31 per cent of their GDP, while it is 50 per cent of the GDP in many parts of Sub-Saharan countries as against 12 per cent in middle-income countries and going down to 1 to 3 per cent in the industrial countries though,

> "the value of the agricultural products of these countries represents 79 per cent of the total market value of world agricultural products .... Globally, agroecosystems produce enough food to provide every person on the planet with 2,757 Kcal each day, which is sufficient to meet the minimum human requirement for nutrition."[44]

As mentioned earlier, rising seas and exposure to extreme weather risks together make agriculture a greater victim to whims of climate extremes. It is already predicted by the IPCC (Fifth Assessment Report 2014)*, observations that the growing incidence of tropical cyclones and hurricanes as consequences of oceans becoming warmer from rising temperature make more and more people subject to capricious weather. It is estimated people facing climate-related hazards will amount to:

> "344 million exposed to cyclones;
> 521 million exposed to floods;
> 130 million exposed to droughts;
> 2.9 million exposed to landslides ... Increased exposure to droughts is of particular concern in Sub-Saharan Africa, though other regions, including South Asia and Latin America, could also be affected. Agricultural production is likely to suffer in these regions, especially those dominated by rain-fed production. In Sub-Saharan Africa, in the areas suitable for agriculture, the length of growing seasons and the yield potential of food staples are all projected to decline.... By 2020, between 75 million and 250 million more people in Sub-Saharan Africa could have their livelihoods compromised by a combination of drought, rising temperature and increased water stress."[45]

On the other hand, floods, tropical storms, a temperature-rise of 3°C-4°C will affect 134-332 million people in the coastal areas of Lower Egypt, Vietnam, and Bangladesh with 18 per cent of land, the latter getting inundated by one-metre rise in sea-level, besides the islands of Maldives with 80 per cent of its area lying less than 1 metre above sea level, Pacific Islands of Fiji, Samoa and Vanuata, the islands in the Caribbean where an increase of sea level by 1 metre would permanently submerge 11 per cent of the lands in Bahamas.

Needless to say, in response to climate change, regional variations in agricultural performances will slow down. In general, climate change will increase the risks to and reduce the productivity of developing country agriculture, making them more dependent on imports from the rich countries, while

---

* IPCC Fifth Assessment Synthesis Report: Climate Change 2014 Synthesis Report.

agriculture in the developed countries will be boosted by increase in the length of the growing season, thereby it will change the course of global trade. Thus, by 2020s agricultural potential is likely to increase by 8 per cent due to longer growing seasons in the developed countries, but decline by 9 per cent in the developing countries, with Sub-Saharan Africa and Latin America experiencing greatest losses. India provides another example of contrast as a victim of climate change where rainfall is going to increase with intense concentration during monsoon periods in already rain-abundant areas, making parts of the country subject to great risks of floods while large areas receive less rainfall. Such drought-prone areas, comprising Andhra Pradesh, Gujarat, Madhya Pradesh and Rajasthan with an increase in temperature by 3.5°C by 2050, will experience a decline 8-9 per cent in yield for water-intensive crops, such as rice. As a whole for India, with a rise in temperature by 2-3°C there will be a decline in net farm-revenue by 9-25 per cent.[46]

According to the projections of IPCC (2014), the resilience of many ecosystems will be undermined by climate change, and the rising CO_2 levels will reduce biodiversity. Temperature increases above 2°C leading to unprecedented losses of biodiversity and the collapse of ecological systems will initiate coral, wet sand land forest systems suffering from rapid losses. The 'Millennium Ecosystem Assessment Report 2005' found 60 per cent of all ecosystem services are already degraded or being used unsustainably. Such losses apply mainly to mangrove swamps, coral reef systems, forests and wetlands. Agriculture along with population and industrial development joining together quicken the process of environmental degradation. The serious implications of climate change is recorded in the previous three decades by the shift in isotherms,

> "moving towards the North and the South Poles at a rate of about 56 kilometres per decade. Species are attempting to follow their climatic zones. Changes in flowering seasons, migratory patterns and the distribution of flora and fauna have been detected across the world. Alpine forests are being pushed towards higher altitudes, for example. Climate change has already contributed to the loss of species and global

> warming in the pipeline will add to the loss. But far greater impacts will take off at 2°C over pre-industrial levels. This is the threshold at which predicted extinction rates start to rise. According to the IPCC, 20-30 per cent of plant and animal species are likely to be at increased risk of extinction if global average temperature increases exceed 1.5-2.5°C, including polar bears and fish that feed on coral reefs. Some 277 medium or large mammals in Africa would be at risk in the event of 3°C warming."[47]

During this century, warming oceans and rising acidification destroying much of coral, with devastating social, ecological and economic consequences already destroyed on an extensive scale, with half of the system is in decline. Coral is very sensitive to any change and even 1°C rise in temperature

> "cause corals to expel the algae that supply most of their food, resulting in breathing and sudden death of the coral.... The 50,000 km^2 of coral reef in Indonesia, 18 per cent of the world's total, is deteriorating rapidly and rise of temperature 2°C will further hasten the process... the collapse of coral system would represent a catastrophic event for human development in many countries. Coral reefs are not only just havens of exceptional biodiversity, but also a source of livelihoods, nutrition and economic growth for over 60 countries. Most of the 30 million small-scale fishers in the developing world are dependent in some form on coral reefs for maintaining feeding and breeding grounds. More than half of the protein and essential nutrients in the diets of 400 million poor people living in tropical coastal areas is supplied by fish."[48]

Besides, they support tourism in Indian Ocean and the Caribbean and thus play an important role in economic social as well as ecological life.

Similarly, global warming is of greater significance for Russia with the thawing of its permafrost covering about 60 per cent of its land area already having accelerated the winter flows of major rivers, with grave consequences for coastal and river-bank settlements. No infrastructure provides immunity from climatic forces. So far, no measures have been found to be fool-proof against the vagaries of nature, such as combating sea-level rise, increasing temperatures, droughts, increased floods, risks of catastrophic hurricanes and typhoons. Eventually, each of this emerging as the result of global warming may be mitigated once the rate of warming is controlled, which makes itself almost an unachievable target, particularly in view of the extremely unreasonable attitude of some rich countries taking greater interest in saving interest of power-lobbies using coal. The emission of unremitting greenhouse gases cannot be halted as long as it is effectively cut down. Various approaches to come to an agreement with firm commitment on actions for reducing the rate of emission has so far not been fully successful, particularly with the withdrawal of the US in its support. Infrastructure for mitigating the effects of climate change adopted by some countries are far from all-pervasive, rather going for a partial remedy, such as proposals for the construction of water gates and culverts for saving road networks in Cambodia does not consider increased risks of flooding; or, creating of a coastal buffer zone in regions vulnerable to strong surges, or raising an 800 kilometre network of roads between 0.5 to 1 metre to counter sea-level rise in Bangladesh. Similarly, the government in Mekong Delta, having taken up a comprehensive strategy for reducing disaster risks which includes strengthening drainage systems, reinforcing dykes and trenches around human settlements and agricultural areas, and supporting the restoration of mangrove areas, or, investment in projects to meet water shortages and the threat of flooding and measures to check soil erosion. Each of these exhibits a limited perspective without making real effort mitigating the more rigorous effects of climate change.

Agriculture for Development

In order to survive as a force for continuing development and guaranteeing a device for meeting the challenges of food security in the world, agriculture needs to sustain productivity and income-growth in the face of declining prices of grains and traditional products by way of diversifying in high-value horticulture, aquaculture and low-protein livestock (non-ruminant) in response to growing demands for such food items in the developed as well as developing countries. The global food-supply system requires close monitoring and new investments to speed up productivity, making productive systems more sustainable and adaptive to climate change, mainly with the introduction of new varieties of crops with shorter growing periods as well as more resistant to pests and diseases.

It needs to be pointed out that the performance of agriculture has been quite impressive, the gross domestic product (GDP) expanding by an average of 2.0 per cent a year between 1980 and 2004, exceeding population growth of 1.6 per cent a year as mentioned earlier, resulting from increasing productivity which brought down the real price of grains by about 1.8 per cent in the world market during this period. However, it may be interesting to observe that developing countries experienced faster agricultural growth, 2.6 per cent per year, 1980-2004, than industrial countries registering 0.9 per cent a year, the former accounting for 79 per cent of overall agricultural growth, their share of world agricultural GDP rising from 56 per cent in 1980 to 65 per cent in 2004, while it was 21 per cent for the industrial countries in 2004. Both Asia and the developing world in general have contributed to their growth through productivity gains rather than expansion of agricultural land, and in East Asia rates of cereal yields increased by 2.8 per cent annually in 1961-2004 against 1.8 per cent in industrial countries.

The major engines of growth have been intensified through,

"widespread use of irrigation, improved crop varieties and fertilizers, when irrigation facilities expanded through the 1990s and into the 2000s, bring 39 per cent of the crop area in South Asia under irrigation, 29 per cent in East Asia and the Pacific, but only 4 per cent in Sub-Saharan Africa. At the same time, since 1960s, 80 per cent of the cereal areas in South and East Asia has been brought under improved varieties of crops, increasing from less than 10 per cent in 1970, but they account for only 22 per cent of the cereal area in Sub-Saharan Africa in 2000. Similarly, the use of chemical fertilizer has also increased in developing countries, rising from about 10 per cent of global share in 1960 to over 60 per cent used now, in which Asia farmers take the lead, jumping from 6 kilograms per hectare in 1961-63 to 143 kilograms per hectare in 2000-02 more than the industrial countries,"[49] helping create at least 20 per cent growth in developing-country agriculture over a period of past three decades (Fig. 1.6).

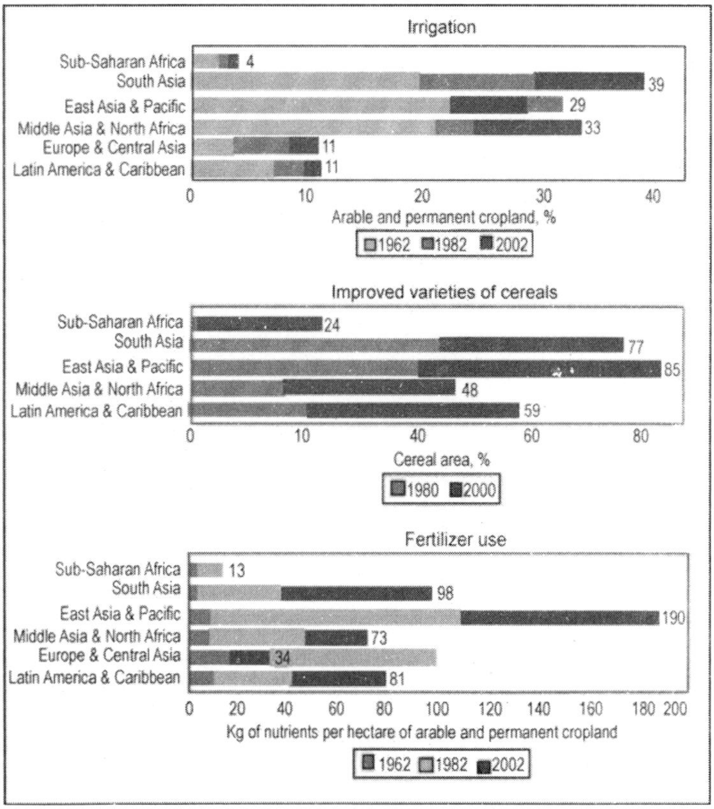

Fig. 1.6: Regional Variation in the Expansion of Inputs for Agricultural Production

Source: Evenson and Gollin 2003: FAO 2006a.

As mentioned elsewhere in this chapter, agriculture has prospered in the developing countries, taking an increasing role in economic welfare of its population through revolution in horticulture, aquaculture and livestock accounting for a growing share of international trade. However, among major handicaps for future expansion of agriculture to ensure increase in food productivity and thereby ensure food security, land is the most important factor though further expansion of this in Asia is highly restricted. Nevertheless, much better prospect in this regard lies in Latin America, Central Asia and Europe because of lower population densities and a declining agricultural population. Such expansion involves high environmental costs, as in Latin America as well as in Sub-Saharan Africa, making inroads into forests, woodlands and grazing lands, a highly expensive job. On the other hand, as indicated earlier, such an encroachment is far from welcome as it entails factors like pollution, salinization and soil degradation from poorly managed intensification projects, which is already making globally 5 to 10 million hectares of agricultural land lost to agriculture. Among other constraints threatening agricultural system are acute water scarcity, climate change combined with high energy prices which make the future somewhat uncertain but this can be overcome largely by way of adopting risk-mitigating measures like 'better water-control' and use of drought-tolerant varieties of seeds.

Incidentally, as very clearly pointed out earlier in this chapter, water management takes a determining role in sustaining as well as enhancing agricultural production and while irrigation takes place in,

> "18 per cent of the cultivated land in the developing world, it produces about 40 per cent of the value of agricultural output."[50]

However, many countries in the developing world are already experiencing serious and worsening water scarcity.

> "Globally, about 15-35 per cent of total water withdrawals for irrigated agriculture are estimated to be unsustainable—the use of water exceeds the renewable supply. ... As a result of excessive withdrawals, such major rivers as the Ganges, the Yellow River, Amu Darya, Syr Darya, Chao Phraya, Colorado River, and Rio Grande may not reach the sea during part of the year.

> Other well-known consequences of unsustainable irrigation are the degradation of the Aral Sea in Central Asia and the shrinking of Lake Chad in Western Africa and Lake Chapala in Central Mexico."[51]

Overuse of groundwater for irrigation has led to an alarming situation, particularly in India and China with the largest areas under groundwater irrigation, withdrawals having increased from less than 20 cubic kilometres to 250 cubic kilometres since 1950s. Reliance on groundwater for irrigation is high as well in Middle East and South Asia. The open-access nature of groundwater subjects it to depletion and contamination by municipal, industrial and agricultural users as well as saline water intrusion (Fig. 1.7).

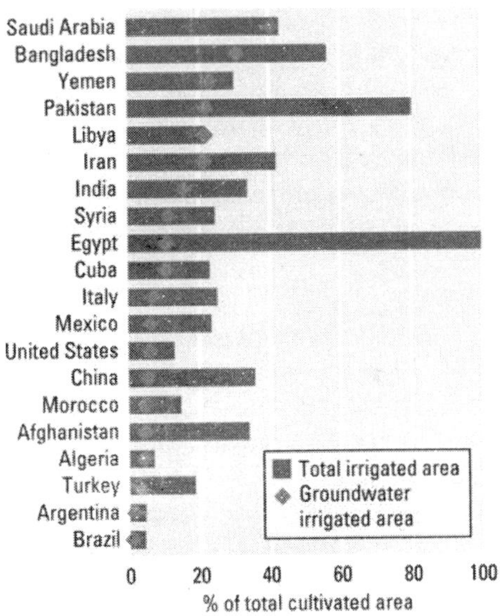

Fig. 1.7: Dependence on Groundwater Irrigation in the Middle East and South Asia

Source: FAO AQUASTAT World Bank: World Development Report 2008.

Another problem is land degradation which has taken a serious turn in irrigated areas giving rise to salinization and waterlogging, the former more common in arid and semi-arid areas, making about 40 per cent of irrigated land areas in Asia subject to salinization, while excessive irrigation combined with insufficient drainage in humid areas makes waterlogging a great problem, resulting in decline in agricultural productivity.

On the whole, intensification of high-input farming, in general, is suffering from injudicious use of inputs, such as water for irrigation, fertilizers and pesticides, causing indirect damage to ecosystems, with excess nitrates used for farming entering water systems and becoming responsible for inadvertent poisoning of humans and other life-systems by pesticides. The algal bloom, destruction of wetlands and wildlife habitats are caused by the run-off from fertilizers used for farming. Besides, productivity growth is also slowing down, resulting from soil-health degradation, pest and weeds. High-input farming has also reduced biodiversity and genetic diversity in crops grown.

Remedies for such malfunctions can be achieved by way of broadening the genetic base and devising means to keep 'ahead of crop-evolving pests and diseases.' At the same time, a more diversified system requiring less chemical fertilizers and pesticides, introduction of alternative cropping patterns such as 'mixed legume-cereal systems' are likely to sustain agricultural productivity.

A sustained agricultural productivity also includes management of intensive livestock system, its development spurred by technological change in animal breeding, nutrition and health consequent to rising per capita incomes and urbanization increasing demand for more animal protein. The emergence of specialized livestock units on a grand scale in Asia, in and around urban or peri-urban areas, ultimately came to be environmental threats in the form of pollution of water and soil with animal waste infusing nitrogen, phosphorous and highly toxic heavy metals such as cadmium, copper and zinc, besides spreading animal diseases (avian'flu) sometimes as threats to human life, requiring culling of existing stock of animals on a massive scale. In order to avoid environmental hazards linking human health alternative strategies to be evolved includes indentification of areas that can absorb higher livestock densities,

"with GIS technology, superimposing current farming

> systems and their balances on ecologically sensitive areas, prevailing human population densities, and infrastructure ... Command and control measures might include limiting the size of livestock farms (Norway), limiting the livestock density per farm (Germany), and introducing minimum distances between farms (Spain), or, between farms and the nearest waterway (Brazil)."[52]

Strategies for improvements of agriculture in less favoured areas requires recourse to advanced technology to make agriculture profitable, to stop resource degradation and improve livelihoods based on better management of natural resources, conserve scarce water and control erosion along with restoration of soil fertility and use of few external inputs, such as fertilizers, need proper attention. On the other hand, less-favoured areas including lands with low agricultural potential because of poor climate and soil and topography and areas having higher agricultural potential but hindered by poor access to infrastructure and markets, low population density, or social as well as political marginalization, generally located on hill sides and mountain regions or arid and semi-arid areas, have to be used with care in regard to agricultural practices, choice of crops and inputs. As a matter of fact, such lands account for 54 per cent of the agricultural area and 31 per cent of the rural population of the developing countries.

Changes in the cropping system using plants more tolerant of drought and poor soil conditions with greater resistance to pest and diseases significantly boost productivity, stabilize yields, making farming system 'more resilient'. Better management of water, soil and crop doubles productivity in rain-fed areas when investment in water harvesting and small-scale irrigation both acting as catalytic agents, increase profitability.

In this context, it may be interesting to mention that,

> "the advent of tubewell and treadle-pump technology in the 1990s was behind the successful transformation in South Asia's poverty triangle—Bangladesh, Eastern India and Nepal's Terai region. Small farmer-controlled irrigation using simple low-cost technologies, river diversion, lifting with small (hand or rope) pumps from

> shallow groundwater or rivers, and seasonal flooding—also enjoys local success in Africa, especially for high-value horticulture (Burkino Faso, Mali, Niger and Tanzania, for example). However, these projects require social capital and community action."[53]

Lastly, the success of agriculture for development greatly depends on sustainable use of 'natural resources such as water, forests, soil conservation, genetically diverse crops and animal varieties and other ecosystem services.' Availability of better technologies and better ways of water and farm inputs' management make intensive farming more sustainable.

In this context it is apprehended that the existing character of food production may undergo necessary changes with time in near future, as dictated by the changing food habits of people, the latter having emerged in recent years under the pressure of growing urban markets in the form of processed/semi-processed food supplied mostly by supermarkets in urban retail markets comprising restaurants, hotels, eateries making a booming business. The growing habits of people in the urban areas, irrespective of the developed or developing countries, of eating outside the home quite frequently turning out as a noticeable practice of avoiding home cooking, particularly with young people with the couple spending endless hours in job-work, has given rise to the business of catering to the varied tastes and requirements shouldered by the supermarkets providing food items of the farmer's choice, often defined by the size, shape and sometimes even colour of the products. Such qualified demands naturally will ultimately have their effects on the types of products produced by the farmers, influencing the character of the productive systems in the long run, very difficult to presume resulting from the changing food system, particularly in urban areas.

The likely impact may be assumed from the growing markets of the processed/semi-processed food, the share of which has increased in the upper middle-income-countries from less than 40 per cent to 50 per cent, while in high-income countries it grew from 72 per cent to 75 per cent between 2001 and 2014. In comparison, the demand for processed/semi-processed food has been much lower in lower middle-class-income countries, growing from 22 per cent to 27 per cent between 2001 and 2014, but without any change between 2008-2014. In contrast, the distribution of fresh food through supermarkets has remained below 50 per cent in high-income countries, below 30 per cent in upper-middle-income countries and around 10 per cent in low-middle-income countries during the last 10 years, which is a clear indication of declining trend of cooking food at home.[54]

Undoubtedly, the growing habit of eating outside home is becoming a characteristic feature of urban life, not only on festive occasions but one as a general rule, in order to avoid the hassle of cooking food at home in a fast-life with more time spent outside than at home, and particularly very convenient for those living 'single' to buy cooked/semi-cooked food, the nature of which ultimately determines the productive policy of agriculture in the countries involved.

However, regional specialities cannot be estimated from these figures. There is no doubt that rapid urbanization in Latin America,

> "has led to profound changes in food production and distribution systems, with supermarkets now account for more than 50 per cent of grocery sales. In much of Asia, most food purchases in urban areas are now made in supermarkets. Even in East Africa, the share of purchased food in total consumption is just below 60 per cent. (Comparatively) hypermarkets, large supermarkets and convenience stores account for 93 per cent of consumer purchases in North America but play a much more modest role in Europe (50 per cent), Latin America (46 per cent), Middle East and Africa (38 per cent) and Asia (37 per cent)."[55]

Putting aside any speculation about the emerging character of agriculture in its productive form under the growing pressure of recent changes in food systems focused primarily on urban areas which, obviously, is going to be the home of the major section of global population (over 66 per cent by 2050: UN 2014 Revision), we need to consider food not only in the light of inevitable requirement of mankind but also consider the fact that as a right of everybody. The challenge emerges particularly from the situation that prevails in India today, though the same is applicable to many other countries as well as existing within the whole of the developing world.

In considering the right to food, India poses the most questionable status noting the catastrophic nature of nutritional situation in India where, according to the facts revealed in the second report of National Family Health Survey (1998-99),

> "47 per cent of all Indian children are undernourished, 52 per cent of all adult women are anaemic and 36 per cent have body mass mix (BMI) below the cut-off 18.5 commonly associated with chronic energy deficiency (International Institute of Population Sciences 2000). These nutritional deficiencies have devastating consequences for the well-being and future of the Indian people. To start with, hunger and undernourishment are intrinsic deprivations and severely diminish the quality of life. Further, under-nutrition is associated with reduced learning abilities, greater exposure to disease and other impairments of individual and social opportunities."[56]

This nutritional situation in India, as such, is 'a sort of silent emergency' as stated by Dreze in a democratic country like India, and he considers the right to food

> "is one of the most basic economic and social rights that are essential to achieve economic democracy, without which political democracy is at best incomplete. Indeed, there is an obvious sense in which mass hunger is fundamentally incompatible with democracy in any meaningful sense of the term. ... The right to food is nowhere near being realised in India. In fact, under-nutrition levels in India are among the highest in the world."[57]

In other words, in India the 'right to food', the most basic moral as well as fundamental of all rights for existence, being denied to a large section of the population makes the status of democracy hollow as well as a mockery and cannot be claimed to have been achieved as yet.

NOTES

Note A

The World Resources Report:

"....considers five main types or categories of eco-systems: grasslands, forest, agro eco-systems, freshwater systems and coastal ecosystems. together, these five major ecosystem types cover most of the Earth's surface and render the bulk of the goods and services people derive from ecosystems....Divisions between ecosystems are less important, however, than the linkages between them. Grasslands give way to savannas that segue into forests. Freshwater becomes brackish as it approaches a coastal area. Polar, island, mountain and even urban ecosystems blend into and add to the mix. All these ecosystems are tightly knit into a global continuum of energy and nutrients and organisms—the biosphere in which we live.

The benefits that humans derive from ecosystems can be direct or indirect. Direct benefits are harvested largely from the plants and animals in an ecosystem in the form of food and raw materials. These are the most familiar 'products' an ecosystem yields—crops, livestock, fish, game, lumber, fuel wood and fodder. Genetic resources that flow from the biodiversity of the world's ecosystems also provide direct benefits by contributing genes for improving the yield and disease resistance of crops, and for developing medicines and other products.

Indirect benefits arise from interactions and feedback among the organisms living in an ecosystem. Many of them take the form of services, like sea erosion control and water purification and storage that plants and soil microorganisms provide . ı a watershed, or the pollination and seed dispersal that many insects, birds, and mammals provide. Other benefits are less tangible, but nonetheless highly valued: the scenic enjoyment of a sunset, for example (such as watching sunrise at Tiger Hill in Darjeeling Himalayas or Kanchenjunga at the rising sun in Darjeeling, West Bengal, India), or the spiritual significance of a sacred mountain or forest grove. Every year, millions of people make pilgrimages to outdoor holy places, vacation in scenic regions, or simply pause in a park or their gardens to reflect or relax. As the manifestation of nature, ecosystems are the psychological and spiritual backdrop for our lives...

Urban and built-up areas now occupy more than 471 million ha—about 4 per cent of land area.

Source: UN, World Resources 2000-01, People and Ecosystems: The Fraying Web of Life: 11 and 24.

Note B

One of the most encouraging results about expanding agriculture in India is provided by recent development as well as expansion of a particular variety of fruit—mango in West Bengal. Already famous for a number of very good qualities of mangos grown in some of the districts—Malda, Murshidabad, Nadia, North and South 24-Parganas, Medinipur and Hooghly districts etc.—the most recent experimental project of growing a particular variety of mango, called 'Amrapali', in Bankura district has been highly successful. Grown in six drought-hit, completely barren lands of South Bankura has witnessed a bumper crop this year, producing 18,000 metric tons, and the largest orchard at Damodarpur village covering about 26,880 cubits, is already finding market in Dubai, Hong Kong and Malaysia, E.U. and the U.K. expecting a much larger international market. The total production this year, including all important varieties, has come to 40 per cent more than in the previous year. Land under mango is expanding further, even in Purulia district, another drought-hit district, with 6,000 hectares of land has so far been converted into mango culture.

Source: The Statesman, Kolkata Issue (India) 14 and 15 June 2014.

Note C

The Global Environmental Footprint of Expanding Livestock—

"During the decade 1994-2004, world trade in soybeans doubled. Seventy per cent of the global increase in export went to China, where total meat production rose from 45 million to 74 million tons over the period, generating rapid expansion in demand for feed grains, Argentina and Brazil... providing more than two-thirds of the increased global exports of soybeans.

Rapid growth in exports from Argentina and Brazil has been supported by bringing new land under cultivation, often at the expense of forests and woodland ... in Brazil planting an additional area (between 1990-2000 and 2004-2005) of 54,000 square kilometres—an area larger than Costa Rica—much of it displacing ecologically important savanna woodland and forest. The mean actual deforestation rate in the Amazon from 2000 to 2005 (22,392 km^2 per year) was 18 per cent higher than in the previous five years (19,018 km^2 per year), partly the result of agricultural expansion."

Source: The World Bank, *The World Development Report 2008,* Washington, World Bank, 2008.

NOTE D

"China has quietly inaugurated one of the biggest engineering projects of all time: the South-North Water Diversion, a $ 48 billion, 1500 miles network of canals and tunnels designed to divert 44.8 billion cubic metres of water annually from the country's humid south to its parched, industrialized north ... China's booming economy over the past three decades, coupled with a long-held mandate to 'grow first, clean up later', has been cataclysmic for the country's once beautiful lakes, rivers and aquifers. More than half of China's 50,000 rivers have vanished during the past two decades according to the first national census of water, published last year. About 70 per cent of its remaining freshwater is polluted."

Source: Jonathan Kaiman, *The Guardian* (UK). 13 December, 2014.

NOTE E

World Needs 'Greener' Water Policies as Demand Rises: UN.

"Governments should focus on "*greener*" policies to improve the supply and quality of water as climate change and a growing global population threaten the water security of billions, the United Nations said today.

In its 2018 World Water Development Report, the UN calculated that an estimated 3.6 billion people—nearly half of the global population—live in areas where water can be scarce at least one month per year. And this number could rise to 5.7 billion by 2050, the report warned.

If we do nothing, some five billion people will be living in areas with poor access to water by 2050, said UNESCO Director General, Audrey Azoulay, at the presentation of the report in Brasilia.

This report proposes solutions that are based on nature to manage water better. ... Global water use has increased by a factor of six over the past century and *continues to grow steadily at a rate of about one per cent per year*. And use is expected to rise significantly due to population growth, economic development and changing consumption patterns, among other factors. *The vast majority of the growing demand for water will occur in countries with developing or emerging economies* .... At the same time, the global water cycle was intensifying due to climate change, *with wetter regions generally becoming wetter and drier regions becoming even drier.* 'Ecosystem-friendly'—so-called *grey* or man-made water infrastructure, such as reservoirs, irrigation canals and treatment plants, were no longer sufficient to meet these challenges, said the Editor-in-

Chief, Richard Connor. There is increasingly limited room to build more reservoirs because of silting, environmental concerns and restrictions, as well as the fact that in many developed countries the most cost-effective and viable sites had already been used, the UN argued.

"In many cases, more ecosystem-friendly forms of water storage, such as natural wetlands, improvements in soil moisture and more efficient recharge of groundwater could be more sustainable and cost-effective than traditional grey infrastructure, such as dams. Nature plays a unique and fundamental role in regulating the different functions of the water cycle," Connor said. "The report said that green solutions were already showing great potential."

Source: The Statesman, Kolkata Issue (India). 20 March, 2018.

NOTE F

"The chain of events that links melting Arctic with weather to the south begins with rising global temperatures causing more sea ice to melt. Unlike on the continent of Antarctica, melting ice here exposes dark ocean, which absorbs more sunlight than ice and warms further. This feedback loop is why the Arctic is heating up faster than the rest of the planet. This in turn narrows the temperature difference between the Arctic and lower latitudes, which is crucial because it is the temperature gradient between them that drives the jet stream's winds, which streak around the Pole at up to 250 mph about five miles above the surface. The connection between vanishing Arctic ice and extreme summer weather in the northern hemisphere is probable. ... Blocking patterns, slow meanders of the jet stream, have been firmly linked to some devastating events including the 2010 summer floods in Pakistan which killed 2000 and affected 20 million. These blocking events have also been linked to summer deluges in the UK leading to flooding in 2007 and 2012. Greenland also experienced an extreme year in 2012, with record melting flushing water into the ocean and accelerating sea level rise. The loop of air that sat on Greenland that year may also be linked to one of the biggest disasters of recent years: Hurricane Sandy, which killed 233 people and cost $ 75 billion. ... Another consequence of the fast melting of the Arctic ice raises the possibility that there may be even worse extreme weather to come, according to a few scientists, titanic Atlantic superstorms and hurricanes barrelling across Europe. The melting of Greenland is pouring about 250 billion tonnes a year of water into the ocean. As a result, the current that drags warm water up the Atlantic is weakened."

Source: Carrington, Damian, Rapid Polar Warming Behind Dramatic Rise in Extreme Weather, in *The Guardian* (UK) 20 December, 2016.

Note G

"More of a giant France-size glacier in Antarctica is floating on the ocean ... raising fears it could melt faster as the climate warms and have a dramatic impact on rising sea-levels. The Totten Glacier (as it is called) is one of the fastest-flowing and largest glaciers in Antarctica ... enormous amount of water it could unleash. ... Glaciers are the huge bodies of dense ice that slowly move down valleys, mountains and slopes under their own weight over many centuries, sculpting the earth below as they go. ... Totten Glacier contains enough ice to raise global sea-levels by about three metres (9.8 feet) if it all melted. Since the 1900s the global sea-level has risen by around 20 centimetres and by the end of the century it's projected to rise by up to one metre or more."
Source: The Statesman, Kolkata Issue (India), 21 March, 2018.

REFERENCES

1. United Nations, World Resources 2000-2001: *People and Ecosystems: The Fraying Web of Life*. p. 53.
2. *Ibid*. p. 57.
3. Kerbs, John, *Food: A Very Short Introduction*, Oxford University Press, Oxford, UK. 2013. p. 2.
4. *Ibid*., pp. 4-5.
5. *Ibid*., pp. 9-10.
6. *Ibid*., pp. 11-12.
7. Rhoades, Robert S. (1991), The World's Food Supply at Risk, in *National Geographic*, Washington, Vol. 179, No. 4, April: 77 and 79.
8. Kerbs, John (2013), *Food: A Very Short Introduction*, Oxford University Press, Oxford, UK. p. 13.
9. Rhoades, Robert S. (1991). The World's Food Supply at Risk, in *National Geographic*, Washington, Vol. 179, No. 4, April: p. 83.
10. United Nations, World Resources 2000-2001: *People and Ecosystems: The Fraying Web of Life*. p. 24.
11. *Op. cit.*
12. United Nations, *World Resources 2000-2001: People and Ecosystems: The Fraying Web of Life*. p. 27.
13. The World Bank, *The World Development Report 2008. Agriculture For Development*. Washington World Bank, 2008, pp. 2-3.
14. *Ibid*., p. 4.
15. Patnaik, Utsa (2014). (Fourth Printing), *The Republic of Hunger and Other Essays*. Three Essays Collective, New Delhi. p. 58.

16. *Ibid.*, p. 60.
17. *Ibid.*, p. 73.
18. *Ibid.*, p. 74.
19. *Ibid.*, pp. 75-76.
20. The World Bank, *The World Development Report 2008*, Washington World Bank, 2008. p. 50.
21. *Ibid.*, p. 51.
22. *Ibid*; p. 60.
23. *Ibid.*, p. 58.
24. Dyson, Tim 1996. *Population and Food: Global Trends and Future Prospects*, Routledge. p. 115.
25. The World Bank, *The World Development Report 2008*, Washington World Bank, 2008. p. 191.
26. *Ibid.*, p. 64.
27. Natarajan, P.M., ex-member of presently defunct Planning Commission, Government of India, in *The Statesman*, Kolkata Issue (India), 20 May, 2016.
28. Milman, Oliver (2016). For Native Hunters, Choice will be to Move or Starve, *The Guardian* (UK), 20 December.
29. Carrington, Damian, and Helen Pid (2016). Major Floods in the UK Likely Every Year, Expert Warns, A Year after the Deluge, York is still Counting the Cost, *The Guardian* (UK), 26 December.
30. Dogra, Bharat (2016). Farming in the Days of Climate Change, in *The Statesman*, Kolkata Issue (India), 5 June, 2016.
31. India Drying Out: Study, The Statesman News Service, *The Statesman*, Kolkata Issue (India), 16 April, 2016.
32. The World Bank, *The World Development Report 2008*, Washington, World Bank, 2008. p. 65.
33. Harvey, Fiona (2016). Arctic Special: Cutting Soot Fastest Way to Slow Global Warming Say Experts, *The Guardian* (UK), 21 December.
34. The World Bank, *The World Development Report 2008*, Washington World Bank, 2008, p. 66.
35. FAO, *The State of Food Insecurity in the World*. Rome: FAO. 2008. pp. 6-7.
36. *Ibid.*, p. 19.
37. IPCC, *Climate Change 2014 Synthesis Report*: IPCC Fifth Assessment Synthesis Report. p. 74.
38. Stern, Nicholas (2009). *A Blueprint for a Safer Planet: How to Manage Climate Change and Create a New Era of Progress and Prosperity* Boley Head, London. p. 30.
39. UNDP. *Human Development Report 2007/2008: Fighting Climate Change: Human Solidarity in a Divided World*. pp. 95-96.
40. UN, *World Resources 2000-2001, People and Ecosystems: The Fraying Web of Life*. p. 56.

41. *Op. cit.*
42. *Op. cit.*
43. UN, *World Resources 2000-2001, People and Ecosystems: The Fraying Web of Life*. p. 59.
44. *Ibid.*, p. 60.
45. UNDP. *Human Development Report 2007-2008: Fighting Climate Change: Human Solidarity in a Divided World*. pp. 98-99.
46. *Ibid.*, pp. 92-93.
47. *Ibid.*, p. 102.
48. *Ibid.*, p. 104.
49. The World Bank, *The World Development Report 2008*, Washington World Bank, 2008. pp. 50-51.
50. *Ibid.*, p. 182.
51. *Op. cit.*
52. *Ibid.*, p. 190.
53. *Ibid.*, pp. 193-194.
54. FAO. 2017. *The Future of Food and Agriculture: Trends and Challenges.* Rome. pp. 106-107.
55. *Ibid.*, 107.
56. Dreze, Jean (Ed.) (2017). Social Policy, from *Economic and Political Weekly* 39 (17), 24 April, 2014. Swan. p. 182.
57. *Ibid.*, p. 193.

2
Food Sovereignty: Feeding the Hungry

Scramble for Food

The availability of food most crucial for human life security cannot be belittled, as pointed out by John Krebs (2013)* in his, *Food: A Very Short Introduction,* when there were 3,600 hungry mouths to feed born in almost every 20 minutes, or about six new babies born every second and three people die, and world population increased by about 180 mouths per minute, rising most likely to over nine billion by 2050, compared with 6.8 billion in the early 21st century.

Thus, the most pertinent question is—will there be enough food to feed over nine billion people by 2050?

As Krebs (2013)† points out, all our food we eat ultimately comes from the sun.

> "Plants capture photons of light energy and use them to power a chemical reaction, photosynthesis, that combines water and carbon dioxide into glucose, which in turn provides the energy to support almost every other living thing on the planet. In addition to solar energy, plants need various nutrients. Nitrogen, phosphorus and potassium are needed in the largest quantities, followed by calcium, magnesium and

---

* John Krebs, *Food: A Very Short Introduction,* Oxford, Oxford University Press, UK, 2010.

† *Ibid.*

> sulphur in smaller quantities, and the so-called trace elements needed in tiny amounts. These are zinc, manganese, boron, molybdenum, iron, chlorine, and copper. Without sufficient supplies of nutrients, plant growth is stunted, hence farmers often add them in the form of fertilizers or manure....The final and crucial ingredient for plant growth is water, the availability of which may increasingly limit future food production in many parts of the world."[1]

This makes a very strong reminder that upsetting any part of this process will hit hard on food production, curtailing the feeding capability of the world population. Any critical evaluation of the existing situation for agricultural growth providing food for mankind has to be considered against the role of many ecological disasters including pollution of ground and surface water with nitrates particularly flowing from fertilizers used for crop production. Further, there is contamination of food, nutrient depletion in farms raising crops, besides accumulation of nutrient wastes to dangerous levels in large-scale animal-rearing facilities and routine use of antibiotics in factory-raised livestock increasing spread of antibiotic resistant microbes. In fact, most of these problems arise from such attitudes when the entire system of agricultural production is driven primarily by the motive of earning profit rather than feeding people.[2]

Such a highly prejudiced view did not improve the situation even long after the end of colonial rule in many of the countries in the developing world, or the Global South which in reality has been treated as a "World Farm" for a minority of the global consumers concentrated in the 'Global North', consisting of the industrial countries giving rise to 'Socially Constructed Food Security', resulting from 'redirection of food production' as well as its circulation giving rise to permanent hunger experienced by over 1 billion people (about 14 per cent of world population).[3]

Quite evidently, this led to the worst food crisis in the world in 2007-08, doubling the price of maize, rising by 50 per cent for wheat, by almost 70 per cent for rice, the food price increasing 75 per cent by 2005, bringing down world's grain reserves to its lowest ever. The reasons for this alarming situation may be traced to, according to experts in the field, intensification of energy, and food demand fuelled further by oil price at its highest. Added to this was the factor of greater purchasing power of 1 billion new consumers in twenty middle-income countries comprising South Korea, Mexico, Turkey and Poland, in addition to China and India (with 40 per cent of this total) contributed to the rise in food prices. The food situation aggravated further with extreme weather patterns and ecological stress, as observed by John Vidal in *The Guardian* (UK) on 9 November, 2007. As claimed by Michael (2010),

> "...the planet's water, land, air, plants, animals and fish stock were all in 'inexorable decline'. According to the UN's World Food Programme (WFP), fifty-seven countries, including 29 in Africa, 19 in Asia, and 9 in Latin America, have been hit by catastrophic floods. Harvests have been affected by drought and heat waves in South Asia, Europe, China, Sudan, Mozambique and Uruguay."[4]

Interestingly, before colonial rule, village-level food reserves were larger and grain prices were 'insulated' from speculation. But, laying down of the transport system, including the railroads, and improved communication facilities offered by the telegraphy during the colonial rule, enabled local merchants to transfer grain from drought-stricken hinterlands to hoarding centres from where they were exported, which rising from 3 to 10 million tons annually, 'an amount equivalent to the annual nutrition of 25 million people', caused death of about 12 to 29 million people during this period. It strikes as a great anomaly that India was exporting food while famines were raging in the country. Even a century later the situation had not changed during the 'Raj' when occurrence of Bengal's famine in 1943 coincided with food being diverted for commercial uses.[5]

The situation of food constraints did not change much even after the end of colonial rule. The post-colonial states, particularly in the West, adopted a development model, expanding cash-cropping systems based on imported technology, and luxury consumer goods demanded by the growing urban market. Between 1950 and 1997 the rural population in the world declined by about 25 per cent while today almost 63 per cent of world population live in or around urban centres. This prompted the emergence of supermarkets, after ousting the traditional markets (local shops) as outlets of smaller traders, dislodging many of them from business and encouraging corporate farming spreading its tentacles in many developing countries as well, such as in Argentina, Brazil, China, India, Mexico, Pakistan, the Philippines, South Africa, Taiwan and Thailand. Asia has taken lead in this global process, 'accounting for two-thirds of meat consumption' fed on Brazilian supply while transforming China from a net exporter of soybeans to the world's largest importer of soybeans from Brazil, with large-scale conversion of its pastures for the production of soybeans.

All this had the most devastating effects on small producers everywhere, compelling them to take shelter in urban slums or earning a living elsewhere, while control of agricultural production ensuring food security was slowly slipping into corporate or agribusiness hands, bringing in fundamental structural transformation in world food. The system is characterised by continuous displacement of staple crops, meant for direct human consumption, with those of export values. This clearly led to the emergence of a higher exploitative situation of 'trade liberalisation and export agriculture' and as its immediate impact, 20 to 30 million people around the world lost their land primarily used for agricultural production practised by small landholders supplying local markets. On the other hand, the capitalist export-based agriculture made a severe encroachment into the lands of various poor countries in the form of land-grab. This has already taken a serious turn,

> "creating a 'scramble for Africa', in particular where the South Korean firm, Daewoo Logistics is negotiating a deal to buy a 90-year lease on as much as 1.3 million hectares of arable land in Madagascar, half the size of Belgium, aiming to produce 5 million tons of corn a year by 2023, and produce palm oil from a further lease of 120,000 hectares (296,000 acres).... The government and corporations in some 'cash-rich-land-poor' countries, mostly in the Middle East, are making similar efforts to

own long-term access to food, buying up land in poor countries."[6]

Some of the major countries affected by 'land grab' are the Philippines (1,243,000 ha); Indonesia (1,625,000 ha); Pakistan (900,000 ha); Sudan (1,078,117 ha); Laos (700,000 ha); Mongolia (270,000 ha); altogether 7,623,675 ha worldwide, and apart from South Korea, major countries involved in acquiring land outside are China (2,090,769 ha), United Arab States (1,282,000 ha), Saudi Arabia (1,610,117 ha) and Japan (324,262 ha).[7]

This, undoubtedly, is the most revealing fact about the entire process of land grab taking place at the cost of local farmers' own food. Regrettably, crops such as maize, palm oil etc. produced on land grabbed are primarily destined for the production of biofuel; in other words, instead of enhancing food production, ensuring food security for humans, the products are turned into commercial ventures for making profit, creating more hungry mouths and, in combination with rising prices of food available in the market, lead to food riots taking place in far-flung countries across the world in 2007-08, such as Italy, Uzbekistan, Morocco, Guinea, Mauritania, Senegal, West Bengal, Indonesia, Zimbabwe, Burkina Faso, Cameroon, Yemen, Jordan, Saudi Arabia, Egypt, Mexico, Argentina and Haiti.[8]

As a consequence of rise in food prices but no increase in the volume of food imports, bills for rice, wheat and vegetable oils in least developing countries rose more than three times that of 2000, as reported by the United Nations, "adding 75 million people to the ranks of hungry people, and drove an estimated 125 million people in developing countries into extreme poverty."[9] The major factor taking a leading role in creating food crisis and corresponding rise in food prices between 2006 and 2008 is diversion of cereals, such as maize and palm oil, for the production of biofuel and, as reported by The World Bank economist, production of biofuels by the US and Europe was responsible for 140 per cent rise in food prices between 2002 and 2008. For example, production of biofuel/agrofuel is targeted to increase by over eight times from 4.7 billion gallons in 2007 to about 36 billion gallons in 2022 and there were already 135 ethanol (biofuel) refineries in operation in 2007 when 74 more were being built or expanded, using 30 per cent of the corn for the production of ethanol. Interestingly, even Mexico, the home of corn, had been converted to a 'corn-importing economy', where the peasant agricultural economy has been destroyed by the introduction of unilateral liberalisation of agricultural trade in the 1980s and the North American Free Trade Agreement (NAFTA) in the mid-1990s by way of converting land under domesticated corn, forced Mexico into a position of importer of the cereal. Another country, mentioned earlier in Chapter I, the Philippines turned from a net food exporter into a net food importer since the mid-1990s, the reason for which lies in its subjugation to a 'structural adjustment programme' involving a 'massive reduction of funding for rural programmes' where the ruling authorities ignored the basic fact that it was peasant agriculture which so long played a key role in the country's economic development. Instead, the authorities allowed land to be rented out to foreign interests to produce agrofuels and food with export values for foreign markets.

Similarly, Africa, on the whole, did not fare well either, importing about 25 per cent of its requirements. As in Mexico and the Philippines, structural adjustments involving drastic reduction or elimination of fertilizer subsidies ultimately turned relatively underpopulated Africa from a net food exporter in the 1960s to a chronic food importer, pushing it into export-oriented agricultural production, earning foreign exchange utilised for meeting fast-rising foreign debts. The results were highly symbolic, having been experienced by many of the developing countries as the victims of 'structural reformation and trade liberalisation policies' happening in Africa as well, where

> "coffee growers, in Southern Africa and West Africa were driven out of business by the dumping of subsidised beef from the European Union. Cotton growers in West Africa were displaced from world market by highly subsidized U.S. cotton....(Further) structural adjustment in the 1980s dismantled the elaborate system of public agencies that provided farmers access to land, credit, insurance inputs, and co-operative organization."[10]

The dynamics of capitalist transformation, transferring

agricultural responsibilities into the hands of corporate agribusiness houses, was at the root of growing food crisis, impacting food security very hard, particularly in the developing world. These developments termed as 'depeasantisation' has quite often led to the death of marginalised farmers losing permanently a way of making a living out of it, which made a cultural identity for them for generations. What really happened is compelling the peasant farmers to depend on costly seeds and costly chemicals and thus breaking them under relentless pressure of industrial farming. Many farmers engaged in it could not take the shock of this abrupt perpetual severance from their age-old practice and preferred taking their own life. India presents a case of an estimated 150,000 farmers having taken recourse to suicide over the last few years, beginning from 1998.

However, in spite of this sheer calculated madness, if one can call this practice of forcible transformation as represented by capitalistic industrial agriculture and the cruelty of the whole system upsetting the peasant agriculture, the latter is still continuing to be the backbone of global food production system, feeding over a third of the global population and is not at the root of food crisis. On the contrary, the responsibility lies with corporate agriculture as, according to reports,

> "...research shows that small farms are much more productive than large farms if total output is considered rather than yield from a single crop. Small integrated farming systems that produce grains, fruits, vegetables, fodder and animal products out-produce yield per unit of single crops such as corn (monoculture) on large-scale farms..... Industrial agriculture has created the absurd situation whereby between production, processing, distribution and preparation, ten calories of energy are required to create just one calorie of food energy. Conversely, it is the ability to combine productivity and ecological sustainability that constitutes a key dimension of superiority of peasant or small-scale agriculture over industrial agriculture."[11]

Factors like ecological destabilisation associated with capitalist industrial agriculture makes its case quite inferior to peasant agriculture since,

> "...the average food item journeys some 1,300 miles before becoming a part of a meal. Fruits and vegetables are refrigerated, waxed, coloured, irradiated, fumigated, packaged and shipped. None of these processes enhances food quality but merely enables distribution over great distances and helps increase shelf life."[12]

In this context, one, however, may refer to the emergence of urban agriculture taking a strong foothold in agricultural economy, ensuring food security in an appreciable measure, initiating a new movement termed as 'repeasantisation'.

The beginning of neo-liberal economic reforms in 1991 have given rise to a deep agricultural depression in India, associated with a sharp decline in per capita grain output and grain consumption, consequently increasing unemployment.

Food Sovereignty and the Right of Peasants as the Major Food Suppliers

As a backlash of the growing industrial control on the process of food production worldwide, a protest movement started in the name of 'Food Sovereignty', which is defined as the

> "right of nations and peoples to control their own systems, including their own markets, production modes, food cultures and environments has emerged as a critical alternative to the dominant neo-liberal model for agriculture and trade."[13]

The idea emerging as a guiding principle, food sovereignty was discussed as the major theme at the International Conference of La Via Campesina held on April 18-21, 1996, in Tlaxcala, Mexico, where it was agreed that the concept of food security is directly 'linked to democracy and justice', demanding putting the control of productive resources such as land, water, seeds and natural resources, in the hands of those who produce food. La Via Campesina was a trans-national agrarian movement started in 1993 constituted by small-scale farmers, farm workers and indigenous communities as an alternative to neo-liberal capitalist forum, now representing 184 organisations from 69 countries, voicing radical opposition to globalisation of an industrial and neo-liberal model of agriculture. Food sovereignty, as its major issue, La Via Campesina advocates it as the standard model for food production and rural development. The abject failure of the policy of neo-liberal globalisation in reducing poverty and eradicating hunger is demonstrated by the fact that the number of hungry people has swelled to exceed one billion alongside the number of people without food having increased by 25 per cent since the mid-1990s prompted the movement of La Via Campesina to take over the control of food security against the powerful advocates of the industrial lobby, such as the World Bank, the International Monetary Fund (IMF), and the World Trade Organisation (WTO) enforcing neo-liberal domination. In consequence, the right of peoples controlling the food system prevailed in pursuance of this ideal and La Via Campesina later took the initiative to work in collaboration with the World Forum on Food Sovereignty held in Cuba (2001) and the NGO/CSO Forum on Food Sovereignty (2002) in Rome to further strengthen the issue of Food Sovereignty.

However, the major question is whether it is possible for Food Sovereignty to address the multiple problems affecting food and agriculture around the world ensuring—

> "sufficient and healthy food for everyone and provide livelihoods for peasant farmers while redressing decades of environmental degradation caused by industrial agriculture. ... (Undeniably) the theory and practice of food sovereignty has the potential to foster dramatic and widespread change in agricultural, political and social systems related to food by posing a radical challenge to the agro-industry model of food production. The transformation envisioned entails a changing relationship to food resulting from an integrated, democratized, localized food production model."[14]

The democratisation of food policy, as visualised in food sovereignty points out at another very important angle, such as it stops violence against women, who play a key role in food production and procurement, food preparation, family food security and food culture. Data in Table 2.1 for 2003-2005 showing the proportion of women in the agricultural labour force around the world makes it clear that women's direct participation in agricultural work exceeds half (51 per cent and over) in at least 26 out of a total of 133 countries for which data is

Table 2.1: Share of Women in Agricultural Labour Force in per cent of the Total (2003-2005)

Number of Countries	*As % of the Total*
28	0—25
77	26—50
26	51—75

Note: (a) Lowest 0% in Hongkong and Kuwait,
(b) Highest of 70.5% in West Bank and Gaza,
(c) Very High: Turkey (64.2%) and Jordon (69.1%), and
(d) In 20 of the Third group of countries the proportion does not exceed 59.8%.

Source: Compiled from: The World Bank, 2008: Agriculture for Development, Table on 'Agricultural and Rural Sector Variables: pp 320-321, in Table A1. World Development Report, 2008: Agriculture for Development, The World Bank.

available, reaching the highest of 70.5 per cent in West Bank and Gaza, and varies between 26 and 50 per cent of the labour force in 77 countries. It is quite important to note that the principle of food sovereignty has already reached the official international stage and is acknowledged as "the path to ensure people's human right to food and food security". As mentioned by Wittman *et al.* (2010),

> "food sovereignty acts as a counterforce to economic pressures from corporate agribusinesses which is undermining a healthy food system and diverting food into other uses such as production of agrofuels continues further commodification, capitalization and corporatization of agricultural production."[15]

Right to food is the most basic of all human claims emphasizing freedom from hunger which came to be challenged economically as well as politically since the World Food Conference in 1974 hosted by the FAO, attended by the representatives of 135 countries, when right to food, freedom from hunger and food security for all made the primary issue. The conference was held in response to the world food crisis beginning in 1972, resulting from a poor harvest in several parts of the world. Food security stood for ensuring a steady supply of food emphasizing national-level supplies. Sen (1981) pointed out that "the national-level availability of food does not necessarily mean house-level food access." In this regard Sen (1981), in one of his most authoritative works, entitled 'Poverty and Famines' considers ownership or entitlement to food is "one of the most primitive rights" which, however, is denied in many cases caused by artificial scarcity, often in the form of high prices when available food is diverted forcibly to other uses as it happens on occasion, creating a situation of famine such as the Great Bengal Famine in 1943 when access to food was severely curtailed for common people, leading to the death of "about 1.5 million people".[16]

The dramatic increase of food prices (corn, wheat, rice, soy beans) in 2007 and 2008, though climbing down in the second half of 2008 yet remaining at about double of those in the early 2000s, did not benefit the farmers but, instead, it became highly beneficial to the middlemen and more so to the global corporations. In consequence, it brought the two agricultural systems—that of the small-farmers against those of industrial monocultures—into direct clash. Significantly, the latter does not produce food for the local consumers (whether it is India, Brazil, Thailand, Spain or in the US) since its principle objective is to export, or the produce is converted into ethanol or biodiesel to 'feed cars instead of human beings'. At the same time, the agribusiness technology uses,

> "heavy machinery, mega-irrigation, insecticides, herbicides, fungicides and chemical fertilizers. The monoculture technology actually produces far less per hectare than does diversified small farm agriculture and, in the process, destroys the productive capacity of the

> land: soils are eroded, compacted, sterilized and increasingly infertile and pests become resistant to ever-increasing doses of insecticides. This kind of agriculture is heavily dependant on petroleum.... Thus we urgently need the kind of ecologically sound farming practices that are far more compatible with small farm agriculture."[17]

Alternative to this ecologically destructive process of agribusiness is provided by the small farmers and peasants' agriculture producing food for local consumers, farming on land almost double in proportion to that used for agribusiness in their hands with overwhelming interest in providing food unless they are driven away by agribusiness and industrial monoculture. Hence, family-farming catering to requirement of food as the major objective, giving a life of dignity to the producer, needs to be revitalised for which measures like land reforms need to be taken up with an objective of taking land away from export-agriculture conducted by 'elites' and transferred into the hands of small peasant-farmers. To make this revolutionary process really effective, there has been a global alliance of 'family-farmers, peasants, landless rural workers, indigenous people, rural youth, and rural women' into what is known as La Via Campesina, as mentioned above, which has proposed,

> "an alternative policy paradigm called food sovereignty... a concept of economic and social human rights, which includes right to food, but it goes further, arguing that there is a corollary right to land and a right to produce for rural peoples. Food sovereignty argues that feeding a nation's people is an issue of national security—of sovereignty... If the population of a country must depend for their next meal on the vagaries and price swings of the global economy, on the goodwill of a super power not to use food as a weapon, or on the unpredictability and high cost of long-distance shipping, then the country is not secure, neither in the sense of national security nor in the sense of food security. Food sovereignty thus goes beyond the concept of food security, which says nothing about where food comes

> from or how it is produced. To achieve genuine food sovereignty, people in rural areas must has access to productive land and receive prices for their crops that allow them to make a decent living, while feeding their nation's people."[18]

Redistributive land reforms take an important role in sustaining development based on poverty reduction, economic development, food production and environmental protection. Arguably, land reform is not only good for economic development but it also becomes an effective tool in stemming the flow of rural people into already over-burdened urban areas and can effectively address the problem of rural underemployment, absorbing people in gainful activities based on utilising rural products, as used to happen in rural India prior to colonial rule which went into extremes of cruelty to shut down the family-based plants famed for ages for their inimitable products in textiles, metals as well as food items including invaluable spices enjoying high demand in the world market.

Record numbers, exceeding a billion people worldwide, suffered from the pangs of hunger in 2008 as a direct consequence of wrong-doings of the capitalist industrial agriculture, leading to food wars, mentioned earlier, when global food prices, as reported by The World Bank, rose by 83 per cent over the period of three years—2006 to 2008, increasing 45 per cent in just nine months, as FAO reports. Interestingly, according to the same source, there had been record grain harvests in 2007 and there was excess food in the world to feed everyone in 2008, 'at least 1,5 times of the demand'. As a matter of fact, food production rose steadily at over 2 per cent a year over the last twenty years against the rate of population growth having declined to 1.4 per cent per year and, as such, population was not outstripping food supply. But, according to Holt-Giménez (2010),

> "over 90 per cent of the world's hungry are simply too poor to buy enough food. High food prices are a problem because nearly 3 billion people—half of the world's population—are poor and near-poor. Around half of the people in the developing world earn less than

> two dollars a day. Nearly 20 per cent are extremely poor, earning less than one dollar a day. Many of those officially classified as poor are subsistence farmers who have limited access to land and water and cannot compete in global markets. In addition, the diversion of large quantities of grains and oil crops for the growing industrial feed lots in the emerging economies, as well as the diversion of land and water for green agrofuels, has put significant pressure on markets for many basic foods."[19]

It is not, therefore, surprising that the major agrifood monopolies derived huge profits out of the chaotic situation when the earnings increased by 42 per cent for corporate houses, like Archer Daniels Midland, 45 per cent for Monsanto, 86 per cent for Cargill's, while it was 1,200 per cent for Mosaic Fertilizer in the last quarter of 2007, when the global food crisis was at its highest.

Bulldozing the rights of the small peasant farmers all the world over, capitalist agricultural expansion went on from which even the small farmers in the Global north were not spared. The overall control of the big industrial farms has come to a frightening level when the top three seed companies—Monsanto, Dupont and Syngenta—together have 39 per cent of the global commercial seed market, placing them into the hands of unwilling producers, including the small peasant farmers. However, it is quite heartening to note that despite the interests of the peasant, small landholder farmers having been bulldozed, the absolute number of them in the Global South has remained unbelievably stable over the last forty years, providing significant amount of food, as high as 90 per cent of all food produced in Africa.

All this led first to 'de-peasantisation' followed by 're-peasantisation' in the process of re-establishing the most dependable role of the peasant agriculture in solving the prevailing food crisis. The responsibility in this regard was taken up by the international federation, La Via Campesina (The Peasant Way) defining first, in 1996, that food sovereignty wants to re-democratise and transform our food systems into the hands of the people's forum rather than corporate monopolies, taking decisions on the overall responsibility of production, processing, distribution, marketing, as well as consumption. In this context, it is quite relevant to mention that for decades, pressure of the capitalist agriculture has stubbornly been resisted by peasant agriculture, saving the native seeds from destruction and replaced by GM seeds. The peasant farmers have worked hard to diversify their crops, 'protect their soil, conserve water and establish markets'. The

> "small holders working with movements like Campesino a Campesino (Farmer to Farmer) of Latin America, and NGO networks for farmer-led sustainable agriculture like Participatory Land Use Management (PELUM) of Africa, and the Farmer Field Schools of Asia have restored exhausted soils, raised yields, and preserved the environment using highly effective agroecological management practices on hundreds and thousands of acres of land. These practices have given them important measures of autonomy in relation to the industrial agri-food system and have increased their environmental and economic resilience, buffering them from climate-induced hazards and market volatility."[20]

The emergence of the international peasant movement, La Via Campesina, made up almost entirely by marginalised groups consisting of landless workers, small farmers, share croppers, pastoralists, fisherfolk and the peri-urban reaffirmed the call for food sovereignty, confirming the rights of the people to control their own food system, as explained elsewhere in this chapter, demand a perpetual end of land grabs by industrial agriculture for agrofuel and foreign food production consisting of value-added crops, giving stress on the findings of UN's International Assessment of Agricultural Knowledge, Science and Technology for Development (IAASTD), sponsored by five UN agencies and The World Bank. Over four hundred scientists and development experts from eighty countries participated in this seminal assessment process asserting on the,

> "adoption of locally appropriate and democratically controlled agroecological methods of production relying

on local expertise, local germ plasm, and farmer-managed local seed systems."[21]

The importance of local farmers may really be appreciated from the fact that people engaged as full-time workers in agricultural work as a profession exceeds 50 per cent of the total workers in at least 8 countries of the world (Table 2.2) and exceeding 25 per cent, varies between 26 and 50 per cent in another 19 countries, but data are not available for 48 out of 133 countries. The highest participation takes place in Madagascar (78 per cent), while it is 69.1 per cent in Uganda, 59.9 per cent in Vietnam, 52.7 per cent in Kyrgyz Republic, 44.6 per cent in Indonesia, 44.4 per cent in Thailand etc., which bring out the role of agriculture in these countries.

Table 2.2: Agricultural Workers as per cent of the Total (2002-2004)

Number of Countries	*As % of the Total*
58	Below 25
19	26-50
8	51-75

Note: Data not available for 48 countries out of a total of 133 countries

(a) Highest: 78% in Madagascar

(b) (i) Uganda: 69.1%

(ii) Vietnam: 59.9%

(iii) Kyrgyz Republic: 52.7%

(iv) Indonesia: 44.6%

(v) Thailand: 44.4%

(vi) Kazakhstan: 34.8%

Source: Table A1: Agricultural and Rural Sector Variables, in World Development Report, 2008: Agriculture for Development, The World Bank.

Campesino a Campesino, or a Farmer to Farmer, approach has resulted in dramatic success in agricultural practices in many of the developing countries. In Guatemala, for instance, the combination of organic matter to soils including green manures, crop diversification, integrated pest management, biological weed control, reforestation and agrodiversity management along with soil and water conservation techniques gave exceptionally higher yield ranging between 100-400 per cent. Cuba exemplifies another success story, where the agroecological practices of the small-holder transformed much of its agriculture from 'high external input, large-scale systems' to 'smaller, low-input organic systems' developed into over 100,000 small-holder ownership and thus overcame food crisis. The system of Rice Intensification (SRI) developed in Madagascar has hugely benefited about a million farmers over two dozen other countries in raising yield to as high as eight metric tons per hectare. Similar results of improved cereal yields by 50 to 100 per cent have been achieved with agroecological apparatus, improving food production and ensuring household food security in seventeen African countries.[22]

Undoubtedly, food sovereignty making a cause for the small farmers worldwide, particularly in the Global South, makes a very strong case resisting the growing push of industrial monopolistic agriculture giving greater importance to export crops, including transgenic crops, encouraging rapid expansion of biofuel crops like maize, sugar cane, soybean, oil palm, eucalyptus etc., increasingly re-shaping world agriculture and food crisis in the face of climate change with deteriorating effects on cropping systems. In combating the situation of emerging food crises another Green Revolution is no-solution as previous experience of environmental damage accompanied by dramatic loss of biodiversity and traditional knowledge including local seeds will lead to a greater disaster.

In this context, we may again turn to the basic issue of food sovereignty as a basis of success in saving biodiversity, largely represented by uncultivated plants available all around the cultivated areas, which turn into food with available technology of cooking in the rural households. The meaning of agriculture, in fact, takes an altogether different character as considered in the background of both Bangladesh and the dry Deccan Plateau in India, two cases of climatic contrasts. Such as,

> "On both the flood plains of Bangladesh and the dry lands of the Deccan Plateau in India, village women cannot imagine the preparation of food for their family members or the raising of livestock without the leafy greens, grasses, roots and tubers, leaves of trees, fruits,

> small fish, molluscs and other items collected from the borders between fields, along roadsides, in small patches of forest or fallow lands, in ponds and other water bodies as well as in the cultivated fields and homesteads ... The very act of collecting uncultivated biodiversity and using it to prepare food or feed livestock brings women into a distinct relationship with cultivated and uncultivated spaces and the gifts of nature... providing a new territory where food, ecology and culture converge."[23]

As such, food sovereignty as a concept focuses on the development of 'ecological production systems that are localised rather globalised'. According to the authors, *'Food Sovereignty and Uncultivated Biodiversity in South Asia: Essays on the Poverty of Food and the Wealth of the Social Landscape (2007)**, the proposals of 'Nayashakti Movement'in Bangladesh and the Dalit Sanghams of the Deccan, express serious doubts about the strategy of organic agriculture as a part of food sovereignty concept, since it may give rise to another form of commercial monoculture. In contrast, food sovereignty should insist on relying on local determinants of food production utilising seeds, soil amendments and agricultural implements generated locally, ensuring the capacity of the communities to go into production systems independently. They want women in the community to become the caretakers of local seeds, ensuring free flow of genetic resources 'within and between farming communities' with resistance against seeds pushed by corporates. As such,

> "producing food ecologically and creating the conditions for the conservation of the gifts of nature is a way of relating to people, the external environment and other life forms that is ethical and peaceful by intent and design ... In this context, food is not perceived strictly as

* Farhand Mazhar, Daniel Buckles, P.V. Sathees and Farida Akhtar, *Food Sovereignty and Unchallenged Biodiversity in South Asia: Essays on the Poverty of Food and the Wealth of the Social Landscape.* (International Development Research Centre, Academia Foundation, 2007).

> a physical entity independent of the social relations that define where and how it is produced, distributed and consumed. Rather, food is a joy of life, produced and eaten not only to satisfy hunger but also to savor and share with others in the community."[24]

The opinion expressed here points out at a very important issue, such as how much land and water are required to sustain the food production system using the prevailing technology or, in other words, the ecological footprint which, as estimated, amounts to be 9.57 hectares per person, the highest in the US and 0.5 per person, the smallest in the world, for Bangladesh.

However defined, there is no escaping the fact that the small-holder farmer has a built-in resilience for adapting to changing climate, pests and diseases. The traditional management of farms with their 'raised fields, terraces, polycultures (growing a number of crops in the same field), and agroforestry systems represent a successful indigenous agricultural strategy etc. promoting biodiversity, sustained yields round the year without the use of agrochemicals and thus representing an ecological, biodiverse, local as well as 'socially' just very much traditional agricultural system feeding the world for centuries. People today across the world are fortunate to have thousands of such small traditional farms in the Global South forming the basis of food sovereignty, emphasising small farmers' access to land, water and native seeds handed down through generations with in-built resistance to local pests and diseases, enjoying local autonomy, local markets, local production-consumption patterns, energy as well as technological sovereignty utilising farmer-to-farmer networks.[25]

Evidently, the role of small farmers as key actors for regional food security is brought out by the fact that in the late 1980s there were about 16 million small farming units, occupying nearly 60.5 million hectares, or 75 million or about two-thirds of its total rural population. The average size of these small farm units is about 1.8 hectares and together they provided 41 per cent of agricultural output for domestic consumption. For example, Brazil alone has 4.8 million small family-farmers, or 85 per cent of the total number of farmers occupy 30 per cent of the total agricultural land of the country, controlling about 33 per cent of the country's land sown to maize, 61 per cent under beans and 64 per cent under cassava, producing 84 per cent of the total cassava and 67 per cent of all beans for the country. Over 50 per cent of the land under food crops, such as maize, beans, barley and okra in Ecuador is produced by small farmers and, in Mexico, the small farmers occupy 'at least 70 per cent' of the land growing maize and 60 per cent for beans, practising intercropping while polyculture is a common practice among small traditional farmers in Latin America for much of its staple crops.[26] Small farmers hold an equally important place in the agricultural economy of Africa, 33 million of such farms representing 80 per cent of all farms in the continent. Women form a significant proportion of African farmers and two-thirds of these farms are below two hectares in size, based mainly on the use of local resources and produce majority of the grains, besides almost all root, tuber, plantation and the majority of legume crops. However, despite increase in imports of food in recent years, small farmers still produce most of Africa's food. Similarly, Asia presents another very strong case of the role played by small farmers, where China alone accounts for almost half of the world's small farms, using 193 million hectares of agricultural land and has nearly 75 million rice farmers still following the age-old (over 1000 years) agricultural methods. India comes next to China, with 23 per cent of the world's small farms, followed by Indonesia, Bangladesh and Vietnam in successive order of importance, representing majority of the 200 million rice farmers in Asia, few of them having more than two hectares of land in possession.[27]

Further, contrary to general assumption, small farms are much more productive than large farms in consideration of total output, such as maize yields amounting to 3.5-6.3 tons obtained from per hectare of land under traditional agriculture in Mexico and Guatemala (compared to not exceeding 4 tons per hectare in the US), sufficient to meet the annual requirements of food for a typical family of 5-7 people. Incidentally, as practised for different crops under traditional agriculture, give a higher return of crops unlike single crop, and intensive use of fewer resources gives a larger profit to the small farmers, thus building up strong economies, allowing people in South to stay with their families, in the countryside, thereby reducing city-ward flow of rural migrants.

The key factor of traditional agriculture practised by smallholders is its diversified farming system, is its stability and less vulnerability to catastrophic loss, such as drought, since crops grown in diversifying combination in polycultural systems exhibit greater yield stability under a stressful situation. This was demonstrated by a study of 360 communities spread over Nicaragua, Honduras, and Guatemala, hit by Hurricane Mitch, which showed that crops under traditional agriculture experienced much less damage than conventionally produced crops, strongly indicating farmers' resilience and capability. The most remarkable aspect of traditional agriculture is sustaining of its underlying potentials, such as,

> "raising cereal yields from 50 to 200 per cent, increasing stability of production through diversification, improving diets and income, and contributing to national food security, exports and conservation of natural resource base and biodiversity."[28]

This was further substantiated by a study sponsored by the UN, known as AKST (The International Assessment of Agricultural Knowledge, Science and Technology) recommending greater stress and strengthening of traditional agriculture which will further prove to be highly contributory to adapt to environmental stresses while maintaining and increasing productivity and at the same time improving soil quality, protect biodiversity based on better management of water nutrient, pests, and climate change.

However, significant structural changes are the urgent requirements for stabilising the process of this ecological change in agriculture, which largely depends on social movements for creating political will among decision-makers. According to La Via Campesina, in order to protect the livelihoods, jobs, people's food security and health, as well as environment, food production has to remain in the hands of small-scale sustainable farmers and should not be left under the control of large agribusiness companies or supermarket chains. The most essential approach should take into account that industrial agriculture, model of large farms, increase poverty, low wages, rural-urban migration, hunger and environmental degradation.

On the contrary, the concept of food sovereignty needs to be taken as alternative to neo-liberal approach, putting faith on an inequitable international trade to solve the world's food problem focusing on local autonomy, local markets, local production-consumption cycles, energy and technological sovereignty and farmer-to-farmer networks. Altieri (2010) convincingly reiterates his firm conviction about the viability of traditional agriculture keeping trust on the policy-makers stressing on the point that,

> "moving towards more socially just, economically viable and environmentally sound agriculture will be the result of the co-ordinated action of emerging social movements in the rural sector in alliance with civil society organizations that are committed to supporting the goals of these farmers' movements. As a result of constant political pressure from organised farmers and others, politicians will, it is hoped, become more responsive to developing policies that will enhance food sovereignty, preserve the natural resource base, and ensure social equity and economic agricultural viability."[29]

Turning again to food sovereignty as a movement, it emerges as a strategic challenge to the 'hegemonic neoliberal concept of food security', bringing change against the neoliberal system of 'dumping' of food 'artificially cheapened' through huge subsidies to the producers of the North, into the markets of the South, besides encouraging exports of value-added food fulfilling the tastes of the Northern markets and thus dismantling the farm sector in the Global South as a repetition of the colonial time, when farming practices were dictated under pressure suiting North's demands.

In this perspective, the basic concept needs to be reiterated that "agricultural land first and foremost, is for producing food, food for people"[30] and these simple words have a background of an intense struggle to establish the rights of people to the ownership of land, the small farmer, who tilled in a situation when much of the land remained concentrated in the hands of large landowners lying idle or under-used. In this respect, Venezuela is one of the most successful countries in the world in transferring almost 2.7 million hectares of such idle lands

(*Latifundios*) into the hands of small farmers, with a wide range of support in credit, technical assistance to social services and access to market (for example, agricultural credit increased significantly from about $ 164 million in 1999 to about $ 7.6 billion in 2008), making an overall increase of 24 per cent in food production since 1968, making it self-sufficient in its requirement of the two most important grains—corn and rice—production of them having increased 132 per cent and 71 per cent respectively since 1968, besides approaching self-sufficiency in some of the other staple food, including beef, chicken and eggs. Further, small-scale agriculture nurtured with government support has brought the country—Venezuela—to a position to export pork and corn in near future, particularly supporting other neighbouring countries lacking adequate food to feed their people. All the achievements are sufficient indications and a strong reminder of the process of transition from 'food dependence to food sovereignty', made possible from a transformation of capitalistic, industrial agriculture into small-farmer agriculture.[31] In addition to the peasant and family farm sector, there are about 50 million individuals belonging to some seven hundred different indigenous groups who live and utilize the humid tropical regions of the world. About two million of these live in the Amazon and Southern Mexico.

Altieri (2010) believes that, according to the primary theme of La Via Campesina, food production has to remain in the hands of peasant farmers as a safeguard to 'protect livelihoods, jobs, people's food security and health as well as the environment', without leaving the small-scale sustainable peasant farmers to the control of agribusiness companies and supermarket chains. For making it feasible, genuine agrarian reforms need to be implemented giving the farmers rightful access and control over land, water, agro-biodiversity etc. which are of vital importance for communities for meeting growing food demands.

In this regard a correct approach for making agriculture sustainable is advocated to avoid application of chemical pesticides, since they destroy non-target organisms in the soil such as beneficial insects, natural predators, and create environmental pollution, besides developing insect resistance and contamination of ground water through prolonged use. In contrast, the use of beneficial soil microorganisms, such as 'Plant Growth Promotion Rhizo Bacteria' (PGPR), as biofertilizers have proved as efficient soil microbes of sustainable agriculture, enhancing plant growth and yield, holding great promise for improvement of yield as well as quality of crops.

> "In order to alleviate poverty and make certain that we are able to continue with feeding an ever-increasing population, we need a socio-economic biotechnology (taking into consideration following facts) invoking a new biotechnology revolution.... Such a new biotechnology revolution has to take into consideration:
>
> 1. that farming in developing countries is profoundly different from developed countries, with crops like cassava, rice, soybean, sago etc.
> 2. that farms are small and should stay small, with minimum mechanisation but more intensive and integrated farming.
> 3. that single crop production must make way to a multi-product farming, including livestock on the farm.
> 4. that we use existing biotechnological techniques to develop biotechnological industries using biomass such as sago palm and cassava
> 5. combine the biomass waste, excessive amounts of agroindustrial wastes with human and animal waste treatments for novel products and renewable energy production....
>
> "It is very surprising, for example, that agricultural biotechnology development so far has totally ignored plants such as cassava and the sago palm as a starch resource, as they are hardly known in developed countries. Cassava can yield up to 65t/ha with a 65 per cent starch content in marginal soils and the sago palm can easily produce 25t of starch/ha in swampy areas unsuitable for any other crop. Both crops are ideal for obtaining a variety of by-products ranging from biofuel, bioplastics, biodetergents, biolubricants to bio-pharmaceuticals. The establishment of biorefineries will diversify rural farming, keep people employed in the

> rural areas and will also increase the income of the individual farmer, helping in the alleviation of poverty."[32]

For making this conception effective, food sovereignty in theory and practice is the only alternative, stressing on the rejection of imposition **agriculture without farmers**, thereby trying to rebuild a diversified agricultural system replacing capitalistic industrial agriculture in an attempt to arrest environmental degradation and provide healthy food to people and doing away with the triple crisis created by energy, intensive industrial agriculture, such as,

> "displacing local food production for almost 50 per cent of humanity, deepening fossil-fuel dependency in an age of peak oil, and generating roughly a quarter of greenhouse gas emission."[33] (See Note A)

Undoubtedly, the importance of food sovereignty with its methods of sustainable food production has the capability of addressing the 'food, energy and climate crises simultaneously' and act directly taking up the challenges of three major constraints affecting a successful programme for agriculture, such as food insecurities, fossil-fuel dependence and global warming. As Michael (2010) observes, food sovereignty has emerged as a very dependable solution to the 'contradictions of an agro-industrialization movement with its aggressive policies involving food distribution, inequality, monoculture, population redundancy, environmental degradation and fossil fuel dependence. In the backdrop of a monopolistic, people-unfriendly drive of the capitalistic agriculture, food sovereignty recognising people's right to food at an affordable price and available locally makes it a democratic approach involving the policy of sustaining the life of common people with their entitlement to the basic need of food adequate for maintaining health, with emphasis on sustainable use of natural resources without jeopardizing the requirements of future generations. In combination of small-scale farmers, pastoralists, fisherfolk, indigenous peoples food sovereignty represents a congregation of people tuned to an idea of a food system based on democratic principles making a sustainable agroecological approach to the development of the production system completely free of the coercive policy of corporate agriculture, which displaces "people, knowledge and culture and induce hunger and malnutrition in the name of an abstraction (the market)"[34], that is making the productive system primarily an export-oriented process.

Interestingly, among many challenges to be encountered is climate change and as a protective measure the agrochemical and biotechnology firms, namely BASF, Monsanto, Bayer, Syngenta and Dupont have already patented over 500 varieties of climate-resistant genes, already controlling 57 per cent of the global seed market which, if adopted, will have a disastrous effect on farmers' sovereignty by replacing the local seeds, with their built-in resistance to climate change. Use of locally available seeds generated through agricultural practices of generations, having gone through all climatic situations, are admirably suitable with their ecological, economic, social and cultural relevance greatly favoured by local farmers.

As a matter of fact,

> "the continuous exchange of seeds for local crop varieties circulates genetic resources from one field to another within a village territory and beyond. The dynamic management of local resources enhances the stability of traditional agrosystems, increases the adaptation potential of local crops to evolving environmental conditions and limits the risks of genetic erosion. Seed transactions also help ensure that land is not left fallow for lack of seeds, thus avoiding soil erosion and increasing the soil's organic matter content and water retention capacity."[35]

Thus, the defining idea of food sovereignty is a concept of food taken as a basic human right to be realized in a system where food sovereignty is guaranteed and should be treated as the,

> "right of each nation to maintain and develop its own capacity to produce its basic foods respecting cultural

> and productive diversity. We have the right to produce our own food in our own territory. Food sovereignty is a precondition to genuine food security."[36]

In order to achieve it, the rural economies have to be created in all countries based on the guiding principle of food sovereignty in which women play a central role having an inherent right to resources for 'food production, land, credit, capital, technology, education and social services', keeping the idea in mind that long-term food security depends on those who produce food and care for the environment. Finally, considered as a basic human right, it should provide every human being access to safe and nutritious food in sufficient quantity for maintaining a healthy life with full human dignity and every country should accept food as a constitutional right. For making this right mandatory, each country should make genuine agrarian reforms giving landless and farming people, particularly women, ownership of land with full legal control over it free of any discrimination, with access to all facilities helping unfettered development of the entire productive system with an ultimate goal to reach all the people.

NOTES

Note A

The Food Sovereignty movement's Terra Preta Declaration at the FAO World Food Summit in Rome, June 2008, stated:

"The serious and urgent food and climate crises are being used by political and economic elites as opportunities to entrench corporate control of world agriculture and the ecological commons. At a time when chronic hunger, dispossession of food providers and workers, commodity and land speculation, and global warming are on the rise, governments, multilateral agencies and financial institutions are offering proposals that will only deepen these crises through more dangerous versions of policies that originally triggered the current situation ... Small-scale food producers are feeding the planet, and we demand respect and support to continue. Only food sovereignty can offer long-term, sustainable, equitable and just solutions to the urgent food and climate crisis."

Source, Michael, Philip, "Food Sovereignty in Movement: Addressing the Triple Crisis" in *Food Sovereignty: Reconnecting Food, Nature and Community,* Edited by Hannah Wittman, Annette Aurelie Desmarais and Nettie Wiebe. 2010. Pambazuka Press, Books for Change. International Publication House. p. 170.

REFERENCES

1. Krebs, John (2013). *Food: A Very Short Introduction,* Oxford University Press, p. 89.
2. Magdoff, Fred and Brian Tokar (Eds.) (2010). *Agriculture and Food in Crisis: Conflict Resistance and Renewals,* Monthly Review Press, New York. pp. 15-16.
3. Michael, Philip (2010). The World Food Crisis in Historical Perspective, in Fred Magdoff and Brian Tokar (Eds.) *Agriculture and Food in Crisis: Conflict Resistance and Renewals,* Monthly Review Press, New York. pp. 51-52.
4. *Ibid.,* p. 53.
5. *Ibid.,* p. 55.
6. Bhattacharya, Bimalendu (2014). *Geography of Deprivation: An Unfair World,* Concept Publishing Pub. Ltd. New Delhi. p. 23.
7. *Ibid.,* p. 25.
8. Michael, Philip (2010). "The World Food Crisis in Historical Perspective," in Fred Magdoff and Brian Tokar (Eds.) *Agriculture and Food in Crisis: Conflict Resistance and Renewals,* Monthly Review Press, New York. p. 61.
9. Bello, Walden and Mara Baviera (2010). "Food Wars," in *Agriculture and Food in Crisis: Conflict Resistance and Renewals,* Monthly Review Press, New York. p. 33.
10. *Ibid.,* p. 42.
11. *Ibid.,* p. 47.
12. *Op. cit.*
13. Wittman, Hannah, Annette Desmarais & Nettie Weibe (2010). The Origins and Potential of Food Sovereignty, in *Food Sovereignty: Reconnecting Food, Nature and Community.* Edited by Hannah Wittman, Annette A. Desmarais & Nettie Weibe, Pambazuka Press, Books for Change: International Publication House. p. 2.
14. *Ibid.,* p. 4.
15. *Ibid.,* p. 10.
16. Sen, Amartya (1981). *Poverty and Famines* (12th Impression), Oxford University Press, Oxford, UK. p. 52.

17. Rosset, Peter (2010). "Fixing Our Global Food System: Food Sovereignty and Redistributive Land Reforms", in *Agriculture and Food in Crisis: Conflict Resistance and Renewals,* Edited by Magdoff and Tokar, Monthly Review Press, New York. p. 190.
18. *Ibid.,* pp. 191-192.
19. Holt-Giménez, Eric (2010). "From Food Crisis to Food Sovereignty: The Challenge of Social Movements," in *Agriculture and Food in Crisis: Conflict Resistance and Renewals,* , Edited by Magdoff and Tokar, Monthly Review Press, New York. pp. 209-210.
20. *Ibid.,* pp. 212-219.
21. *Ibid.,* p. 215.
22. *Ibid.,* pp. 215-218.
23. Mazhar, Farhad, Daniel Buckles, P.V. Sathees and Farida Akhtar, (2007). "Food Sovereignty and Un-Challenged Biodiversity" in *South Asia: Essays on the Poverty of Food Policy and the Wealth of the Social Landscape,* International Development Research Centre, Academic Foundation. p. 2.
24. *Ibid.,* p. 65.
25. Altieri, Miguel A., Agroecology, Small Farms and Food Sovereignty, in *Agriculture and Food in Crisis: Conflict Resistance and Renewals,* Edited by Magdoff and Tokar, Monthly Review Press, New York. 2010. p. 255.
26. *Ibid.,* p. 257.
27. *Ibid.,* pp. 256-257.
28. *Ibid.,* p. 263.
29. *Ibid.,* p. 266.
30. Schiavoni, Christina and William Camacaro (2010). "The Venezuelan Effort to a New Food and Agriculture System", in *Agriculture and Food in Crisis: Conflict Resistance and Renewals,* Edited by Magdoff and Tokar, Monthly Review Press, New York. p. 272.
31. *Ibid.,* pp. 278-281.
32. Haggag, Wafaa M., Haballa Essam and Lashin, S., Microbial (2015), "Biotechnology: Role in Sustainable Agriculture and Environmental Management", in *Biotechnology, Agro-Ecology and Environment,* edited by Avnish Chauhan, Pawan Kuman Bharti and Anubhuti Sharma. Discovery Publishing House Pvt. Ltd. New Delhi. 2015. pp. 28-29.
33. Michael, Philip (2010). "Food Sovereignty in Movement: Addressing the Triple Crisis" in *Food Sovereignty: Reconnecting Food, Nature and Community,* Edited by Hannah Wittman, Annette Aurelie Desmarais and Nettie Wiebe. Pambazuka Press, Books for Change. International Publication House. pp. 170-171.
34. Michael, Philip (2010). "Food Sovereignty in Movement:

Addressing the Triple Crisis", in *Food Sovereignty: Reconnecting Food, Nature and Community*, Edited by Hannah Wittman, Annette Aurelie Desmarais and Nettie Wiebe. Pambazuka Press, Books for Change. International Publication House. p. 174.

35. *Ibid*. p. 177.
36. Wittman, Hannah, Annette Desmarais & Nettie Weibe (2010). "The Origins and Potential of Food Sovereignty", in *Food Sovereignty: Reconnecting Food, Nature and Community*. Edited by Hannah Wittman, Annette A. Desmarais & Nettie Weibe, Pambazuka Press, Books for Change: International Publication House. p. 197.

3

Is there Enough Food for Feeding the Growing Global Population?

Lester R. Brown, described by the *Washington Post* as one of the world's most influential thinkers, observed in 2012 that the

> "world is in transition from an era of food abundance to one of food scarcity, with global grain reserves having fallen by one-third over a decade resulting in a double escalation of food price (Brown, 2012). In his words, 'food is the new oil, and land is the new gold'."[1]

As reported by FAO (2008)* mentioned earlier in Chapter I of this book, the rising food prices, doubling between 2007 and 2008, pushed more people into foodless days, adding 75 million more in 2007 and bringing the total number to 923 million worldwide, which was likely to increase further and continuing well into 2008 made the situation worse.[2] According to this report the progress in reducing the share of hungry people in the developing world from about 20 per cent in 1990-92 to less than 16 per cent by 2003-05 has been thrown 'into reverse', bringing it down to 17 per cent by soaring prices (FAO, 2008). By mid-2008 real food prices were 64 per cent higher than their 2002 level, while one can find similar situation not earlier than early 1970s in response to first international oil crisis, as mentioned before. In this connection one needs to be cautioned that rise in the price of petroleum is just one

---

* FAO, *The State of Food Insecurity in the World 2008: Undernourishment Around the World: High Food Prices Another 75 Million Hungry* (Rome).

of the factors affecting food prices when among the others responsible for pushing prices up were the growing demands of food depending on consumption behaviour as caused by rising income level leading to greater demand for protein-rich food particularly involving meat and dairy products dependent on using cereals as feed. Moving up the food chain mainly in the countries of Asia along with production shortfalls connected with weather events, such as in 2005-2009, including droughts and floods, bringing down cereal production falling by 3.6 per cent in 2005 and 6.9 per cent in 2006. Over and above the rapid and steep rise in the price of petroleum, more than tripling between 2003 and 2008, tripling the prices of fertilizers and doubling the transport costs in 2006-2008, raised the cost of production of cereals, with highly detrimental effects, especially for those of the small-scale farmers. Added to this with greater harmful impact was the emergence of the biofuel industry making ever-growing demands on crops like maize, sugarcane, oilseeds, cassava and palm oil diverted into ethanol for feeding cars but not human beings. The most frightening prospect of such a situation is further revealed in the fact that biofuel production concentrated mostly in the US, using 32 per cent of the total production of grains, 127 m tons out of 400 m tons (Brown, 2012), as a measure for staving off the burden of rising petroleum prices, was going to utilize 100 million tones of cereals (4.7 per cent of global cereal production) in 2007-2008. (FAO, 2008).*

Reviewing the situation, it is not difficult to assume that the prospect of improvement is not very bright because of the unrelenting pressure on high-protein food including 3 billion people moving up the food chain consuming more and more meat, milk and eggs, making an ever-increasing demand for cereals as animal feed. Interestingly, among the emerging economies, China has taken the leading role with the greatest consumption of meat in the world, double of what is consumed in the US.

Factors responsible for making food situation very critical have been summed by Brown (2012)† in the following words:

---

* *Ibid.*

† Lester R. Brown, *Full Planet, Empty Plates: The New Geopolitics of Food Security*. (New York, London, W.W. Norton & Company, 2012).

> "Population growth (adding 219,000 everyday or almost 80 million every year), the rising consumption of livestock and poultry products, and the use of grain to fuel cars together raised the world growth in grain consumption from an average of 21 million tons per year from 1990 to 2005, to 45 million tons per year from 2005 to 2011. Almost overnight the annual consumption in grain doubled."[3]

In the backdrop of this situation the immediate question that arises is, if there is enough possibility of increasing grain production commensurate with drastic change in consumption behaviour which, in all possibility, is likely to keep its ever-increasing tendency in pursuance of conditions going to remain unaltered. As mentioned earlier, there is hardly any further scope for cereal expansion in the absence of good cultivable land in the world, and a look at Table 3.1 indicates the possibility of increasing grain production with extension of irrigation facilities. According to Brown (2012)*, instances of using irrigation as

Table 3.1: Factors Affecting the Future Supply of Cereals, around 1991

Region	*Potential Arable Land (m. hectares)*	*Cropland 1991 (m.ha)*	*% of Potential Arable land is cropped*	*% of Cropland that is irrigated*
Sub-Saharan Africa	815.7	142	17.4	2.9
Middle East	72.3	70.2	97.1	16.7
South East	230.2	227.6	98.9	33.2
Far East	235.9	185.2	77.9	38.1
Latin America	889.6	153.3	17.2	10.9
Europe/FSU	N.A.	366.9	–	10.1
North America/Oceania	N.A.	282.2	–	7.7
World	–	1441.6	–	16.8

Source: Tim Dyson, 1996.

a very important tool since the earliest civilizations of Euphrates-Tigris and Indus Valley has played a leading factor in the spectacular expansion during the second half of the twentieth century, having tripled between 1950 to 2000, from 200 m acres

* *Ibid.*

of irrigated land in the world to about 700 m acres , though followed by a much slower expansion in its coverage since the turn of the century, expanding only 9 per cent between 2000 and 2009. This drastic reduction is further linked to fast depletion of groundwater resources, the rate of use far from reciprocated by the rate of replenishment.

> "Roughly 40 per cent of the world grain harvest is grown on irrigated land. The rest is rain-fed. Among the big three grain producers—China, India and the United States—the role of irrigation varies widely. In China, four-fifths of the grain harvest comes from irrigated land. For India it is three-fifths and for the United States, only one-fourth. Asia, where rice is the staple food, totally dominates the world irrigated area."[4]

The next most important input consists of fertilizers and among them nitrogen fertilizers "were found to be crucial for improving crop production" (Kerbs, 2013). According to Kerbs (2013), this was discovered Sir John Bennet Laws, an English landowner and entrepreneur in 1843 that addition of nitrogen fertilizer increases crop yields.

> "The Canadian scientist Vaclav Smil has estimated that only half the world's population at the end of the 20th century could be fed were it not for the Huber Bosch process (that) combines nitrogen, 78 per cent of the Earth's atmosphere, with hydrogen (in making ammonia)."[5]

But genetic engineering may prove to be a very important tool holding a great promise for expansion in agricultural production by way of developing new strains of seeds resistant to pests and diseases tolerant to soil acidity or soil salts and can withstand wider range of climatic conditions.

Quite evidently, environmental constraints on increasing food production are of serious concern since

> "air pollutants such as near-surface ozone, sulphur dioxide and peroxyacetyl nitrate (PAN) can reduce productivity substantially because they are directly toxic

> to crops. For instance, it has been estimated that ozone in the lower atmosphere caused a 5-10 per cent loss of US crops during 1980s.... Depletion of the stratosphere ozone shield is another threat to future increases in food production. The thinning of the ozone layer allows increased amounts of dangerous ultraviolet-B (UV-B) radiation to reach the surface."[6]

However, rapid climate change poses to be a great threat to crop production than ozone depletion and any reduction in precipitation in the central parts of the northern continents, representing the world's principal breadbasket now, will be disastrous. Another effect of global warming is rise of sea level, resulting salinization of a coastal aquifers hitting hard on irrigation facilities apart from changing the ecosystems of the coastal wetlands and estuaries, which will damage oceanic fisheries.

Undeniably, environmental degradation in the form of deforestation, desertification, wetland destruction, toxic pollution of air, water and land along with emission of greenhouse gases into the atmosphere pushing us to biophysical limits are caused by man in the struggle for feeding the growing population (Ehrlich 1993).

As a way out of this complicated situation, when crop production cannot keep pace with population growth, it is felt necessary, first of all, to stop current losses amounting to be as high as 40 per cent of the global harvest through better storage and transport facilities besides saving crops from rodents, insects, fungi and other organisms. It is suggested further that conservation of soil and water should get topmost priority by way of avoiding destruction of ecosystems and efforts are to be made to restore productivity of degraded land. The method adopted in Australia to reclaim salinized land by replanting local vegetation which "lowers water tables and permits rain to flush salt below the root zone of the wheat"[7] seems to be very effective, along with the policy of restoration of agro-ecology and integrated pest management systems which needs to be taken up seriously. However, the responsibility of providing food for all cannot be accomplished as long as the hungry people do not have purchasing power in their abject poverty.

In a revaluation of agriculture it shows that it has the capability of lowering the rate of poverty in general since it happens to be the dominating sector of activity in regions where poverty prevails. However, it may be argued that as back as Adam Smith (1766-1834) it was considered that agricultural productivity was bound to slow down compared with development in manufacture due to impediments faced by the farmer. But the situation improved in recent times and the labour productivity has been found to be more important source of growth in agriculture than in non-agriculture as exemplified by three types of countries—agriculture-based countries, Transforming countries and urbanized countries (World Bank, 2008).

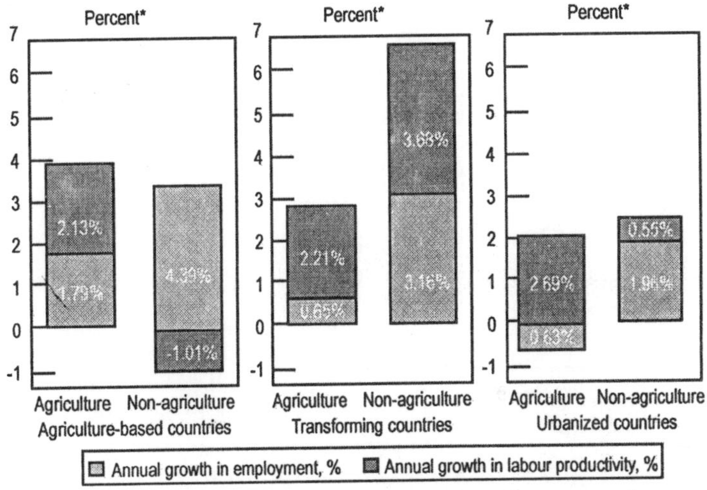

Fig. 3.1: Labour Productivity has been a More Important Source of Growth in Agriculture than in Non-Agriculture

Source: World Bank: World Employment Report 2008.

As such, agriculture no longer remains as a backward sector and, instead, can be a dynamic sector and developing countries have achieved much faster agricultural growth (2.6 per cent a year) than industrial countries (0.9 per cent a year) between 1980-2004. The World Bank (2008) has identified three complementary pathways out of poverty in which farming takes an important role, and other two pathways are represented by labour and migration. The decline in rural poverty in many countries, such as in Tanzania, is cited as the most successful in moving out of poverty where

> "farmers who diversified their farming activities by growing food crops for their own consumption and non-traditional cash crops (vegetables, fruits, vanilla) as well as raising livestock. People who remained in poverty were those who stuck to the more traditional farming."[8]

Similar cases of success in escaping poverty based on agricultural activities are provided by countries like Uganda with improving the productivity of land diversifying into commercial crops, like coffee production, and Niger showing instances of 'more sustainable cultivation practices' along with increasing income from agroforestry. Though rural poverty rates remain frustratingly high in South Asia (40 per cent in 2002) and Sub-Saharan Africa (51 per cent), many of the Asian countries have made impressive progress in infusing new trends in their agricultural activities as a link to reduction in rural poverty. Instances of this are provided by Vietnam, with 'land reform and trade and price liberalization', Bangladesh, with rising farm and rural non-farm earnings and lower rice prices resulting from new technologies (World Bank, 2008)[*] and

> "Ghana's growth and poverty reduction over the past 15 years is Africa's new and important success story ... In 2001-05 agriculture outperformed the service sector, growing at 5.7 per cent a year, faster than overall GDP at 5.2 per cent. Agricultural growth has been mainly due to area expansion, with yields increasing modestly at 1 per cent. Since 2001, a significant part of productivity gains has been in cocoa. Cocoa production, although accounting for only 10 per cent of total crop and livestock production values, contributed about 30 per cent of agricultural growth. Ghana has also enjoyed strong growth in horticulture (almost 9 per cent of total exports in 2006) driven mostly by pineapples."[9]

---

* The World Bank, World Development Report 2008: Agriculture and Development: p. 73.

However, in this respect, China holds the most illustrious record in poverty reduction achieved through agricultural reforms, bringing it down from 53 per cent in 1981 to 8 per cent in 2001. Steps like introduction of the household responsibility system in 1978, assigning rights of individual plots of land to the user, improvement in procurement prices by the government for the products of the farmers along with partial price liberalization acted as greater incentives for higher yields giving higher income to the farmer. Among other countries of the developing world having used agricultural development as an instrument for poverty alleviation, India and Indonesia are prominent where income from non-agricultural sector having an indirect effect on rural income played an important role for poverty reduction between 1970 and 2000. It is interesting to observe that migration has a double way of poverty alleviation—both for those who migrate and those left behind receiving money from abroad from migrated family members, which also is the case in El Salvador and Nepal. In some countries, nevertheless, rural poverty did not decline despite agricultural growth. They are Bolivia and Brazil, where the entire growth was concentrated in the hands of industrial agriculture giving greater thrust on export-oriented products controlled by the corporates (World Bank, 2008).*

Is Available Food Enough for Growing Global Population?

The World Bank Report 2008 makes a very cautious observation in this regard, saying that

> "The world is generally food secure, producing enough to meet the dietary needs of today's global population although future global food security should not be taken for granted because of uncertainties from growing resource scarcity and climate changes. Yet 850 million people remain undernourished ... The highest incidence of undernourishment is in Sub-Saharan Africa where

---

* The World Bank, *World Development Report 2008: Agriculture and Development:*

> one in every three persons suffers from chronic hunger. The greatest number of undernourished is in South Asia (299 million), closely followed by East Asia (225 million)."[10]

As a matter of fact, lack of access to food is a greater problem than availability of food. As Nobel Laureate Sen (1981) observed,

> "starvation is a matter of some people not having enough food to eat, and not a matter of there being not enough food to eat."[11]

Among the people affected by malnutrition,

> "about half of the hungry are small-holders; a fifth are landless; and a tenth are agropastoralists, fisherfolk and forest users; the remaining fifth in urban areas. Today, agriculture's ability to generate income for the poor, particularly women, is more important for food security than its ability to increase local food supplies. Women more than men, spend their income on food in households."[12]

Which was also the observation of Dr. Muhammad Yunus of Bangladesh, winning Nobel Prize for establishing the movement of Grameen Bank, providing small credits to women. It is necessary to mention that, apart from the role of horticultural products and livestock in improving diet quality, addition of

> "biofortification is enhancing staple crop varieties and improving diet quality with high levels of vitamins and minerals through crop breeding and biotechnology."[13]

All this leads to the most challenging question—if all the food produced in the world is sufficient to feed the growing world population. In this connection Sen, writing in 1981, is quite specific about the question.

> "As far as the present is concerned—rather than the future there is no real evidence of food supply falling behind population growth for the world as a whole,

> even though this has been observed for a number of countries. There is no outstripping of food growth by population expansion even when we look at the global picture leaving out the United States, which has been such a large supplier of food to other countries. The 'balance' in the future will depend on a variety of economic and political conditions, but there is as yet no indication that world population expansion has started gaining on the growth of world food supply."[14]

The most pertinent question, already answered some time back by Sen (1981), is more relevant today with increasing population which, according to the estimates of the UN World Urbanization Prospects; The 2014 Revision is likely to reach 9.5 billion by 2050, making an addition of 2.2 billion. We may ask if food production can keep pace with this growing population. So far the balance has been maintained, but at what cost? This has been maintained since the time of Thomas Malthus (1766-1834) at a tremendous cost involving natural capital critical to agriculture and, as pointed out by some authors it involves an annual loss of roughly 24 billion tons of top soil (Ehrlich *et al.*, 1993)*, trillion of gallons of ground water besides jeopardising the lives of innumerable other organisms involved in the services of ecosystems crucial to food production and, as such, of immense interest to humanity. Accordingly, the major impediment in keeping up with population growth does not depend directly on food production itself but, as mentioned before, the availability of food at the right time and at the right place, both making a necessary condition for food security. As experience shows, agricultural production growing faster for four decades prior to 1990s failed to feed people, particularly in developing countries, not because of availability but the poor could not buy the food, which means lack of purchasing power of these people came to be the major handicap in satisfying their hunger.

In evaluating the emerging situation in this regard one has to consider assessments made by different experts in the field from time to time. For example, summarising their opinion, it

---

* Paul R. Ehrlich, Anne H. Ehrlich and Gretchen C., Daily, Food Security, Population and Environment", *Population and Development Review* 19, No. 1, March, 1993.

may be said that continuing expansion of harvest in a 'finite' world is faced with following problems 'categorized' as major biophysical impediments. They include—

> "(1) losses of farmland to other uses because of population pressures and limits to the amount of suitable new land that can be brought into production; (2) diminishing opportunities to irrigate additional farmland, associated in part with limits to freshwater supplies; (3) erosion and degradation of soils; (4) biological limits to yield (production per hectare) increases, already seen in little-understood caps on yields in rice and possibly other crops (but not yet in corn or potatoes; (5) limits to or diminishing marginal returns from the application of fertliizers; (6) problems associated with chemical control of pests; (7) declining genetic diversity of crops themselves and of their wild relatives; (8) the possibility of depressed yields from increased ultraviolet B radiation; (9) reduced yields from a variety of air pollutants (including those causing acid precipitation) that are toxic to crops; (10) the substantial possibility of agricultural disruptions and reduced production due to rapid climate change and sea-level rise; and a general decline in the free services supplied to agriculture by natural eco-systems."[15]

At the same time, it has been observed by Ehrlich *et al.* (1993)* that about 17 per cent of the land surface of the earth used by 5.5 billion people (at that time) is utilized for crop production, and the remaining land used for non-agricultural purposes, or lying vacant, was marginal for any further agricultural expansion, as proved by the fact that the area under crop increased from 593 million hectares in 1950 to 720 million hectares in 1990—an increase of 21 per cent though the production has increased by 139 per cent resulting from an increase in average yield, being more than double per hectare—from 1 ton to 2.3 tons per year.

However, the declining soil quality has turned out to be a major handicap in realising its potential for better production. As a natural process, while soil is generated in centimetres per

---

* *Ibid.*

millennium its rate of erosion rises up to centimetres per decade and globally, as pointed out above, 24 billion tons of top soil is lost annually in excess of natural rate of soil regeneration, the remaining top soil getting lost 'at an average rate of 7 per cent per decade which slowly turns agricultural practices unsustainable (Ehrlich *et al.*, 1993).*

The loss of biodiversity is another highly sensitive issue making an irreplaceable part of the earth's resource capital providing support to human civilization with services essential to agriculture, such as,

> "maintenance of gaseous composition of the atmosphere; moderation of climate; control of hydrologic cycle; recycling of nutrients; control of the great majority of insects that might attack crops; pollination; and maintenance of a vast genetic library containing many millions of kinds of organisms from which humanity has withdrawn the crop and livestock species on which civilization was built and which potentially could (if preserved) provide benefits in the future. Indeed, that library holds the raw materials with which plant geneticists work. Yet biodiversity resources are being lost at an accelerating rate that may cause the disappearance by 2025 of one-quarter of all species now existing on Earth."[16]

Rhoades (1991),† speaking in a similar vein a little earlier (1991), was more specific to call it genetic loss and, as mentioned in Chapter I, estimated that by the middle of the 21st century, one-quarter of the world's 250,000 plant species will vanish, resulting from deforestation, shift to monoculture, overgrazing, water-control projects and urbanization, and warning us that, "the diversity of our genetic resources stand between us and starvation on a scale we cannot imagine."[17]

---

* Paul R. Ehrlich, Anne H. Ehrlich and Gretchen C. Daily, "Food Security, Population and Environment," *Population and Development Review* 19, No. 1, March 1993.

† Robert C. Rhoades, "The World's Food Supply at Risk," *National Geographic,* Washington, Vol. 179, No. 4, 1991.

Agricultural production and its expansion have a close relationship with two other inputs—fertilizers and irrigation. Their pivotal role is indicated by increase in the use of chemical fertilizers ten-fold between 1950 and 1990 giving, however, a three-fold increase in global grain production during the same period does not make a very strong justification in support of their use, already showing records of a diminishing return of their use in developed countries. Apart from the polluting effects of surface and groundwater, they have a capacity to damage forests and natural ecosystems by way of disrupting the nutrient cycles besides being sources of greenhouse gases. On the contrary, use of cow-dung and compost have proved to be a much better way of enhancing fertility of soils. Further, growing resistance of pests to pesticides is turning out as one of the major handicaps for food production, particularly when previously harmless pests are transformed into deadly ones 'through broadcast use of pesticides.'

As already pointed out, another 'Green Revolution' is no solution for increasing food production as it will lead to a greater disaster for its damaging role to biodiversity and loss of traditional resilient seeds.

Vaclav Smil, the noted Canadian scientist, gave a very straight answer to the question—if the Earth can feed its growing population almost in the same vein in 1993 as was done by Sen (1981). Reviewing the opinion of all the experts in the field, Smil sounded very positive in observing that—

> "current global food production is sufficient to provide adequate food for the world's population. Even if all the poor world's populations would raise their health status and activity level to those prevailing in rich countries the average 1990 global food energy consumption would have to increase by only 60 per cent, and it would still remain well below the available mean supply. This conclusion starkly confirms that the current pattern of malnutrition and hunger is unrelated to food availability but, instead, a function of global entitlements to food."[18]

In support of the statement made above, Smil mentions that in making any assessment of food one has to take into account the amount of grains, some 700 million tons, fed to the domestic animals along with post-harvest losses equivalent to about another 600 Kcal/day, and losses during distribution and retail amounting to about 800 Kcal/day, taken together bringing down the total amount of food available for direct human consumption. In this connection Smil (1994) gives us a comprehensive idea about the availability of food (Table 3.2). In this regard it seems to be very optimistic about the prospect of an expanded food supply from more efficient management of land, water and nutrients along with cutting down losses and wastage mentioned before. According to him, the developed countries with their population nearly stable have opportunity of producing more food without going into any major change

Table 3.2: Estimated Global per capita averages (Kcal/day) of food harvests, availabilities, losses, consumption, and requirements in 1990

	Global Average	*Sub-Totals*
Edible Crop Harvests	4600	
Cereals		3500
Tubers		300
Pulses		100
Vegetables, Fruits, Nuts		150
Oils		350
Sugar		200
Animal Feed	1700	
Grain		1300
Grain Milling Residues		300
Other Crops and Processing Residues		100
Apparent Postharvest Losses	600	
Food Availability		
FAO Total	**2700**	
Plant Foods		2300
Animal Foods		400
FAO's Food Balance Sheets plus 3 per cent	2800	
Apparent Distribution, Retail, Institutional and Household Losses	800	
Food Consumption	2000	
Food Requirements		
No Stunting	2050	
No Stunting and High Activity Levels	2200	

Source: Vaclav Smil (1994), [the data calculated and estimated by the author from data in FAO (1993)] and Bender *et al.* (1993).

while the poor countries have a better prospect, making proper use of available techniques and taking greater care in choosing the right time for planting, as exemplified by the fact that 'earlier or more timely planting of soybeans can increase yields up to 50 per cent.' Besides when to plant, it is also equally important to know 'how to plant' which matters a lot, such as,

> "optimum density of corn seeding raises yields by as much as 2.5t/ha, denser seeding improve wheat yields, and narrow rows can bring another ton of soybeans per hectare. Returning to crop rotations is another well-proven low-cost strategy in some regions. Rotations were the mainstay of all highly productive traditional agroecosystems. Their rapid decline, and even outright abandonment, during the past two generations should be seen as an aberration. Their environmental advantages have been well documented by long-term field experiments. They include, above all, reduced soil erosion and run-off, benefits of symbiotic nitrogen production by legumes, better soil tilth, and an interruption of weed, insect and crop disease cycles."[19]

Smil advises further inclusion of leguminous crops giving greater attention to the productivity of edible cultivars boosting protein supply, predicting an average increase in crop yields by 20 per cent during the period of next 50-60 years.... In his opinion, timing takes a very critical role in the application of fertilizers which should coincide with the periods of the highest nutrient need, minimizing field losses. Application of urea 'broadcast onto rice fields' while in dry land row cropping application to every second row are advised. At the same time it has been observed that effective supply of nitrogen has raised the yield of wheat from 18-37 per cent in Greece to 52-65 per cent in England and it is expected that the gains in production will be at least 30 per cent during the next two to three generations. Further, this should be supplemented by more efficient practices of irrigation such as replacing traditional ridge-and-furrow irrigation by irrigating every other furrow, coupled with timing, can save one-third of water used otherwise. Moreover, better matching of crops has been found to be a very effective alternative method and, as has been found, sorghum replacing corn lowers water requirement by 10-15 per cent. Similarly, sunflowers replacing soybeans saves 20-25 per cent of water (Smil, 1994).*

In short,

> "consistently conservative estimates supported by well-documented possibilities concerning more efficient use of agricultural resources, more careful treatment and storage of harvested crops, and more healthy ways of eating reveal that in 1990 world agriculture had recoverable inefficiencies equivalent to about 60 per cent of actual food consumption. This would be enough to feed—without stunting—an additional 3.1 billion people, a total global population of about 8.4 billion instead of 5.3 billion, without cultivating more land, and without increasing fertilizer and water inputs. If everybody were to receive 2,200 Kcal/day, the total would be reduced to 7.7 billion people, 2.4 billion above the 1990 total."[20]

The scope of further area expansion of arable land being limited, the lacuna can be overcome with the introduction of greater multiple cropping system to enhance cereal production. But as Dyson (1996) points out—

> "there had been expansion of harvested area even in some land-scarce countries in the 1980s in the Middle East, such as Syria, Morocco, Sudan, Iraq, Saudi Arabia and Egypt, the enlargement amounting to an average of 1 per cent per year during 1970-1990, done partly through increased multiple cropping, reclamation and enlarged irrigation facilities. Making a critical assessment of development in food production Dyson seems to be convinced that issues of distribution (of food) apart, in the year 2020, the global agricultural system probably will be producing enough, at least in aggregate terms."[21]

---

* Vaclav Smil, How Many People Can the World Feed? *(Population and Development Review Vol. 20, No. 2,* June 1994)

However, grain production falling behind the rate of population growth since 1984 is attributed to overproduction of cereals in the developed world which could largely be avoided. Nevertheless, food production in all other regions of the world kept ahead of population and since early 1980s farmers in three regions have diversified their production, switching out of cereals to more remunerative food (or non-food crops), bringing changes in diets raising per capita consumption of food. Undeniably, population growth plays the most critical role, creating greater demand for food, behind expansion of world food production and it is predicted by Dyson (1996) that nearly 3 billion tons of cereal will need to be produced in 2020 for satisfying global requirement, primarily based on a modest expansion through multiple cropping along with larger inputs of fertilizers and irrigation facilities.[22]

However, the overall situation does not seem to be prospective in the beginning of the present century and Brown (2004 Reprint) finds it is going to be difficult and beyond the means of the human society to feed all the people of the world. Despite the highly impressive gain in grain production in the world during the last half of the twentieth century, which nearly tripled, increasing from 631 million tons in 1950 to 1,835 million tons in 2000, a double of that from the beginning of agriculture some 11,000 years ago until 1950, it could not cope with population growth (Brown, 2004 Reprint), leaving 1.1 billion people undernourished and underweight out of 1.3 billion living in poverty in the world, as estimated by the World Bank, 72 per cent of them living in the rural areas. These rural poor—

> "live not on the productive irrigated plains but on the semi-arid/arid fringes of agriculture, or in the upper reaches of watersheds on highly erodible, steeply sloped land. Eradicating hunger depends on stabilizing those fragile ecosystems."[23]

It is further to be noted that most of the world's poor live in countries with rapidly growing population, such as India with hungriest people on earth. India, with about 90 million of its farms having less than 2 hectares of land each on average containing about 540 million people altogether, nearly half of India's total population, is not in a position to fully feed their families of 6 members on average. The situation in Bangladesh is not better either, where farm-size on average falls below one hectare. It, rather, still is worse in Africa recording the world's fastest population growth.

Another major handicap is growing water shortage, already very serious in India, Pakistan, in the Middle East and in semi-arid Africa, despite the fact that irrigated areas in the world have tripled—increasing from 90 million hectares in 1950 to almost 270 million hectares in 2000. Competition for the dwindling supply of water between industry and agriculture is unseemly as the former can always pay much more for water than the latter. Besides, overpumping from aquifers makes it more undependable as well as far more expensive in countries like China, India and the United States, as aquifers are fast getting depleted (Brown, 2004 Reprint).*

Raising water productivity depends much on irrigation efficiency, including practices like furrow, flood, overhead sprinkler, and drip irrigation. Replacement of flood irrigation with periodic flood (as for rice) will save water while a shift from high pressure to low-pressure overhead sprinkler system can boost irrigation efficiency from 65 per cent to 80 per cent. The drip irrigation technology developed in Israel has proved to be the most efficient system reducing water use by 30-70 per cent, as observed by Sandra Postel and her colleagues, raising yields by 20-90 per cent with steady supply of water. According to Brown (2004 Print),† Postel reports that India can profitably take advantage of drip irrigation for an estimated 10 million hectares of her agricultural land. Another way of gain in food production is to shift to more water-efficient crops, such as wheat replacing rice.

In Brown's opinion, a broad strategy undertaken for eradicating hunger requires superhuman efforts since,

> "food security may depend as much on efforts of family

---

* Lester R. Brown, *Eco-Economy: Building an Economy for the Earth* (Orient Longman, 2004).

† *Ibid.*

> planners as on farmers and as much on the decisions made in ministries of energy that shape future climate trends as on decisions made in ministries of agriculture."[24]

In terms of control over food availability, stabilizing population, specifically in the developing countries, takes topmost priority. Eradicating hunger can not be achieved in a world which is already heavily handicapped with supply of land having become a scarce resource, water for irrigation is dwindling with fast depletion of aquifers, chronic negligence in stopping huge wastage of food, due to poor storage facilities, poor transport network along with exposure to rodents, insects and the like adding to the loss. Efforts need to be made for raising water productivity for which multiple cropping systems may prove to be highly beneficial, made possible by training farmers in water-harvesting methods. At the same time, in order to minimize soil erosion reducing crop-yields, high erodible land needs to be reverted back to grassland or trees, as done in the United States, along with the practice of conservation tillage ultimately contributing to raise productivity. Further, another very important practice, represented by feeding crop residue to ruminants, as done in India and China makes a substantial saving of grain for human feed (Brown, 2004 Reprint).*

Food Availability and Continuing Hunger/Malnutrition

In finding out the present status of the poor, suffering constantly from hunger or malnutrition, we have to be sure about the degrees of poverty. Jeffrey Sachs (2005) distinguishes between the degrees of poverty,

> "extreme (or absolute) poverty, moderate poverty, and relative poverty. Extreme poverty means that households cannot meet their basic needs for survival. They are chronically hungry, unable to access healthcare, lack of amenities of safe drinking water and

---

* *Ibid.*

> sanitation, cannot afford education for some or all of the children, and perhaps lack rudimentary shelter—a roof to keep rain out of the hut, a chimney to remove the smoke from the cook stove—and basic articles of clothing, such as shoes. Unlike moderate and relative poverty, extreme poverty occurs only in developing countries. Moderate poverty generally refers to conditions of life in which basic needs are met, but just barely. Relative poverty is generally construed as a household income level below a given proportion of average national income."[25]

As estimated by the World Bank economists Shaohua Chen and Martin Ravallion, people earning an income of $ 1 per day measured at purchasing power parity (PPP) are classified as extreme poor, while those earning $ 1-2 a day are considered as moderately poor. (Sachs, 2005).*

In this connection, the development of economic prosperity intimately connected with the level of regional economy defining poverty makes an interesting study. It appears that though the world population growth only rose slowly from about 230 million in A.D. 1 to perhaps 270 million by A.D. 1800, there had virtually been no change in living standards on a global scale, thereby making no division between rich and poor. However, the whole picture changed very fast during the succeeding period, the global population increasing over six times in the following two centuries, reaching an astounding 6.1 billion at the beginning of the third millennium along with world's per capita income rising even faster, increasing almost by nine times between 1820 and 2000 (Note A), followed by wide disparity in per capita income, which during this period had been almost twenty-five-fold in the US and fifteen-fold in Western Europe. At the same time, it is interesting to observe that world food production 'more than kept up' with the growing world population during this period, made possible by improved farming technology, and the total economic activity in the world leaped 49-times during the

---

* Jeffrey D. Sachs, *The End of Poverty: How We Can Make It Happen In Our Life Time* (Penguin Books, 2005).

past 180 years (Sachs, 2005).*

Nevertheless, the widening gap between the rich and poor is a new phenomenon, a product of modern economy beginning from 1820, when all regions were poor at the beginning, the gap between the rich and poor was a ratio of four to one in per capita income between the world's leading economy of that time, the United Kingdom, and the world's poorest economy, Africa. The gap widened further through time, becoming twenty to one between the US, the richest economy by 1948, and Africa, the poorest region.[26] (Note B)

It may be noted that the world was remarkably poor until the mid-1770s, with life expectancy low, children dying in vast numbers in all countries, many of the latter afflicted by waves of epidemics of smallpox, measles and the Black Death of Europe making life uncertain. But the whole situation dramatically changed almost overnight with the beginning of Industrial Revolution setting forth a new era of human activity through a—

> "combination of new industrial technologies, coal power and market forces related to the Industrial Revolution. The Industrial Revolution, in turn, led to the most revolutionary economic events in human history since the start of agriculture ten thousand years earlier. Suddenly, economies could grow beyond long-accustomed bounds without hitting the biological constraints of food and timber production. Industrial production grew rapidly, and the power of economic growth spilled out from Great Britain to all parts of the world. Societies the world over were fundamentally changed, often tumultuously."[27]

Before going on to analyse the revolutionary changes brought in the world economy by the aforesaid 'great transformation', one may feel tempted to find the forces behind making Great Britain as the venue for the start of 'Industrial Revolution' and why it was not China which had been the technological leader for the world for about a thousand years,

---

* *Ibid.*

between A.D. 500 and A.D. 1500. Or, why not other centres of power in Europe, or Asia? According to economic historians, at that point of time when 'Industrial Revolution' surfaced, the British society—

> "was relatively open with more initiative and social mobility than most other societies of the world ... (with) strengthening institutions of political liberty ... (the) Parliament and its traditions for free speech and open debate were powerful contributors to the uptake of new ideas. ... Critically Britain became one of the leading centres of Europe's scientific revolution. After centuries in which Europe was mainly the importer of scientific ideas from Asia, European science made pivotal advances beginning in the Renaissance. ... With Britain's political openness, speculative scientific thinking was given opportunity to thrive, and the scientific advances on the continent stimulated an explosion of scientific discovery in England. The decisive breakthrough came with Isaac newton's *Principia Mathematica* in 1687, one of the most important books ever written. ... (Besides) Britain had several crucial geographical advantages. ... as an island close to continental Europe, Britain enjoyed low-cost sea-based trade ... had extensive navigable river ways for internal trade, enjoyed a highly favourable environment for agriculture, with a combination of plentiful rainfall, an ample growing season, and good soils. Another critical geographical advantage was Britain's proximity to North America ... provided vast new territories for food production and raw materials such as cotton for British industry ... Britain remained sovereign and faced lesser risk of invasion than its neighbours ... (Lastly) Britain had coal, and with the invention of the steam engine, coal freed the society from energy constrains that had limited the scale of economic production throughout human history .... Geography enabled Britain to benefit from trade, productive agriculture, and energy resources in vast stocks of coal. Other parts of the world were not as fortunate to have this confluence of favourable factors."[28]

All this laid out the stage for heralding a new epoch, a dramatic rise in economic and technological advances in Britain during the late 18th and early 19th centuries, between 1760 to 1840/1850, called the Industrial Revolution. Initiated by the use of steam engine, for the first time providing power for newly developed machines previously performed by human hands, it was a great invention particularly for the cotton textile industry, followed by "great changes in related industries such as metallurgy, particularly in the construction of steam engines and machine tools."[29] Since then, it has become a historical process, associated with further innovations, described as the 'second' Industrial Revolution when it first spread into Europe, while the internal combustion engine or atomic energy or the computer suggest 'third', 'fourth', or 'fifth' Industrial Revolution (*Encylopaedia Americana*).

The modern economic growth closely connected with 'Industrial Revolution' in Britain, as its geographical root, did not remain confined and its diffusion occurred in three different forms, spreading into its colonies in North America, Australia and New Zealand, all of them located in temperate zones providing almost similar settings for farming and other economic activities as those of Britain making it easier—

> "to transplant British technologies, food crops, and even legal institutions into these new settings. Those new homes of economic growth were literally a New England, in the case of North America sea coast, or a 'western offshoots', in the phrase of Angus Maddison. Ideologically, the imperial powers and colonizers considered North America and Oceania to be empty places, despite the presence of native inhabitants in both regions. By slaughtering, cornering, or removing these native inhabitants from their lands, England's new colonizers fuelled a huge expansion of population and subsequent economic growth of North America and Oceania."[30]

Similar diffusion also took place into Europe and later from Europe to Latin America, Africa and Asia giving rise to turmoils in many situations, based on exploitation of local resources, as in

Africa, and, especially in India, destroying its export-economy particularly based on cottage-level products, its manufacturing skills in textiles of inimitable quality competing with machine-made products of England. Hence, growing pressure, mostly disruptive in nature, involving the economic efforts of colonized countries gradually widened the gap between the rich and poor, the latter obviously representing the colonized people. According to Sachs,* the modern economic growth during the past two hundred years triggered by Industrial Revolution brought 'phenomenal gap between the richest and poorest', and poverty gripped all of the world dividing it into four broad groups as per annual income. The rich income-group with an earning of above $ 20,000 per capita included countries like the United States, Canada, Western Europe, Japan, Australia and New Zealand. Countries like most of East Asia (such as Korea and Singapore), Central Europe, the former Soviet Union, and Latin America fell within the middle-income group with per capita income of $ 4000 and $ 20,000. With per capita income of $ 2000 and $ 4000 in parts of South America, South Asia and East Asia placed them within the upper-end of the low-income group while Sub-Saharan Africa and South Asia represented the poorest countries, with per capita income falling below $ 2000 (Sachs).†

On the whole, it makes about five-sixths (of 6.3 billion) people living above the level of poverty. It has been argued, poverty itself is a trap, keeping people immersed in it without a way of escape. The most pertinent question in this regard is—why? The answer is as simple as the fact that poverty is caused by a 'lack of capital leaving no money from income to be invested for future.' To be more specific, it is the lack of transport, paved roads, power generation, irrigation channels that hampers any development. Besides, the human capital being very low, the hungry, disease-ridden and illiterate villagers struggle for survival. Hence, to get out of such a situation what is needed is more capital, including physical, human and natural, for investment which can improve the

---

* Sachs, Jeffrey D. (2005). *The End of Poverty: How we can make it Happen in Our Lifetime*. Penguin Books. p. 30

† *Ibid.*

economy and take people out of poverty in the long run (Sachs, 2005).

The natural capital is unknowingly depleted by the poor as a means of living by way of cutting down forests to be used as fuel, as mentioned before, exhausting the soils of their nutrition with excessive use of land without replenishment, mining the minerals, energy and metal deposits ceaselessly, as well as overfishing, leaving the people in a desperate condition. Comparing with this situation it is, rather, quite alarming to notice that while not a single country in North America, Western Europe and East Asia failed to achieve economic growth between 1980 and 2000, it was just the reverse in the developing countries where forty-five countries registered negative growth in GDP per capita though thirty-six other countries enjoyed economic growth. Reasons for such contrasting results as explained by Sachs (2005)* are quite simple. It was possible for some countries to escape the poverty trap by way of adopting a particular policy. The most determinant, it seems, is food productivity. Countries that started with high cereal yield per hectare and that used high levels of fertilizer input per hectare, are the poor countries that tended to experience economic growth. Countries that began with very low yields in 1980 are the countries that tended to experience economic decline between 1980 and 2000. The poverty trap is mainly a rural phenomenon of peasant farmers caught in a spiral of rising populations and stagnant or falling food production per person (Table 3.3).

Table 3.3: Comparative Position of East Asia and Sub-Saharan Africa in regard to Social and Economic Factors in 1980

	East Asia	*Sub-Saharan Africa*
Crop Yield (kg/hectare)	2016	927
Irrigated Land (% of Cropland)	37	4
Share of Crop Area Planted to modern varieties	43	4
Adult Literacy (%)	70	38
Infant Mortality Rate (per 1000 live births)	56	116
Total Fertility Rate (birth per woman)	3.1	6.6

Source: Jeffery D. Sachs (2005) (Calculated from World Bank Data).

* Sachs, Jeffrey D. (2005). *The End of Poverty: How we can make it Happen in Our Lifetime*. Penguin Books. p. 30.

However, it is not at all difficult to find that the benefit of higher production does not reach all people in a country equally, as in Latin America where some of the countries in central and southern parts, like Ecuador, Guatemala, Paraguay and Peru, experienced decline, as a result of their geographical difficulties as well as social conflict besides being afflicted by natural hazards such as earthquakes, droughts, floods and landslides. Along with the international price fluctuations affecting their economy hard for export items like copper, fishmeal, coffee, bananas etc. and all these joining together in their unrelenting push for people into poverty trap. Asia presents another case where poverty persists in the midst of economic growth because of uneven development, as in China and India, such as the hinterlands in China with backward economy as compared with coastal areas, while in India the Ganga Plains have experienced less economic growth than the region in the south (Sachs, 2005).*

It is, in fact, rural poverty, as explained earlier, which keeps people trapped in unendurable living conditions and some of these rural people spill over into nearby urban areas in the hope of escaping rural deprivation. However, the problem of taking people out of the rural poverty trap does not seem to be an unsurmountable problem since making improvement in the current status of human and natural capital can be accomplished with concerted efforts from the government through its administrative set-up (the Government-aided elected Rural Administrative Bodies called the 'Panchayat' in India) empowered with legal authority in collaboration with political leaders, taking an un-biased attitude working with all honesty and integrity. When there are funds allocated for each Panchayat Body for developmental works in India, a programme setting priorities need to be drawn up keeping the resources in mind, giving stress on deriving economic benefits in a developmental programme generating employment scope and marketing prospects preferably based on creating local variations in production as determined by available resources so as to make it an interdependent economy (Note C). In brief, what is needed is generation of purchasing capability of the rural people steeped

---

* Sachs, Jeffrey D. (2005). *The End of Poverty: How we can make it Happen in Our Lifetime*. Penguin Books. p. 30.

in poverty, which depends on how fair the human capital can be equipped to productive work. In other words, human capital in the form of skill acquired through proper training (vocational) increases its saleability and the income made strengthens the capability of a person in terms of human capital, which he/she can utilise for the family members in terms of food, education, health, recreation etc. and thus contribute further to the formation of human capital. It, obviously, becomes an ongoing process, constantly adding to building up the economic structure sustaining the healthier progress of the society involved, making people able and independent in choosing their life-style and once for all escape the poverty-trap.

Needless to say that the entire process depends on the goodwill, determination and an honest, integrated as well as serious approach of related government/s in co-operation and full understanding of the situation by the politicians of the country involved, making unbiased efforts at taking the rural population out of poverty trap, which itself is a great economic as well as social drag on the entire society pulling it down all the while, negating whatever good is done otherwise.

Food Situation for Future

Release, if at all it could make happen, of almost a billion people in the rural areas from poverty trap needs to be considered as the most serious venture. But, the most relevant query is, even if people, in the long run, are released from poverty trap, will there be enough food in the world for feeding all the people? The answer is not simple and it is necessary to evaluate the status of food in the perspective of factors in its favour or against it.

The first major obstacle to the production of food in the world, in general, is global warming which was warned by Physicist and Mathematician Albert Bartlett that our entire economy including agriculture is heavily dependent on oil, specifically pointing out that the use of land for agriculture amounts to the concept of 'converting petroleum into food' and in his opinion, the shortages in global food supply during the last several decades 'have been temporarily and artificially kept at bay with petrochemicals'. Magnuson (2013) refers to David

Pimentel of Cornell University, who emphasizes the role of oil in upsetting our bread-basket:

> "As a result of overpopulation and resource limitations, the world is fast losing its capacity to feed itself. ... More alarming is the fact that while the world population doubled in numbers in about 30 years the world doubled its energy consumption within the past decade. Moreover, the use of energy in food production has been increasing faster than its use in many other sectors of economy."[31]

Apparently, both coal and oil had been the major source of energy during the twentieth century, oil finally replacing coal since 1967 while natural gas came to a competing stage as a source of energy during the closing decades of the last century. But, because of fast depleting oil reserves of the US, the production was predicted to fall 63 per cent below its current production peak by 2040 (Magnuson, 2013)* highlighting the importance of looking for other sources as substitute for oil besides making present use of energy more efficient. This has already been accomplished in considerable measure in many countries making effective cut down on energy use. For example,

> "Europeans routinely use 30 per cent less energy per unit of gross national product than Americans do. ... China is now setting the pace in increasing energy efficiency and reducing carbon emissions. ... For example, China will soon start to produce a high-efficiency refrigerator that will use only half as much electricity as conventional models. Some of the worldwide potential for saving energy can be seen in the substitution of compact fluorescent lamps (CFLs) for traditional incandescent light bulbs. The compact fluorescent uses less than one fourth as much electricity

---

* Joel Magnuson, *The Approaching Great Transformation: Towards a Liveable Post-Carbon Economy, Policy,* Press at the University of Bristol, 2013.

> ... lasts 13 times as long. ... Another area with enormous potential for efficiency improvements is automobile fuels."[32]

Perhaps, it is time to turn to other available sources as energy substitute for coal, oil, shales and natural gas which are not only expensive as sources of energy but also high-degree polluters of the atmosphere. Wind offers one of such choices as a worldwide source of energy. Initiated in California in the early 1980s, interest in its development rose fast, its generation having expanded four-fold between 1990-2000, 15 per cent of electricity in Denmark was being supplied by it, Germany taking lead in its production, yielding second place to the United States lowering the price for kilo watt-hour from 38 cent in 1980s to less than 4 cent in 2000, making cheaper than that of oil or gas-fired power in some areas (Table 3.4) (Brown, 2004 Reprint).*

Table 3.4: Wind Energy Generating Capacity in Selected Countries, 2000

Country	Capacity (Megawatts)
Germany	6,113
United States	2,554
Spain	2,250
Denmark	2.140
India	1,167

Source: Brown, 2004 Reprint.

After wind, another fast growing source of energy is sunlight, or solar cells developed first in 1952. Initially costly, its price is coming down fast while utility-wise solar cells have proved far better than any other source of energy since it can be developed in inaccessible regions where any other source of power cannot be accessed. The use of photovoltaic or solar cells on the roof of a building, turning it into a power plant, irrespective of location, using sunlight as its raw material has already become highly popular, and with the cost of production fast coming down as well as its pollution-free status, have made

* Brown, Lester R., *Eco-Economy: Building an Economy for the Earth,* Orient Longman, 2004.

it very popular worldwide. It is quite encouraging to know that the cost of production of solar cells came down from over $ 70 per watt of production capacity to less than $3.50 per watt between 1970s and 2001 (Brown, 2004 Reprint).* According to the same author solar power in Europe can now satisfy the electricity needs of some 15 million households (Brown, 2012).† At the same time another free gift of nature as a source of unlimited power in many locations is geothermal power, an inexhaustible source by itself, producing power indefinitely, if properly used.

> "Produced radioactivity within the earth and by the pressures of gravity, it is a vast resource, most of which is deep within the earth. Geothermal energy can be economically tapped when it is relatively close to the surface, as evidenced by hot springs, geysers, and volcanic activity. The energy source is essentially inexhaustible. Hot baths, for example, has been used for millennia. ... Geothermal energy is much more abundant in some parts of the world than in others. The richest region is the vast Pacific Rim. In the 'East pacific' geothermal resources are found along the coastal regions of Latin America, Central America, and North America all the way to Alaska. On the west side, they are widely distributed in Eastern Russia, Japan, the Korean Peninsulas, China and island countries such as the Philippines, Indonesia, New Guinea, Australia and new Zealand. This buried energy source is used directly both to supply heat and to generate electricity. When used for heat, hot water or steam is typically pumped from underground, heat is extracted, and then the water is re-injected into the earth. Electricity can be generated from hot water pumped from beneath the earth's surface, from steam extracted directly, or from steam produced by circulating hot water into fissures in hot rock below

---

* *Ibid.*

† Brown, Lester R., *Full Planet, Empty Plates: The New Geopolitics of Food Security*, Earth Policy Institute, (New York, London, Earth Policy Institute, W.W. Norton & Company, 2012).

> the surface. Geothermal energy extracted directly can be used for space heating, as in Iceland, where it heats some 85 per cent of buildings; for hot baths, where springs bring geothermal energy to the surface, as in Japan; and for generating electricity, as in Italy in 1904, geothermal energy is now used in scores of countries ... by 1998 it had expanded nearly eight-fold, to 8240 megawatts."[33]

According to the same author, one-fifths of total energy generated in Kenya comes from geothermal energy, while Indonesia has targeted for generation of 9,500 megawatts of geothermal energy by 2025, equivalent to 56 per cent of its total electricity requirements (Brown, 2012).*

Re-evaluation of energy status is intimately connected with reduction in cost of energy for production of food, the demand for which is fast increasing in keeping with population growth and change in dietary habits of people with growing affluence. According to the estimates of The World Bank, 72 per cent of the world's 1.3 billion poor as well as hungry people live in rural areas. Since poverty and hunger go together, they occur faster in countries where population grows faster, as in Indian subcontinent, adding 21 million people a year, expected to add another 900 million by mid-twenty-first century to the 'hungriest on earth' (Brown, 2004 Reprint).† However, one may have some idea about the prevalence of poverty from Table 3.5, giving data on people below poverty line. Out of 134 countries only 21 countries provide data, making it very difficult to get a correct picture when 82 countries do not provide any. The survey year during which the relevant data were collected varies from 1995 to 2004. Among all the 21 countries, those having over 50 per cent of their rural population living below poverty line, the highest rises to almost 82 per cent in Bolivia and in another 7 countries it is above 70 per cent, while in another 12 countries

---

* Lester R. Brown, *Full Planet, Empty Plates: The New Geopolitics of Food Security* (New York, London, Earth Policy Institute, W.W. Norton & Company, 2012).

† Lester R. Brown, *Eco-Economy: Building an Economy for the Earth* (Orient Longman, 2004).

rural people living below poverty line exceeds 40 per cent.

Notably, as estimated by the FAO, the number of chronically undernourished people amounted to 854 million in 2001-03, 820 million of them living in developing countries, 25 million in countries in transition and 9 million in developed countries (Table 3.6) (Note D). The picture of regional distribution shows overwhelming presence of the grossly deprived people concentrated in South Asia, Asia, the Pacific and Africa, which together contains almost 61 per cent of the total chronically malnourished people of the world while South Asia alone, comprising countries like India, Bangladesh, Pakistan, Nepal, Sri

Table 3.5: Population Below the Poverty Line above 50 per cent of the Rural Population

Sl. No.	*Country*	*Survey Year*	*Population Below the Poverty Line above 50% of the Rural Population*	
			Rural	*National*
1.	Bangladesh	2000	53.0	49.8
2.	Bolivia	1999	81.7	62.7
3.	Burkina Faso	2003	52.4	46.4
4.	Columbia	1999	79.0	64.0
5.	Dominican Republic	2004	55.7	42.2
6.	Ecuador	1998	69.0	46.0
7.	Georgia	2003	52.7	54.5
8.	Guatemala	2000	74.5	56.2
9.	Haiti	1995	66.0	–
10.	Honduras	2004	70.43	50.7
11.	Kenya	1997	53.0	52.0
12.	Madagascar	1999	76.7	71.3
13.	Malawi	1997-98	66.5	65.3
14.	Mauritania	2000	61.2	46.3
15.	Moldova	2002	67.2	48.5
16.	Nicaragua	1998	68.5	47.9
17.	Peru	2004	72.1	53.1
18.	Philippines	1997	50.7	36.8
19.	Rwanda	1999	65.7	60.3
20.	Sierra Leone	2003-04	79.0	70.2
21.	Yemen Republic	2004	78.0	68.0

Note: No data for 82 countries.

Source: Compiled from The World Bank 2008: Table 2.

Table 3.6: Geographical Distribution of Undernourished Population (millions) 2001-2003

Region	*Population (millions)*
South Asia	300
Developed Countries	9
Countries in Transition	25
Sub-Saharan Africa	206
Near-East and North Africa	38
Latin America and the Caribbean	52
East Asia	160
Southeast Asia	65

Source: FAO: The State of food for Agriculture 2006.

Lanka etc., contains over 35 per cent of the total, while Sub-Saharan Africa alone sharing a load of 24 per cent of the total represents the case of 'highest prevalence of undernourishment' which, according to FAO's estimate is 32 per cent.

Nevertheless, a glimmer of hope in reducing the overall number of undernourished people is given by the fact that it has reduced from 37 per cent of total population in 1969-71 to 17 per cent in 2001-03 in the developing countries though the decline has slowed down in recent years. Asia and the Pacific have experienced the highest rate of reduction, by 'almost two-thirds' in the past 35 years in contrast to increase in the number of undernourished people in Sub-Saharan Africa during the same period (FAO, 2006) (Figs. 3.2 and 3.3). However, there are sub-regional variations in this respect in the Sub-Saharan Region as except Central Africa all the other sub-regions have made substantial reduction in the prevalence of undernourishment.

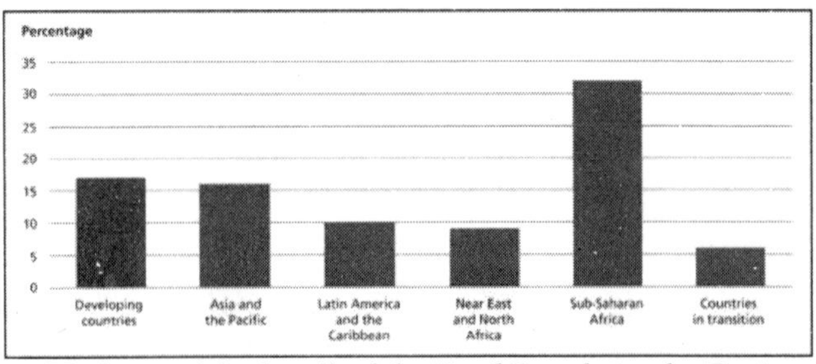

Fig. 3.2: Undernourished as % of the Total Population by Region: 2001-2003

Source: FAO 2006: The State of Food and Agriculture: Food Aid and Food Security.

Since availability of food cannot be dissociated from growth of population it is necessary to point out that the growth has started slowing down since 1960s due to declining birth rates resulting from greater awareness of people—especially in the urban areas as well as the developing economies—boosted further by adoption of family planning measures, bring down the growth rate from world population from 2.2 per cent in 1963 to 1.3 per cent in 1998.

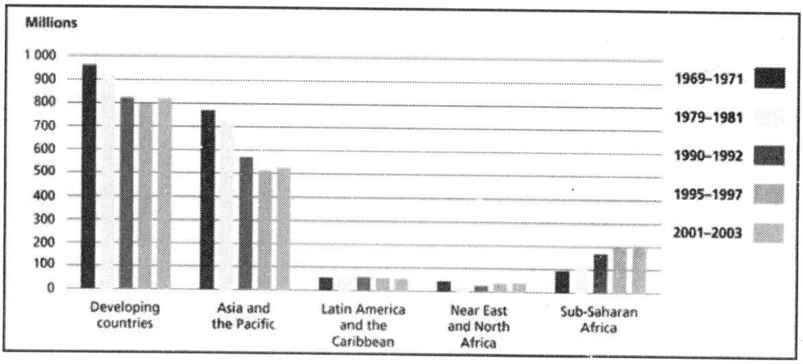

Fig. 3.3: Number of Undernourished People in Developing Countries, by Region

Source: FAO: 2006: The State of Food and Agriculture: Food Aid for Food Security.

> "According to 2002-based projections, prepared by the United Nations (2003), the growth rate is likely to fall below 1.0 per cent during 2015-20 (almost exactly a hundred years since it first exceeded this rate). It is expected not to be much over 0.3 per cent by mid-century—a level not seen since around 1750."[34]

It is rather frightening to know that a 3 per cent rate of growth will actually lead to a 20-fold growth in a century. The most recent U.N. Demographic Projections show world population growing to 9.3 billion (UN World Prospects: The 2014 Revision shows the global population will reach 9.55 billion by 2050). This brings us to a problematic situation given the difficulties in expanding the food supply, such as those posed by water shortages and global warming. We are fast outgrowing the earth's capacity to sustain our increasing numbers.[35]

Stabilisation of population growth nappens to be the most important step ensuring a better position in food supply. The rate of population growth has already shrunk from 2.1 per cent in 1967 to 1.1 per cent in 2011, as mentioned above, and it may further slow down making wider provision of family planning measures already in high demand among women preferring a smaller family having a direct effect on health and well-being of the family. It is very encouraging to note that 44 countries, almost all of them located in both Western and Eastern Europe, containing a total of 970 million, or roughly one-seventh of the global population, with a declining fertility rate have reached population stability. Two other regions are moving rapidly towards this goal. They are East Asia, including Japan, North and South Korea, China and Taiwan, together having 1.5 billion people. As a matter of fact, Latin America has also joined this league and taking effective measures on poverty reduction and family planning. The growth of population has already been arrested and population is slowing down (Brown, 2012).*

On the contrary, virtually growth of population remains strong in the developing countries with least capability of supporting them. Both Indian Subcontinent and Sub-Saharan Africa are going to experience population surges in future and among them Indian Subcontinent faces the worst future where, according to UN (2014 Revision), the total population is going to increase from nearly 1.3 billion in 2015 to over 1.6 billion by 2050, thus making a giant leap of over 34 million within the space of three-and-a-half decades; the position of Pakistan and Bangladesh may be slightly better with population in the former rising from 1.88 million in 2015-16 to 271 million by 2050, while in Bangladesh the population is going to shoot up from a little over 160 million in 2015 to a little less than 202 million by 2050. Altogether, these three countries are going to add another 462 million people to their total between 2015 and 2050 which, by any standard, is abnormally large. Likewise, the total population in Sub-Saharan Africa with a further addition of over 1.1 billion to its total population is a highly frightening prospect.

---

* Lester R. Brown, *Full Planet, Empty Plates: The New Geopolitics of Food Security* (New York, London, Earth Policy Institute, W.W. Norton & Company, 2012).

Poverty alleviation taking up family planning as the most necessary step, making contraceptives easily available and giving greatest priority to education especially for female children, along with providing proper healthcare facilities, are likely to prove, in the long run, as the major pathways for relieving population pressure with declining birth rates as well as fertility rates conjoined with resulting decline in female mortality and infant mortality rates.

Population Puzzle and Food Worthiness

What is of real significance in this context is a proper evaluation of the available resources to assess the major obstacles to the path of providing food for all. The growing population of the world has been a major handicap in this regard. However, it may be encouraging to observe that an assessment brings out the changing scenario in this regard revealing the fact that there are at least 42 countries in the world, out of a total of 233, where population has been stabilized, showing further records of decline between the period 2015 and 2050. Most of them are concentrated in the developed world or, rather, in Europe (Table 3.7), as mentioned before, particularly in Eastern Europe with 9 out of a total of 10 countries, and in Southern Europe where in 12 out of 16 countries population is going to decline. Among other sub-regions having similar records of decline in population between 2015 and 2050, 3 countries of Northern Europe experience the same, while Germany is the lone example in Western Europe with similar record of decline. However, Europe as a whole is going to have a declining population during this period. At the same time, remarkable cases of population decline are presented by Japan and China in East Asia, reducing population by 14.6 per cent and 1.2 per cent respectively, representing the only cases of declining population in the developing world though two other countries in Asia—Georgia and Armenia—have a record of decline by 17.2 per cent and 6.9 per cent respectively during the same period—2015 and 2050. On the other hand, both Latin America (including South America) and the Caribbean as well as North America do not have any large claim in this respect, while Africa provides the lonely example of Mauritius with a decline in population over the period by 1.8 per cent.

Table 3.7: Countries with Decline in Population Growth between 2015 and 2050

Sl. No.	Region/Sub-region/Country	Population (000)		Vol. and Rate of Decline	
		2015	2050	Volume	Rate (%) 2015-2050
Northern Europe					
1.	Estonia	1,280	1,121	-159	12.4
2.	Latvia	2,031	1,674	-357	17.6
3.	Lithuania	2,999	2,557	-442	14.7
Southern Europe		156,157	150,889	-5,268	3.4
4.	Albania	3,197	3,094	-103	3.2
5.	Bosnia & Herzegovina	3,820	3,332	-488	12.8
6.	Croatia	4,255	3,606	-649	15.2
7.	Gibraltar	29	27	-2	6.9
8.	Greece	11,126	10,688	-458	4.1
9.	Italy	61,142	60,015	-1,127	1.8
10.	Malta	431	417	-14	3.2
11.	Montenegro	622	557	-65	10.4
12.	Portugal	10,610	9,843	-767	7.2
13.	Serbia	9,424	7,074	-2,350	2.7
14.	Slovenia	2,079	2,023	-56	2.7
15.	TFYR Macedonia	2,109	1,881	-228	10.8
Western Europe					
16.	Germany	82,562	72,566	-9,996	12.1
Eastern Europe		292,501	244,522	-47,979	16.4
17.	Belarus	9,280	7,359	-1,921	20.7
18.	Bulgaria	7,113	5,077	-2,036	28.6
19.	Hungary	9,911	8,954	-957	9.6
20	Poland	38,222	34,079	-4,143	10.8
21.	Republic of Moldova	3,437	2,484	-953	27.7
22.	Romania	21,579	17,809	-3,770	17.4
23.	Russian Federation	142,098	120,896	-21,202	14.9
24.	Slovakia	5,458	4,990	-468	8.6
25.	Ukraine	44,646	33,658	-10,988	2.4
	Europe	743,123	709,067	-34,056	4.9
	Asia				
	Eastern Asia	1,637,559	1,605,341	-32,218	2.0
26.	China	1,401,587	1,384,977	-16,613	1.2
27.	Japan	126,818	108,329	-18,489	14.6
	Southeastern Asia				
28.	Thailand	67,401	61,740	-5,661	8.4

(Contd.)

Table 3.7: *(Contd.)*

Sl. No.	Region/Sub-region/Country	Population (000)		Vol. and Rate of Decline	
		2015	2050	Volume	Rate (%) 2015-2050
	Western Asia				
29.	Armenia	2,989	2,782	-207	6.9
30.	Georgia	4,305	3,563	-742	17.2
	Latin America and the Caribbean				
31.	Aruba	104	103	-1	1.0
32.	Cuba	11,249	9,392	-1,837	16.5
33.	Grenada	107	95	-12	11.2
34.	Jamaica	2,813	2,808	-5	0.2
35.	Martinique	406	400	-6	1.5
36.	Puerto Rico	3,680	3,611	-69	1.9
37.	Trinidad and Tobago	1,347	1,155	-192	15.4
38.	United States Virgin Islands	107	103	-4	3.7
	Northern America				
39.	Bermuda	66	64	-2	3.0
40.	Greenland	57	50	-7	12.3
41.	Northern Marina Islands	55	52	-3	5.4
	Africa **Eastern Africa**				
42.	Mauritius	1,254	1,231	-23	1.8

Source: Compiled from World Urbanization Prospects: The 2014 Revision: File-5.

Incidentally, countries having stabilized their population and firmly set on the path of decline, show variation in the rate of decline, ranging from the highest of 28.6 per cent in Bulgaria between 2015 and 2050, and Eastern Europe recording all the three highest in the world as a sub-region (16.4%). In this respect, Table 3.8 gives a further interesting insight into the situation, recording the change in population growth in another group of 41 countries spread across the world already having developed signs of stabilization or slow decline of population. On the whole, in 13 of these countries the population is going to decline in near future while in others the population is likely to stabilize in a short while or has already stabilized.

Together, their total population comes to a staggering 2.3 billion, or nearly one-fourth of the total global population by 2050 which, without doubt, is quite a large figure making a hefty cut on food requirement as well as making growingly a reduced demand on world resources and, as such, providing the most agreeable reassurance for future humanity.

However, the prospective situation gets somewhat blurred by the present rate of population growth in two of the developing world's sub-regions—the Indian Subcontinent and Sub-Saharan Africa—with staggering growth records (Table 3.9). Population in Indian Subcontinent is headed to increase from a total of 1,630 million in 2015 to 2,093 million by 2050, making

Table 3.8: Countries with Population Stabilized or with Decline setting in shortly

Sl. No.	*Region/Sub-region/Country*	*Status (between 2015 and 2050)*
Eastern Africa		
1.	Seychelles	Likely to stabilize since 2040
Northern Africa		
2.	Tunisia	Likely to stabilize from 2015
3.	Western Sahara	Similar Status
Southern Africa		
4.	Botswana	Approaching Stabilization
5.	Lesotho	Same
6.	Swaziland	Slowly approaching Stabilization
Eastern Asia		
7.	Democratic People's Republic of Korea	Likely to stabilize from 2040
8.	Mongolia	Slowly Stabilizing
9.	Republic of Korea	Signs of Decline from 2045
South-Central Asia		
10.	Kyrgyzstan	Slowly Stabilizing
11.	Turkmenistan	Same
12.	Uzbekistan	Same
13.	Kazakhstan	Same
Southern Asia		
14.	Sri Lanka	Fast Stabilizing
Western Africa		
15.	Azerbaijan	Signs of Decline since 2040
16.	Bahrain	Strong Signs of Stabilization
17.	Cyprus	Signs of Decline from 2045
18.	Lebanon	Decline from 2050

(Contd.)

Table 3.8: (*Contd.*)

Sl. No.	*Region/Sub-region/Country*	*Status (between 2015 and 2050)*
Eastern Europe		
19.	Czech Republic	Likely to slowly stabilize from 2025
Northern Europe		
20.	Channel Islands	Likely to stabilize from 2045
21.	Faroe Islands	Likely to stabilize from 2035
22.	Finland	Likely to stabilize from 2025
23.	Sweden	Likely to stabilize from 2040
Southern Europe		
24.	San Marino	Likely to stabilize from 2025
25.	Spain	Likely to Decline from 2050
Western Europe		
26.	Netherlands	Likely to Decline from 2040
Latin America and the Caribbean Population in the Caribbean as a whole is likely decline from 2050		
27.	Dominica	Likely to Decline from 2050
28.	Guadeloupe	Likely to Decline from 2045
29.	Caribbean Netherlands	Likely to stabilize from 2030
30.	Curacao	Likely to Decline from 2050
31.	St. Kitts & Nevis	Likely to stabilize from 2045
32.	St. Lucia	Likely to Decline from 2050
33.	St. Vincent and the Grenadines	Likely to Decline from 2050
34.	Turks and Caicos islands	Likely to stabilize from 2040
South America		
35.	Falkland Islands	Stabilized
36.	Guyana	Likely to Decline from 2050
37.	Uruguay	Same
Melanesia		
38.	Fiji	Likely for Decline to start from 2035
Polynesia		
39.	American Samoa	Likely to stabilize from 2035
40.	Wallis and Futuna Islands	All through Stabilized from 2015
41.	Tokelau	Same

Source: Compiled from UN Urbanization Prospects: The 2014 Revision: File- 5.

nearly 29 per cent increase, representing a little less than one-fifth of the total humanity, and together with Sub-Saharan Africa's load of another 2,074 million (UN, 2014), adds up to a formidable 4 billion people, a little less than the half of total

Table 3.9: Growth of Population in Countries with Signs of Decline between 2015 and 2050

Sl. No.	Region/Sub-region/Country	Population (000) 2015	2050	Decline
Northern Europe				
1.	Estonia	1,280	1,121	√
2.	Latvia	2,031	1,674	√
3.	Lithuania	2,999	2,557	√
Southern Europe		156,157	150,889	√
4.	Albania	3,197	3,094	√
5.	Bosnia & Herzegovina	3,820	3,332	√
6.	Croatia	4,255	3,606	√
7.	Gibraltar	29	27	√
8.	Greece	11,126	10,688	√
9.	Italy	61,142	60,015	√
10.	Malta	431	417	√
11.	Montenegro	622	557	√
12.	Portugal	10,610	9,843	√
13.	Serbia	9,424	7,074	√
14.	Slovenia	2,079	2,023	√
15.	TFYR Macedonia	2,109	1,881	√
Western Europe				
16.	Germany	82,562	72,566	√
17.	Netherlands	16,844	16,919	+
Eastern Europe		292,501	244,522	√
18.	Belarus	9,260	7,359	√
19.	Bulgaria	7,113	5,077	√
20	Hungary	9,911	8,954	√
21.	Poland	38,222	34,079	√
22.	Republic of Moldova	3,437	2,404	√
23.	Romania	21,579	17,809	√
24.	Russian Federation	142,098	120,896	√
25.	Slovakia	5,458	4,990	√
26.	Ukraine	44,646	33,658	√
	Europe	743,123	709,067	√
Asia				
	Eastern Asia	1,637,559	1,605,341	√
27.	China	1,401,587	1,384,977	√
28.	Japan	126,818	108,329	√

(Contd.)

Table 3.9: (*Contd.*)

Southeastern Asia				
29.	Thailand	67,401	61,740	√
Western Asia				
30.	Armenia	2,989	2,782	√
31.	Georgia	4,305	3,563	√
Latin America and the Caribbean				
32.	Arguilla	15	15	–
33.	Aruba	104	103	√
34.	Cuba	11,249	9,392	√
35.	Grenada	107	95	√
36.	Jamaica	2,813	2,808	√
37.	Martinique	406	400	√
38.	Puerto Rico	3,680	3,611	√
39.	Trinidad and Tobago	1,347	1,155	√
40.	United States Virgin Islands	107	103	√
Northern America				
41.	Bermuda	66	64	√
42.	Greenland	57	50	√
43.	Northern Marina Islands	55	52	√
Africa				
Eastern Africa				
44.	Mauritius	1,254	1,231	√

Source: Compiled from UN Urbanization Prospects: The 2014 Revision: File- 5.

global population. As Brown (2012)* observes, trapped between low incomes and rising food prices, people are forced to eat less, living chronically hungry and malnourished. Incidentally, the children in these regions are the worst sufferers and having been nutritionally deprived have a stunted growth, often too weak to walk to school if there is one. For instance, in India 48 per cent of children are stunted physically and mentally. Interestingly, according to a report in 'The Guardian (UK)', 4 March, 2016, "nearly half of children in the US live dangerously close to the

* Lester R. Brown, *Full Planet, Empty Plate: The New Geopolitics of Food Security* (New York, London, Earth Policy Institute, W.W. Norton & Company, 2012).

poverty line and more kids today are likely to live in families barely able to afford most basic needs." However, the most redeeming feature in this respect is that, as reported by 'The Guardian (UK)', 16 December 2016, The World Bank has pledged "to step up the fight against extreme poverty" after announcing that tough negotiations with rich countries have left it with a record of $ 76 billion for grants and soft loans to its poorest members over the next three years". ... The IDA (International Development Association) ... intended to support health and nutrition for 400 million people, access to water for 45 million people, training for 9-10 million teachers and immunizations for 130-180 million children. However explained, such measures or financial aid do not go to the core issue of finding the scope of increasing the volume of food basket of the world through more production, to sustain the growing human load. When, according to a recent survey, the international charity, 'Save The Children' conducted in five countries—India, Pakistan, Nigeria, Peru and Bangladesh—24 per cent of families in India, 27 per cent in Nigeria and 14 per cent in Peru experience foodless days due to price-rise (Brown, 2012)*.

Irrefutable evidences provided by 83 out of a total of 233 countries make it evident that pressure on food requirement and also on available resources of nature is on the wane and with time its impact is likely to increase further, with more countries taking population growth as the most serious concern in economic, social as well as political perspective. As mentioned before, according to Brown (2012),† we are now passing through a transition from 'food abundance to food scarcity', when world grain reserves have dropped by one third over the period of last decade against prices having doubled, making its supply more restricted in terms of rising price than availability. Factually, the abrupt doubling of grain price between 2007 and 2008 'left people more hungry than at any time in history'. This, as observed earlier, led to food riots becoming instrumental in

---

* Lester R. Brown, *Full Planet, Empty Plate: The New Geopolitics of Food Security* (New York, London, Earth Policy Institute, W.W. Norton & Company, 2012).

† *Ibid.*

encouraging political strikes of serious implications, such as fuelling the 'Arab Spring'.

The world food stock dropped sharply after 2001, when consumption of food exceeded production, bringing an end to world food security between 2001 to 2011. Most of chronically hungry and malnourished people, almost 1 billion, lived in Indian Subcontinent or Sub-Saharan Africa. In spite of India's burgeoning economy, a section of its people cannot cope with rising prices, where almost 50-70 per cent of family income needs to be spent on food alone, curtailing expenses on health, education, sanitation etc. The addition of about 80 million people annually to the global population is undoubtedly great pressure on food supply, not in keeping with food production when a growing portion of grain is diverted to the production of ethanol. Besides, as Brown (2012) calls it, 'moving up the food chain', is another reason making heavier demands of grain involving almost 3 billion people in the race with ever-increasing demand for animal protein in the form of meat, milk and eggs, which makes greater consumption of grain as animal feed.

Eventually, shrinking land and water availability with increasing non-agricultural use resulting from industrial and urban-industrial spread creating more demand on both land on one hand and fast dwindling water resources on the other, making availability of food for human consumption increasingly uncertain.

Nevertheless, as many experts feel, it is not only the availability of food in adequate amount 'at the right place at the right time' is the crucial factor for satisfying the requirement of all people, both affluent and deprived, but more than anything else it is affordability making for people to buy food for satisfying their requirement which restricts access to it. The most important fact is that, according to the FAO, there had been record grain harvests in 2007, with more than enough to feed everyone in the world in 2008, but, as mentioned earlier in Chapter 2, food production having outstripped population growth for twenty years, increasing by 2 per cent a year against growth of population by 1.4 per cent a year, it is actually the absence of purchasing power of a large section of people, comprising nearly half of the world population were too poor to buy food with less than an income of one to two dollars a day were poor and unable to buy food, which kept them hungry and malnourished.[36]

Undeniably, rising oil prices in recent years have been instrumental in raising food prices all over the world, going beyond the capability of the poor bringing down their purchasing power. According to the World Bank, the agrofuels policies of the U.S. and E.U.—

> "were responsible for three-quarters of the 140 per cent increase in food prices between 2002 and February 2008 ... the most important factor (in the food price increases) was the large increase in biofuels production in the U.S. and the E.U. Without these increases, global wheat and maize stocks would not have declined appreciably, oil seeds prices would not have tripled and price increases due to other factors, such as droughts, would have been more moderate."[37]

As a matter of fact, the US was more interested in the production of agrofuels, ethanol, using increasing amounts of grain crops which, otherwise, would have been available as human-feed. As for example, it made a target of increasing agrofuels production by more than 'eightfold from 4.7 billion gallons in 2007 to at least 36 billion gallons in 2022, besides making huge land-deals—mentioned previously—in so-called land-rich countries like the Philippines, Cambodia and Madagascar for producing crops used in the production of agro-fuels, ultimately converting countries like the Philippines from a net food exporter into a net food importer since the mid-1990s, affecting similarly Mexico, the homeland of corn (maize), turning it into a corn-importing country (Bello and Baviera, 2010).*

Likewise, the Indian food crisis is a direct product of export-import policy mostly imposed by the developed economies on the developing countries, impacting very hard on the production capacity as is revealed in the global decline in per capita output and availability of food grains.

---

* Walden Bello and Mara Baviera, "Food Wars", in *Agriculture and Food in Crisis: Conflicts, Resistance and Renewal,* Ed. by Fred Magdoff and Brian Tokar, Monthly Review Press, New York, 2010.

> "Among the developing countries, China and India, which together accounted for over 30 per cent of world cereal output in the early 1990s, contributed significantly to this global decline. Let us consider the eleven developing countries—China, India, Indonesia, the Philippines, Thailand, Vietnam, Iran, Egypt, Pakistan, Bangladesh and Sri Lanka—which together contributed 40 per cent of world cereal output. Over the thirteen-year period, between 1989-91 and 2003-04 we find a mere 15.6 per cent rise in cereal production from this group, a rate of growth of only 1.1 per cent per year, well below the nearly 2 per cent population growth rate of these countries. At the same time, the output of their export crops have been rising fast, up to ten times faster than food grains, owing to the diversion of land and resources to export crops."[38]

The enforced exports, consisting of fresh vegetables, fruits, flowers, largely replacing traditional exports like sugar, tea, coffee, timber and cotton, led to a decline in the availability of grain—a food for people in affected countries—which was at the root of growing food crisis and consequent price rises lowering the purchasing power of the people and ultimately leading to mass suicides of farmers failing to cover their loans, taking altogether over 160,000 lives over the last decade (Patnaik, 2010).

An emerging situation like this naturally raises the most serious question delving into the future prospect of increasing agricultural production, particularly food grains, with a more efficient use of existing resources in order to reduce the gap between supply and demand. Hence, the most searching question is—does nature offer any further scope of getting more production out of the fast dwindling natural resources taking recourse to much more careful and judicious practices based on experience of gains and failures or unintentional mistakes?

NOTES

Note A

"It was not until the beginning of the nineteenth century that world population attained its first billion (around 1804). Then, while it took some 123 years to add a second billion (1927), the third took only another 33 years, the fourth only 15 years and the fifth and sixth only twelve years each. Looking at it another way, the first millennium saw virtually no net increase from the 300 million people estimated to have been alive around the time of Christ's birth, whereas the second millennium has witnessed a 20-fold growth of population. Perhaps most dramatically, while the first 1900 years from Christ's birth added 1.3 billion people, the last 100 years have added 4.4 billion. ... The fact that world population doubled from 3 to 6 billion between 1960 and 1999 means that its annual rate of growth increase over this period averaged just under 2 per cent."

Source: Peter Daniels, Michael Bradshaw, Denis Shaw and James Sidaway, *An Introduction to Human Geography: Issues for the 21st Century,* Pearson/Prentice Hall, 2005, pp. 88-89.

NOTE B

It is very important to note in this regard that "the economies of Africa have grown at an average rate of 0.7 per cent per year. This difference may not seem like much compared with 1.7 per cent per year in the United States, but over a period of 180 years a small difference in annual growth leads to a huge difference in income levels. With growth of 0.7 per cent per annum, Africa's initial income (roughly $ 400 per capita) increased by little more than three-fold, to roughly $ 1300 per capita as of the year 1998, compared with an almost twenty-nine-fold increase in the United States. Today's twenty-fold gap in income between the United States and Africa, therefore, results from a three-fold gap as of 1820, which was magnified seven times by the difference in annual growth rates of 1.7 per cent in the United States versus 0.7 per cent in Africa."

Source: Sachs, Jeffrey D., 2005, *The End of Poverty: How we can make it Happen in Our Lifetime.* Penguin Books. p. 30.

NOTE C

There is some encouraging news about efforts being made in

agricultural production getting recognition from the central government. It is reported that the West Bengal Government has bagged the "Krishi Karman" (agricultural activity) award from the Central Government this year again, for the fifth time in succession, for increase in cultivation of pulses and registering overall increase in food production in spite of devastating floods of 2014-15.

Source: The Statesman, Kolkata Issue, Kolkata Plus Supplement, 13 April 2017.

NOTE D

It is important to highlight that natural and human-induced catastrophes, which trigger food aid, are currently responsible for around 10 per cent of all hungry and malnourished people in the world; 90 per cent of the hungry suffer from chronic malnutrition. Around 80 per cent of the hungry live in rural areas, half of them are small-holder peasants, another 22 per cent are landless labourers and 8 per cent live by using natural resources, such as pastoralists, fisherfolk etc. The majority of these groups live in extremely marginal conditions, in remote areas without secure access to productive resources, credit and markets and without any formal support by extension services etc. It is extremely important to overcome this marginalisation in order to reduce the number of hungry worldwide. Moreover, it is often the extremely poor and marginalized who are first hit by natural catastrophes. Absence of land reform forces poor and marginal farm households to use land highly vulnerable to catastrophes, such as floods or droughts. National and international agricultural policies have often forced them to migrate to these risk-prone areas. It would therefore be a wrong trend to focus more and more resources on combating catastrophes while failing to address these problems. What is needed is to combat the marginalization of the affected communities and people."

Source: FAO, *The State of Food and Agriculture,* 2006: p. 78.

References

1. Brown, Lester R. (2012). *Full Planet, Empty Plates: The New Geopolitics of Food Security,* Earth Policy Institute, W.W. Norton & Company, New York, London. p. 1.
2. FAO, *The State of Food Insecurity in the World 2008: Undernourishment Around the World: High Food Prices another 75 million Hungry*. Rome: p. 6.

3. Brown, Lester R., *Full Planet, Empty Plates: The New Geopolitics of Food Security*, Earth Policy Institute, W.W. Norton & Company, New York, London. 2012. pp. 9-10.
4. *Ibid.*, p. 58.
5. Kerbs, John (2013). *Food: A Very Short Introduction,* Oxford University Press, p. 92.
6. Ehrlich, Paul R., Anne H. Ehrlieh and Gretchen C. Daily (1993). "Food Security, Population and Environment", in *Population and Development Review* 19, No. 1 (March), p. 17.
7. *Ibid.*, p. 25.
8. The World Bank, *World Development Report 2008: Agriculture and Development*, p. 73.
9. *Ibid.*, p. 47.
10. *Ibid.*, p. 94.
11. *Ibid.*, p. 95.
12. *Op. cit.*
13. *Op. cit.*
14. Sen, Amartya (2008). (Twelfth Impression): *Poverty and Famine: An Essay on Entitlement and Deprivation,* Oxford University Press, p. 158.
15. Ehrlich, Paul R., Anne H. Ehrlieh and Gretchen C. Daily (1993). Food Security, Population and Environment, in *Population and Development Review* 19, No. 1 (March), pp. 6-7.
16. *Ibid.*, p. 9.
17. Rhoades, Robert E. (1991). "The World's Food Supply at Risk", in *National Geographic*, Vol. 179, No. 4 (April 1991): pp. 79 and 84 .
18. Smil, Vaclav (1994). "How Many People Can The Earth Feed?" in *Population and Development Review*, Vol. 20, No. 2 (June 1994): p. 264.
19. *Ibid.*, p. 267.
20. *Ibid.*, p. 272.
21. Dyson, Tim (1996). *Population and Food: Global Trend and Future Prospects*, London, Routledge, p. 133.
22. *Ibid.*, pp. 202-205.
23. Brown, Lester R., *Eco-Economy: Building an Economy for the Earth,* Orient Longman, 2004: p. 147.
24. *Ibid.*, p. 163.
25. Sachs, Jeffrey D. (2005). *The End of Poverty: How we can make it Happen in Our Lifetime*. Penguin Books: p. 20.
26. *Ibid*: pp. 27-29.
27. *Ibid.*, p. 35.
28. *Ibid.*, pp. 33-35.
29. *The Encylopedia Americana* International Edition, 1973, Americana Corporation, New York: p. 122.

30. Sachs, Jeffrey D. (2005). *The End of Poverty: How we can make it Happen in Our Lifetime*. Penguin Books. pp. 30-40.
31. Magnuson, Joel (2013). *The Approaching Great Transformation: Towards a Liveable Post Carbon Economy,* Policy Press at the University of Bristol, p. 19.
32. Brown, Lester R. (2003). *Eco-Economy: Building an Economy for the Earth,* Orient Longman, pp. 100-101.
33. *Ibid.* pp. 110-111.
34. Daniels, Peter, Michael Bradshaw, Denis Shaw and James Sidaway (2005). *An Introduction to Human Geography: Issues for the 21st Century,* Pearson/Prentice Hall, (Second Ed.) p. 89.
35. Holt-Giménez, Eric (2016). "From Food Basics to Food Sovereignty: the challenge of Social Movements", in *Agriculture And Food in Crisis: Conflict, Resistance and Renewal,* by Fred Magdoff and Brian Tokar, Monthly Review Press, New York, p. 209.
36. Bello, Walden, and Mara Baviera (2010). "Food War", in *Agriculture and Food Crisis: Conflict, Resistance and Renewal,* Ed. by Fred Magdoff and Brian Tokar, Monthly Review Press, New York, p. 36.
37. *Ibid.*
38. Patnaik, Utsa (2010). "Origins of the Food Crisis in India and Developing Countries," in *Agriculture and Food Crisis: Conflict, Resistance and Renewal,* Ed. by Fred Magdoff and Brian Tokar, Monthly Review Press, New York, p. 94.

4
Limitations and Opportunities

Quite evidently, it is necessary to explore the possibilities of having a greater return from a more judicious use of existing natural resources so that food production may keep pace with the growth of global population. At the same time one has to take into account the anomalous situation where availability of food does not always mean it reaches everybody without any hindrance, such as poverty barring people's access to food when they are bereft of purchasing power—the money to buy food for himself/herself as well as the family, often because a price rise caused by some unrelated factors makes food unaffordable.

I will talk first about some limitations quite often caused by natural factors which have to be viewed as conditions making productive process gradually inadequate or largely inactive. Facts in this regard are more realistic in terms of our expectations for a better future when we see that in spite of world's farmers having tripled world grain production, raising it from 631 million tonnes in 1950 to 1,835 million tonnes in 2000, almost double that from the beginning of agriculture 11,000 years ago, until 1960, it was overshadowed by the presence of over 1 billion hungry and undernourished people, and the World Bank reporting that, of the 1.3 billion people living in poverty, earning up to $ 1 a day, 72 per cent of whom live in rural areas, obviously of the developing world (Brown, 2004 Reprint).*

A re-evaluation of natural assets offering any further scope

---

* Lester R. Brown, *Eco-Economy: Building an Economy for the Earth* (Orient Longman, 2004).

for boosting agricultural production through more judicious practices demands an assessment of the existing status along with future prospects of greater returns. In this context we need to take up systematically each of the natural assets for assessing how far it can contribute to improve further the scope of agricultural production. Proceeding with one of the most valuable natural assets, the Forest Wealth, Brown (2004 Reprint) points out that,

> "protecting the earth's 3.9 billion hectares of remaining forests and replanting those lost are both essential for restoring the earth's health and providing an important foundation for economy. Reducing rainfall runoff and the associated flooding and soil erosion, recycling rainfall inland, and restoring aquifer recharge depend on simultaneously reducing pressure on forests and on reforestation."[1]

However, only about 290 million hectares of global forest areas are legally protected from logging while a substantial proportion of this natural asset is exploited for various industrial purposes, major part of which is used for making pulp in the industrial countries, or as fuel wood in the developing countries, apart from making furniture and also used as building material. However, if all the major 10 paper-producing countries had followed the example of Germany in recycling, the use of wood pulp to produce paper worldwide would drop by one-third (Brown, 2006).*

Further, taking the example of the Philippines, banning logging particularly in old-growth and virgin forests and thus arresting large-scale flooding, erosion and landslides in particular followed also in a country like India, could save this important natural resource from extinction and this could turn into a very important source of replenishing the world's food-bowl. Brown (2006), quoting Reed Funk, Professor of Plant Biology at Rutgers University, believes that the vast areas of

* Lester R. Brown, *Plan B 2.0: Rescuing a Planet Under Stress and Civilization in Trouble* (New York and London, W.W. Norton and Company, 2006).

deforested land can be used to grow trillions of genetically improved trees for food, mostly nuts, and for fuel. Funk observes that nuts could be used to supplement meat as a source of 'high-quality protein in developing country diets'.

The second most important problem involving the restorative process of nature is to conserve and rebuild soils lost or getting lost through 'clear-cutting, overgrazing and overploughing' (Brown, 2006)* for which planting rows of tree shelter belts have proved to be very effective way to check wind erosion where strip-cropping consisting of planting crops on alternate strips leaving cultivable fallows each year permit soil moisture to accumulate on fallowed strips. Planted strips reduce wind speed which cuts down erosion on the land lying unused. Besides, the practice of conserving tillage including both no-till and minimum tillage, apart from reducing both wind and water erosion helps in retaining water, raises carbon content in the soil, and reduces energy consumption needed for crop cultivation. Incidentally, severe lessons of overploughing and overgrazing are provided by the formation of the 1930s Dust Bowl in the U.S., forcing hundreds of thousands of farm families to leave the Great Plains. A repetition of the same history is provided by erstwhile Soviet Union where the 'Virgin Lands Project', between 1954 and 1960, one which in an effort to 'convert grassland into grainland, exceeding the current grainland in Canada and Australia combined' after some initial success turned into a dust bowl. Kazakhstan, as part of this Virgin Lands Project, saw its grainland peaking at 25 million hectares in early 1980s, reduced to 17 million ha in 2009, declined further, giving an extremely poor yield of hardly 1 ton per hectare—in sharp contrast to 7 tons per hectare in France today (Brown, 2012).† At present, two more dust bowls have formed—one in north-western China and western Mongolia while the other is in the Sahel in Africa, stretching across the continent from Somalia and Ethiopia in the east to Senegal and Mauritania in the west, separating the Sahara Desert from the tropical rainforests in the

---

* *Ibid.*

† Lester R. Brown, *Full Planet, Empty Plates: The New Geopolitics of Food Security* (New York, London, Earth Policy Institute, W.W. Norton & Company, 2012).

south. "Both of these newer dust bowls are massive in scale, dwarfing anything in the world has seen before."[2]

In no-till practice, the seeds are directly drilled into the soil left with its residues of the previous year's cropping undisturbed, the latter becoming resistant to water and wind erosion. The no-till practice proved as a very effective way of conserving nature from natural elements of wind and water in their erosive role, and the practice has thus become very popular as a dependable way of crop production. The no-till area has expanded from 7 million hectares in 1990 to 25 million hectares in 2004 in the US alone, widely used for the production of corn and soybeans. Practised widely in the western world, no-till area covers 24 million hectares in Brazil, 18 million hectares in Argentina, 13 million hectares in Canada and 9 million hectares in Australia. It is also slowly becoming popular in Europe, Africa and Asia as well.[3] (Note A)

On the other hand, for saving cultivable land from advancing deserts, measures adopted in some countries have proved very effective, such as in Algeria where development of orchards and vineyards in the southern part of the country are going to halt desertification of its croplands. In 2005, the Moroccan government pledged to fight severe drought and allocated funds for farmers to convert cereal planted areas into less vulnerable olive and fruit orchards. Nigeria is going to create a five-kilometre wide 'Green Wall' of trees stretching 7000 kilometres to check the inroad of Sahara Desert. Senegal, lying at the western end of this proposed 'Green Wall', is losing 50,000 hectares of productive land each year to the approaching desert. China provides another example fighting the progress of Gobi Desert inland, for which it is paying its farmers in affected areas for planting trees in their croplands, covering altogether 10 million hectares of grainland, representing about one-tenth of China's total grainland area. Inner Mongolia, in order to reclaim land for productive use, uses desert shrubs to stabilize the sand dunes and has succeeded in the process, saving 7,000 ha of land, besides having completely banned rearing of sheep and goats, replacing it with dairy cattle in closed areas, feeding them on corn stalks, wheat straw, some drought-tolerant forage crop resembling alfalfa and thus having increased their number from 30,000 in 2002 to 150,000 by 2007. The programme is likely to double the income of farmers within a decade. Incidentally, the stall-feeding practice has been borrowed from India (Brown, 2006). Nigeria, Africa's most populous country, is losing 868,000 acres of rangeland cropland every year to desertification. The growth of the goat population compared to sheep and cattle is in direct relationship with grassland deterioration when overgrazing changes grasslands into desert shrubs. India is also faced with the problem of expanding deserts. According to Brown (2012)*, with only 2 per cent of the world's land area it has to support 18 per cent of the world population, and 15 per cent of its cattle. According to Indian Space Research Institute (ISRO), 25 per cent of India's land surface is slowly turning into desert, threatening the life of India's cattle population as well as human economy.

The most life-threatening effect of the formation of dust bowls are the generation of dust storms already having suffocating effect on the people with their frequent occurrences. The grave consequences of dust storms having turned into a very common and frequent happening is experienced most in China in late winter and early spring, with an average of ten major dust storms visiting the north-eastern part each year, reaching as far as South Korea, at times leaving people gasping for breath, the intensity of which is increasing fast from an average of 39 days a year in the 1980s, 77 days in 1990s, and 111 days from 2000 to 2011 (Brown, 2012).† The effect of this fast growing ecological catastrophe originating in north-western and north-central China may even spread far, and

> "on April 18, 2001, for instance, the Western United States—from Arizona border north to Canada—was blanketed with dust ... (which came from a huge dust storm that originated in north-western China and Mongolia on April 5th."[4] (Note B)

However, regions more affected by dust storms are in

---

* Lester R. Brown, *Full Planet, Empty Plates: The New Geopolitics of Food Security* (New York, London, Earth Policy Institute, W.W. Norton & Company, 2012).

† *Ibid.*

Africa. According to an expert, dust storms previously a rare occurrence in Sahara, have become a common thing, increasing ten-fold during the last half century invading most countries like Niger, Chad, Northern Nigeria, Burkina Faso and Mauritania, where top soils had been badly eroded. Interestingly, dust storms originating in Africa travel west across the Atlantic and deposit dust in the Caribbean.

> "The 2-3 billion tons of fine soil particles that leave Africa each year in dust storms are slowly draining the continent of its fertility and hence its biological productivity."[5]

Dust storms are a very common feature in India, particularly in the northern plains with increasing frequency in their appearance and that is also the case in Western Syria and northern Iraq where from sometimes they travel eastward into Iran.

Water, having no substitute, is an absolute necessity needed in a vast quantity for production of crops. Food as a highly water-intensive product consumes 70 per cent of the world's fresh water in irrigation. Though use of irrigation goes back nearly 6,000 years it was only in the second half of the twentieth century that it had its rapid expansion, its coverage increasing from about 250 million acres to almost 700 million acres by 2000, though slowing down later 'expanding only 9 per cent between 2000 and 2009' (Brown, 2012). In fact, water has turned into the most scarce natural resource and becoming more and more scarce with its demand increasing in all spheres of production including various forms of human consumption. But,

> "human action alters rivers in numerous ways. Unchecked pollution diminishes water quality and depletes the oxygen that fish and other riverine life need. The introduction of normative species, whether accidentally or intentionally, changes predator-prey relationships and other interactions among native biological communities. One threat to river health looms over the others, a force of ecosystem decline that has quite literally reached geologic proportions resulting

> from the alteration of natural flows by dams, diversions, levees and other infrastructure.
>
> "An estimated 800,000 dams of all sizes now block the flow of the world's rivers. Approximately one-fourth of the global flux of sediment carried by flowing water now gets trapped in reservoirs rather than nourishing floodplains, deltas and estuaries. Swedish scientists Matts Dynesius and Christer Nilsson report that 77 per cent of the large river systems in the United States, Canada, Europe and the former Soviet Union—essentially the northern third of the world—are moderately to strongly altered by dams, reservoirs, diversions and irrigation projects. They warn that, because of the extent of river modifications, key habitats such as waterfalls, rapids, and floodplain wetlands could disappear entirely from some regions, extinguishing many plant and animal species that depend on running-water habitats. Perhaps the most startling finding about the scale of human hydrological impacts is that the weight of impounded waters at high latitudes in the northern hemisphere has slightly altered the tilt of the earth's axis and increased the speed of the earth's rotation."[6]

Postel and Richter further point out that the growing demands for more and more water in step with population and economic growth since the Second World War required for urban, industrial and agricultural uses along with hydrological power generation led to "unprecedented boom in the construction of dams and reservoirs, so much so that the number of large dams (at 15 metres and higher) increased from 5,000 in 1950s to 45,000." (Table 4.1) (Fig. 4.1). According to these authors, about half of the large dams were constructed for irrigation purposes, mostly concentrated in Asia, as in China, India and Japan, contributing directly to 12-16 per cent of global food production (Postel and Richter, 2003). To get a correct idea about the role of dams built so far across almost all the big rivers of the world gives a frightful picture of their role in controlling the flow of fresh water on the one hand and the frightening consequences on the other. Having "girdled with dams, many of

Table 4.1: Worldwide Distribution of Large Dams by Country

Sl. No.	Country	Number of Large Dams	Per cent of World Total
1.	China	22,000	46.2
2.	United States	6,575	13.8
3.	India	4,291	9.0
4.	Japan	2,675	5.6
5.	Spain	1,196	2.5
6.	Canada	793	1.7
7.	South Korea	765	1.3
8.	Turkey	625	1.3
9.	Brazil	594	1.3
10.	France	569	1.2
11.	South Africa	539	1.1
12.	Mexico	537	1.1
13.	Italy	524	1.1
14.	United Kingdom	517	1.1
15.	Australia	486	1.0
16.	Others	4,969	10.4
	World Total	**47,655**	**100.0**

Source: Postel and Richter, 2003.
Note: Large Dam: 15 Metres.

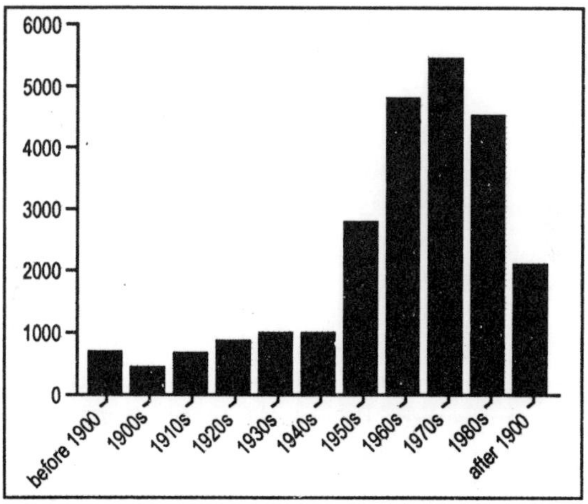

Fig. 4.1: Construction of Dams in the World by Decades (China not included)

Source: World Commission Dams 2001, Sandra Patel and Brian Pichtel, 2003.

the great rivers are now little more than staircases of reservoirs",[7] having 19 dams across only 70 kilometres of the total 2000 kilometres of the Colorado River, US. Damming is the case with many other rivers, such as

> "in France ... (and) elsewhere in Europe, neither Volga, the Weser, the Ebro nor the Tagus has a stretch more than a quarter of its length which has escaped being turned into a reservoir."[8]

This is the case all over the world and as McCully (1998) points out, worldwide 'the combined storage capacity of about 6,000 cubic kilometres, equivalent to over three times the volume of water in all the rivers in the world', inundating more than 400,000 square kilometres, or submerging 0.3 per cent of the global land surface, turns into a greater loss considering the fact that it involves inundation of the floodplains representing the world's most fertile farmland, marshes, forests and wildlife while degrading the most valuable asset for human existence—the freshwater—beside endangering or making extinct one-fifth of the world's freshwater fish and flooding off almost 60 million people from their lands inhabited by them (McCully, 1998).*

Regarding water fast becoming a scarce commodity on earth we have to remember that the major source of our water is rainfall that falls on earth for supplying our system of life such as meeting requirements of agriculture and food production, industrial waste disposal and support of natural and semi-natural ecosystems.

> "The fate of this water (rainfall) is either to be taken up by plants and the soil and then eventually returned to the atmosphere by evapotranspiration, or to drain from the land into the sea *via* rivers, lakes and wastelands. Our primary source of water is runoff diverted by humans for use in irrigated agriculture, in industry and in homes (rural and urban); for consumption of various kinds, and for waste disposal. It is the water of

---

* Patrick McCully, *Silenced Rivers: The Ecology and Politics of Large Dams* (Orient Longman, 1998).

> evapotranspiration that mainly supports forests, rainfed cultivated and grazing land, and a variety of ecosystems. Despite a withdrawal of only 8 per cent of total annual renewable freshwater resources, it has been estimated that 26 per cent of annual evapotranspiration and 4 per cent of accessible runoff is now appropriated by humans."[9]

However, use of water is increasing per capita with changes in lifestyle along with population increases.

It should be noted that already over 2 billion people in the world are affected by water shortages in forty countries of which 1.1 billion do not have sufficient water for drinking purpose while 2.4 billion have no provision for sanitation which is at the root of increases in diseases, poor food quality, conflicts between different users and limitation on many livelihood and productive activities. According to the same source (U.N., 2003)* 'by 2050 at least one in four people is likely to live in countries affected by chronic or recurring shortage of fresh water.' Gravity of the situation is further emphasized by the fact that the minimum annual per capita requirement of 1,700 cubic metres of drinking water necessary for active and healthy life for people is not met in many of the developing countries, the solution becoming more grave in the cities. As mentioned in the Report (U.N., 2003),† per capita water use among the people of the world in general has gone down by one-third between 1970 and 1990 as a result of population growth. It is rather going to be a highly alarming situation when, as suggested by projections,

> "nearly 7 billion people in 60 countries will live water-scarce lives by 2050. Even under the lowest projection, just under 2 billion people in 48 countries will struggle against water scarcity in 2050."[10]

In fact, there cannot be any complacency in this matter

---

* United Nations, *World Water Development Report: World Water Assessment Programme, Water for People, Water for Life* (UNESCO Publishing, Bergham Books, 2003).

† *Ibid.*

looking at the fact that while water consumption has nearly doubled during the last fifty years, the contrast is widening further with the growth of population in developing countries considering the reality that a child born in the developed world consumes '30-50 times the water resources of one in the developing country' (U.N., 2003).

The situation is aggravated further by the quality of water which getting polluted from various sources has already made it highly unsuitable for human consumption in many countries. As reported by the U.N. (2003),* even when there are enough water to meet current needs, increasing rates of pollution of water in rivers, lakes as well as groundwater resources are making it unusable for any purpose. Quite alarmingly, with 2 million tons of human waste disposed of in watercourses a day, other sources of pollution are industrial wastes and chemicals, agricultural pesticides and fertilizers. The resultant incidence of diseases connected with the consumption of polluted water, particularly in the developing countries make half their population exposed to them. As mentioned in the report (U.N., 2003),

> "key forms of pollution include faecal coliforms, industrial organic substances, acidifying substances from mining aquifers and atmospheric emissions, heavy metals from industry, ammonia, nitrate and phosphate pollution from agriculture, pesticide residues (again from agriculture), sediments from human-induced erosion to rivers, lakes and reservoirs and salinization. The situation is particularly bad in developing countries where institutional and structural arrangements for the treatment of municipal, industrial and agricultural waste are poor. Levels of suspended solids in rivers in Asia have risen by a factor of four over the last three decades. Asian rivers also have a biological oxygen demand some 1.4 times the global average, as well as three times as many bacteria from human waste as the global average. They also include rivers that have twenty times more

---

* *Ibid.* United Nations, *World Water Development Report: World Water Assessment Programme, Water for People, Water for Life* (UNESCO Publishing, Bergham Books, 2003).

lead than that in surface waters of OECD countries."[11] (Note C)

Use of Water

An assessment of the use of water by various agencies makes it necessary to find out the demand for freshwater, a finite vulnerable resource in different regions of the world, and as shown in Fig. 4.2, by 2025 it will be the highest in the U.S., followed by Canada. Agriculture, already mentioned earlier, as

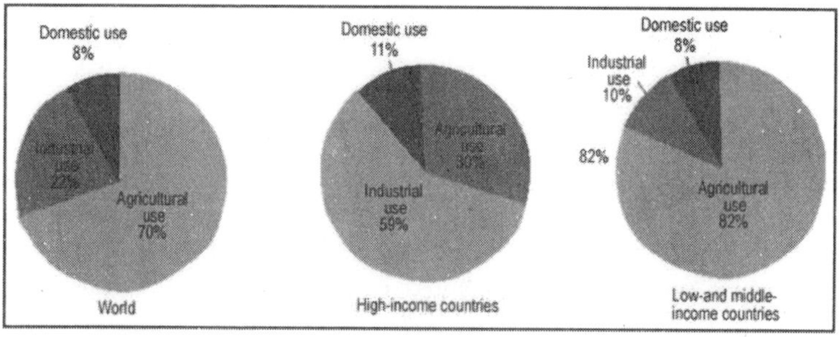

Fig. 4.2: Use of Water for Different Purposes for Different Income Groups

Source: UN World Water Development Report 2003.

the major consumer of fresh water, is going to face a loss in its momentum in expansion and, coupled with depletion of aquifers, is going to experience reduction in irrigated area in some countries. While 40 per cent of the world's grain harvest is grown on irrigated land—mentioned earlier—with four-fifths of it coming from irrigated land in China, three-fourths from India, and only one-fifth from the U.S., Asia dominates the world in irrigated area (Brown, 2012).* The period between 1950 to 1975, coinciding with dam-building spree around the world was, as such, the period of surface irrigation which changed into drilling wells for access to underground storage since the 1970s. The aquifers get their water from rainfall seeping through surface

* Lester R. Brown, *Full Planet, Empty Plates: The New Geopolitics of Food Security* (New York, London, Earth Policy Institute, W.W. Norton & Company, 2012).

and replenishing them to keep their supply as long as the rate of replenishment is not exceeded by overexploitation and thus reducing the rate of irrigation. There are at least 18 countries containing more than half the world's population where the rate of depletion of groundwaters is affecting grain harvest.

According to Brown (2012),* among the countries hit very hard by depleted aquifers are Saudi Arabia, while enjoying wheat self-sufficiency for over 20 years, the government has announced a programme of phasing out wheat production since the beginning of 2008, where wheat production having dropped almost half between 2007 and 2011, the country, in order to avoid food insecurity, went to lease (or buy) land in Ethiopia and Sudan for food production. Yemen is another country facing similar problem with water tables falling by some 2 metres per year, had even to ration the tap water to only once in the capital city when shrinkage of harvest was threatening hunger nationwide. Similarly, in both Syria and Iraq many wells drilled in turned inactive due to falling water tables caused by overpumping which had a severe effect on annual harvest, bringing it down to its one third in Syria, having declined by one-sixth of peak production 2002. Jordan faced a similar fate due to 'unsustainable aquifer withdrawals' (Brown, 2012),† bringing down its harvests from 300,000 tons per year about 40 years ago to mere 55,000 tons today.

> "Thus the Arab Middle East with its high growth of population witnessing a collision between population growth and water supply. Because of the failure of governments in the region to mesh population and water policies, each day now brings 9000 more people to feed and less irrigation water with which to feed them."[12]

Water shortages are also threatening China's harvest where 130 million people in North China Plain, itself a highly

---

* Lester R. Brown, *Full Planet, Empty Plates: The New Geopolitics of Food Security* (New York, London, Earth Policy Institute, W.W. Norton & Company, 2012).

† *Ibid.*

productive area, are fed with grain produced with highly unsustainable supply of groundwater provided by two aquifers—the shallow aquifer, rechargeable but largely depleted, and deep fossil aquifer, depletion of which will force farmers to turn to rain-fed crops. The fall in water table is quite high, the average level being nearly 10 feet in Hebei Province, in the heart of North China Plain, the level being abnormally high, 6 metre in one year around some cities. According to another report, Beijing was drilling from 1000 feet to reach water, five times deeper than 20 years ago (Brown, 2012).*

In this respect India faces a much more grim future where 21 million shallow wells have been drilled by farmers having been given an almost free ride by the government providing heavily subsidized electricity acting as a great impetus in accelerating the rate of withdrawal of groundwater causing fast fall of water level, by 20 feet per year in Gujarat. Other states equally affected are Punjab, Haryana, Rajasthan and Tamil Nadu, in the last of them the falling water table has dried up 95 per cent of the wells owned by small farmers. However, the rich farmers are stalling this frightening prospect by drilling further deep down using modified oil-drilling technology, going as far down as 1000 feet in some locations. The whole operation is highly expensive and energy-intensive. Sadly, where underground resources have gone completely dry, agriculture has turned into a rain-fed practice and drinking water is brought from outside in trucks (Brown, 2012).†

Depleting aquifers along with increasing demand from urban areas in the US have combined to reduce irrigated area from about 9 million acres in 1997 to 8 million acres in 2007 in California, historically the irrigation leader. In Texas, similar drop in irrigated area happened, from 7 million acres in 1978 to 5 million acres in 2007. Other states affected with shrinking irrigated area include Arizona, Colorado and Florida, and among them Colorado seems to be facing the worst, the shrinkage, as predicted, amounting to a loss of 700,000 acres of

---

* Lester R. brown, *Full Planet, Empty Plates: The New Geopolitics of Food Security* (New York, London, Earth Policy Institute, W.W. Norton & Company, 2012)

† *Ibid.*

irrigated land between 2010 and 2050, roughly one-fifth of the state's total (Brown, 2012)* (Table 4.2).

Table 4.2: Countries Overpumping Aquifers in 2012

Sl. No.	*Country*	*Population (millions)*
1.	Afghanistan	33
2.	China	1,354
3.	India	1,258
4.	Iran	76
5.	Iraq	34
6.	Israel	8
7.	Jordon	6
8.	Lebanon	4
9.	Mexico	116
10.	Morocco	33
11.	Pakistan	180
12.	Saudi Arabia	29
13.	South Korea	49
14.	Spain	47
15.	Syria	21
16.	Tunisia	11
17.	United States	316
18.	Yemen	26
	Total	**3,599**

Source: Brown (2012) (Earth Policy Institute, with Populations from U.N. Population Division).

In Mexico, water table is falling by 6 feet or more a year, and farmers in the north-west pumping water from a depth of 40 feet once, has to pump it from over 400 feet now. The over-pumped aquifers providing 58 per cent of Mexico's water needs will soon have a disastrous effect on its food production capability.

The situation of growing scarcity of water has further intensified in Egypt, a country with one of the highest yields of wheat in the world, facing very stiff competition with three more countries sharing the waters of the Nile. The other countries are Sudans—the Sudan and South Sudan, and Ethiopia, all these three upstream countries together occupying three-fourths of the

* Lester R. Brown, *Full Planet, Empty Plates: The New Geopolitics of Food Security* (New York, London, Earth Policy Institute, W.W. Norton & Company, 2012).

Upper Nile River Basin, which are also the targets of land grab, of which South Sudan has already given up 4 per cent of its land area to foreign investors. Any further scope of finding more food for the growing population, likely to reach 101 million by 2025, is going to be an unachievable target while further potential for increasing land productivity appear impossible.

Mekong Basin faces a similar situation where water flow of the river, Mekong, flowing through a number of dams and their reservoirs built by China in its upper reaches, gets reduced and the loss of water volume is further curtailed through evaporation, amounting to about 10 per cent from each reservoir. Finally leaving very little portion of the river water reaching the delta and threatening the down-stream ecosystem, reducing fish populations and people's livelihood (Brown, 2012).*

Another country, Pakistan, is going through a very struggling situation with its principal river, Indus, in keeping up with its dual responsibilities of providing water for its basin, the world's largest irrigation as well as meeting all needs of the entire country leaving hardly any water for the river to reach the ocean.

It is not Colorado, Nile or Indus alone gradually losing irrigation water in sharing it with other non-agricultural uses. Chennai in India provides another glaring example in this regard where,

> as a result of the city government's inability to supply water to many of its residents, a thriving tank-truck industry has emerged that buys water from nearby farmers and hauls it to the city's thirsty residents. For farmers near the city, the market price of water far exceeds the value of the crops they can produce with it. Unfortunately, the 13,000 truckers hauling water to Chennai are mining the region's underground water resources. Water tables are falling and shallow wells have gone dry. Eventually, even the deeper wells will go

* Lester R. Brown, *Full Planet, Empty Plates: The New Geopolitics of Food Security* (New York, London, Earth Policy Institute, W.W. Norton & Company, 2012).

dry, depriving rural communities of both their food supply and their livelihood."[13]

As Lester R. Brown (2012)* acquaints us with the existing conditions to the nature and cause of the current situation in regard to growing water scarcity, the message of its highly alarming consequences are not difficult to comprehend. Quite apparently the humanity all the worldover, irrespective of difference in economic level, is in a direct collision, the greatest challenge of any time since man started growing his own food, such as between growing population (even though having already stabilized or slowly approaching stabilization in many parts of the world) and feeding them (when rising income is already putting increasing thrust on diet-change). In a threatening situation like this countries gradually losing in the race of producing enough food due to fast depleting aquifers through over-pumping, are forced to import food as equivalent to importing water lost in the competition, but this can never be a permanent solution to food security as the total amount of food grown in the world—either in the form of grains or in the form of high-value fruits/nuts etc. or animal protein—is very likely to go down when sufficient water (1000 tons of water is needed for producing 1 ton of grain) is not available. A situation like this happening on an unprecedented scale spells disaster for human society.

In this perspective we need to restore the water-regime of our river systems so that we can derive the benefits to our advantage. In saving water one needs to be reminded that,

> "water is fundamental for life in human dignity. It is a prerequisite to the realization of all other human rights ... adopted by the Covenant on Economic, Social and Cultural Rights (CESCR) in November 2002, is a milestone in the history of human rights,"[14]

the most important basis of which is not only entitlement to food, but easy access to it. Based on this primary requirement of humanity, one is amazed to find in how many ways water acts

---

* Lester R. Brown, *Full Planet, Empty Plates: The New Geopolitics of Food Security* (New York, London, Earth Policy Institute, W.W. Norton & Company, 2012).

as a saviour of mankind (including all sorts of other lives), such as

> "water has the pivotal role in mediating global ecosystem process, linking together the atmosphere, lithosphere and biosphere by moving substances between them and enabling chemical reactions to take place. Not only is it essential for maintaining living organisms, but its physical properties allow it to be used by humans for energy generation, transport and waste disposal, and in a variety of industrial processes. Access to a sufficient amount of good-quality water is essential to human health; productive freshwater ecosystems are crucial to the livelihood of fishers and other littoral communities; and healthy freshwater systems provide a range of services to people worldwide."[15]

One needs to be cautioned that it is high time for the humanity to be actively conscious about imperilling life unless it behaves with the simple logic that even though freshwater ecosystem represents less than one per cent of all the habitat area on earth, compared with about 28 per cent by terrestrial ecosystems and 71 per cent by marine ecosystems, the freshwater ecosystem's role in human life is much more critical than that of others since,

> "species/richness relative to habitat extent is greater in freshwater ecosystem than either of the other two. Home to 2.4 per cent of globally known species but comprising only 0.8 per cent of earth's total habitat area, freshwater ecosystems have a higher species density than either terrestrial or marine ecosystems."[16]

It, thus, becomes imperative that the loss of freshwater will lead to the loss of a significant share of the variety of freshwater life which, as a matter of great concern, is already happening everywhere around us, as claimed by researchers in this field during recent decades when

> "at least 20 per cent of the world's ten thousand freshwater fish species have become endangered,

threatened with extinction, or have already gone extinct. A significant, but known, share of mussels, birds, amphibians, plants and other species that depend on freshwater habitats are also believed to be at risk."[17] (Note D)

Undoubtedly, human life directly dependent on the various species becomes equally endangered with their loss and gradual shrinkage of this source of food likely to reach highly critical level as life-support for the growing population. It is pointed out that at least 123 species of North American freshwater fish etc. have already gone extinct size 1900 and it has been estimated that as the most investigated ecosystems in the world, the rate of extinction of fish species—averaging half a per cent per decade—is likely to increase to 3.7 per cent, five times more than the rate of extinction of animal species of terrestrial ecosystems. (Postel and Richter, 2003).* Interestingly, the US freshwater ecosystems as the leading habitat for the three hundred known species of freshwater mussels, snails and salamanders etc. and with about eight hundred species of freshwater fish, ranks as seventh in freshwater fish diversity in the world. Equally victims are the tropical rainforest freshwater ecosystems, suffering from the loss of species diversity. However, individually wild Atlantic salmon have significantly dwindled in number and at least 214 salmon and steelhead stocks are at a risk of extinction (Postel and Richter, 2003). As reported, historically more than two thousand rivers on both sides of the Atlantic ocean had the wild salmons but, according to the WWF (World Wildlife Fund), they have completely disappeared from more than 300 river systems stretching from countries like Germany, Switzerland, Belgium, the Netherlands, the Czech Republic and Slovakia, while it is likely for them to vanish soon from the rivers of Portugal, Poland, Estonia, the United States and parts of Canada. The only countries which still have about 90 per cent of healthy wild Atlantic salmon are Scotland, Iceland and Norway.

---

* Postel, Sandra and Brian Richts, (2003). *Rivers for Life: Managing Water For People and Nature,* Island Press, Washington, Cavelo, London.

> "Overfishing, dam construction, other river engineering projects, pollution, and commercial salmon farming, which spreads disease and erodes the gene pool of wild populations."[18]

are responsible for this disaster. (See Note E)

We need to get out of this worsening situation of water becoming a more and more scarce commodity to meet growing human demand, including that of escalating food production commensurate with population increase.

In this context an assessment of the life-support services provided by rivers, wetlands, and other freshwater ecosystems shows their crucial role in human life (Table 4.3). Further, one feels highly curious about the economic value of all these services taken together which, as suggested by Postel and Richter (2003), may be made based on the following principle. Such as, the monetary value of freshwater fish consumed may be on the basis of 'the market value of commercial catches plus tourism and other receipts related to recreational fishing'. However, it becomes difficult to assess the monetary return available for the cultural and aesthetic values of river fish. But,

> "it is possible to value rivers and other freshwater systems for the water supply services by estimating the cost of replacing natural supplies with de-salted sea water. Substituting the entire volume of fresh water now consumed by the global economy—some 2000 cubic kilometres a year—with desalinated water (assuming this could be done, which is questionable) would cost on the order of $ 3 trillion annually, not counting the expense of distributing the water to users, or the air pollution and climate change impacts of so many energy-intensive de-salting plants. In other words, if river, lakes and wetlands dried up, at least 7 per cent of the entire global gross national product (GNP) would have to be devoted to treating water supplies that nature now provides for free. Many forms of recreation—boating, swimming, and fishing, for instance—would vanish, and these losses might be quantifiable as well.

Table 4.3: Life-Support Services provided by Rivers, Wetlands and other Freshwater Ecosystems

Ecosystem Services	*Benefits*
Provision of Water Supplies	More than 99 per cent of irrigation, industrial and household water supplies worldwide come from natural freshwater systems.
Provision of food	Fish, waterfowl, mussles, clams and the like are important food sources for people and wildlife.
Water purification/Water treatment	Wetlands filler and breakdown pollutants, protecting water quality.
Flood Mitigation	Healthy watersheds and floodplains absorb rainwater and river flows, reducing flood damage.
Drought Mitigation	Healthy watersheds, floodplains and wetlands absorb rainwater, slow runoff and help recharge groundwater.
Provision of Habitat	Rivers, streams, floodplains and wetlands provide homes and breeding sites for fish, birds, wildlife and numerous other species.
Soil Fertility Maintenance	Healthy river-floodplain systems constantly renew the fertility of surrounding soils.
Nutrient Delivery	Rivers carry nutrient–rich sediment to deltas and estuaries, helping maintain their productivity.
Maintenance of Coastal Salinity Zones	Freshwater flows maintain the salinity gradients of deltas and coastal marine environments, a key to their biological richness and productivity.
Provision of beauty and life-fulfilling values	Natural rivers and waterscapes are sources of inspiration and deep cultural and spiritual values; their beauty enhances the quality of human life.
Recreational Opportunities	Swimming, fishing, hunting, boating, wildlife viewing, waterside hiking and picnicking.
Biodiversity Conservation	Diverse assemblage of species perform the work of nature (including all the services in this table) upon which societies depend: conserving genetic diversity preserves options for the future.

Source: Sandra Postel and Brian Richter, 2003.

But humanity would also lose the aesthetic, cultural and spiritual benefits that emanate from sparkling rivers, mountain streams, and the knowledge that a rich diversity of freshwater life exists—losses that cannot be expressed monetarily, but that may be even more important than those that can."[19]

In this context, we may look at another related observation made by Balmford *et al.* (2002),* referring to an estimate made on the 'value of ecosystem goods and services', putting the nature's services in the range of $ 18 trillion to $ 61 trillion, around a rough average of $ 38 trillion, which is similar in size to global gross national product (GNP), updated to US $.[20] Eventually, we have to recognize once for all that the life-sustaining role of the freshwater ecosystem is in dire peril under excessive pressure of growing population, its growing demands with continuing change in human tastes and desires for water, food, energy and other limitless material claims.

> "Meeting the challenge of satisfying human needs while at the same time protecting the health of the aquatic environment will require a much more fundamental shift in how society uses, manages and values fresh water—one that recognizes from the outset the importance of healthy ecosystems and humanity's dependence on them. As the great physicist Albert Einstein observed, you cannot solve a problem within the mind-set that created it."[21]

Any development plan should consider freshwater ecosystems as resources to be exploited for human economy, providing more water for agriculture, industry, transport etc. In order to make this happen,

> "Society ... needs to make what we might call an ecosystem support allocation ...—a designation of the quantity, quality, and timing of flows needed to safeguard the health and functioning of the river systems themselves. This eco-support allocation implies

---

* Andrew Balmford, Aaron Bruner, Philip Cooper, Robert Constanza, Stephen Farbes, Rhys E. Green, Martin Jenkins, Paul Jeffries, Valma Jessamy, Joan Madden, Kat Munro, Norman Myers, Shahid Naeem, J. Pavola, Mathew Rayment, Sergio Rosendo, Joan Roughgarden, Kate Trumper, Economic Reasons for Conserving Wild Nature in *Science Magazine* (American Association for the Advancement of Science, 2002).

> a limit on the degree to which society can wisely alter natural river flows, a limit that we call the sustainability boundary."[22]

On questioning if we can save Earth's rivers, both Postel and Richter (2003) think that it all depends on taking certain absolutely necessary steps. Such as, (a) man must cooperate with nature's cycles which, in other words, mean 'co-exist with aquatic communities, otherwise they will be perpetually lost with their ecological performances; (b) growth of population and consumption are needed to be reduced along with reducing per capita use of water and energy, particularly in the developed countries; (c) raising water productivity requires suitable changes in the conventional flood irrigation to drip irrigation saves water. Besides, changes in dietary habits, from high animal-protein to vegetarian, make noticeable impact on rivers and aquifers when a typical American diet consumes almost 1,970 cubic metres of water (in the form of evapotranspiration) while an 'equally nutritious' vegetarian diet consumes only 950 cubic metres, so that using same amount of energy two instead of one person could be fed; (d) water needs to be treated as a public trust to be preserved for the common good of this as well as future generations; (d) lastly, since

> "each habitat and species in the normal world is a life-support component, performing task we may or may not be aware of or know the value. For our own self-preservation, it makes sense to conserve all the components unless we can say with certainty that a particular piece can be eliminated without causing serious harm. With so many components already gone or at risk, there is a premium now on preserving those that remain (which, in other words, is called by the authors as
>
> an ethic of stewardship toward fresh water and its dependent species, a life-support component performing tasks we may not be aware of or know the value of, is about respecting the beauty and mystery of a natural world we did not create and cannot fully understand but over which we have acquired dominance.'"[23]

Water as one of the most scarce resources in its role in human (all other as well) life is further highlighted by the abysmal situation in regard to its availability for drinking and sanitation purposes in the developing world, in sharp contrast in its availability as well as abuses in the developed world for meeting both the requirements as mentioned earlier. All this undoubtedly brings to focus the limitations of water supply, very strongly indicating that any further stress will deteriorate not only the quantity available but the quality as well. Naturally, demand for more water either for domestic consumption in various forms is untenable under existing conditions. Among all the users, agriculture takes the lion's share, as we know, for irrigation and therefore any further expansion in agriculture not only demands more water, and maybe also more land. In general, for 90 per cent of the global population agriculture is the main source of food while, as estimated, the unmanaged natural systems could provide food for 600 million people. Water makes a critical factor for the production of food consisting mainly of cereals, oils, livestock and fish. It may be interesting to observe that the production of cereals is by far the most important source of food, increased by nearly a billion tons, from 0.94 billion tons between the mid-1960s to 1.89 billion tons in 1998, and according to the FAO predictions, it has to increase by another billion tons to cope with population growth, though according to the same source, less than half of the increased amount of cereals will be used as human food and 44 per cent for animal feed (UN, 2003).

The growth in crop production has been primarily with expansion of arable land which has increased by 12 per cent to about 1.5 billion hectares since early 1960, amounting altogether to 11 per cent of global land surface when global population has almost doubled, from 3.1 billion to 5.9 billion in 1981. However, land per person fell by 40 per cent, declining from 0.43 hectares in 1961 to 0.26 hectares in 1998, but in contrast average land yields in the world increased from 1.4 tons per hectare in 1962 to 2.8 tons per hectare in 1996 (UN, 2003).*

---

* United Nations, *World Water Development Report: World Water Assessment Programme, Water for People, Water for Life* (UNESCO Publishing, Bergham Books, 2003).

Water Requirement for Agriculture

The requirement of water for agriculture is the most crucial factor in assessing if available supply of water is adequate for the required amount of food. At present, dependence on rainfall is greater for food production as 60 per cent of it is rain-fed leaving 40 per cent dependent on irrigation. Composition of meals along with post-harvest losses taken into account, the food intake amounts to an average of 2,800 Kcal per person a day, amounting to a total production of 1,000 m^3 per year. Amount of water needed for the production of food necessary for feeding 6 billion people is estimated to be 6,000 km^3. Most of this comes from rainfall stored in the soil profile and only about 15 per cent of water for crop production is available through irrigation which, on its part, needs 900 km^3 of water (U.N., 2003).[24*]

According to the U.N. 2003 Report, irrigated land representing about one-fifth of the total arable land in the developing world produced about two-fifths of all crops and nearly three-fifths of cereals. On the other hand, the developed world containing only about a quarter of the total irrigated area, or 67 million hectares, records an extremely slow increase in its irrigated land in contrast to irrigation's increase in the developing world. However, irrigation potential varies widely in the developing world depending largely on water availability. For example, a sizeable portion of irrigation potential is already in use in Near East/North Africa, with water being a limiting factor, and in Asia, with land being a limiting factor in both Sub-Saharan Africa as well as in Latin America irrigation potential lies mostly unutilized.

According to FAO's prediction, expansion of irrigation is going to take place in the coming decades particularly in the developing countries, increasing by 20 per cent, or adding 40 million hectares to its total by 2030, and it will take place by converting rainfed agriculture, concentrated mostly in South Asia, East Asia and North East/North Africa. In this perspective, irrigation water withdrawal in the developing countries is likely

---

* United Nations, *World Water Development Report: World Water Assessment Programme, Water for People, Water for Life* (UNESCO Publishing, Bergham Books, 2003).

to increase by about 14 per cent from the current 2,130 Km^3 per year to 2,420 Km^3 in 2030.[25]

As mentioned earlier, water scarcity has already reached a critical stage and will take a more serious turn because of reckless concern for treatment of the natural resources without any concern about this nature's bounty which is not endless, but may be enough provided treated judiciously without interfering with the natural process. As a result, despite a withdrawal of only 8 per cent of total annual renewable freshwater resources, it has been estimated that 26 per cent of annual evapotranspiration and 54 per cent of accessible runoff is now appropriated by humans. As the per capita use increased due to changes in lifestyle (leisure and domestic practices) and population increases, the proportion of appropriated water is increasing. This, coupled with spatial and temporal variations in water availability, means that the water to produce food for human consumption, industrial processes and all other uses is becoming scarce. It has been mentioned before that over 1.1 billion people in 41 countries do not have sufficient drinking water while 2.4 billion go without proper sanitation, leading to diseases, disputes for the share of available water and suffering from limitations for productive activities and thus making half of people in developing countries immersed in water poverty.[26]

Nevertheless, food security can be strengthened with judicial use of water for raising crop productivity, cutting back on the amount of water used for the purpose. Improved technology permitting, 'accurate water application' may go a long way in saving water as the most precious agricultural input. As mentioned earlier, drip irrigation is one of such devices having a great significance in crop production using minimum amount of water. Another technique has been developed involving "crops grown in greenhouses in such a way that water transpired by the plants is not released to the atmosphere but condensed and re-used."[27]

In this context, it will be enlightening to have an idea about how the use of water for different activities, such as agriculture, industry and domestic purposes, vary according to different income groups of countries. This is shown in Table 4.4 and Fig. 4.2.

Table 4.4: Competing Water Uses for main income groups of Countries

	Agricultural Use (%)	Industrial Use (%)	Domestic Use (%)
World	70	22	8
Low Income	87	8	5
Middle Income	74	13	12
Lower Middle Income	75	15	10
Upper Middle Income	73	10	17
Low and Middle Income	82	10	8
East Asia & Pacific	80	14	6
Europe and Central Asia	63	26	11
Latin America & Caribbean	74	9	18
Middle East & North Africa	89	4	6
South Asia	93	2	4
Sub-Saharan Africa	87	4	9
High Income Group	30	59	11
Europe Economic and Monetary Union (EMU)	21	63	16

Source: U.N., World Water Development Report, 2008.

Indian Status

India, as the second largest country in total population among the developing countries as well as globally, may give us some idea in regard to her present agricultural status. The water resource potential of India has been estimated at 1,869 billion cubic metres which includes replenishable ground water getting charged on annual basis. The irrigation potential, using modern techniques involving "integrating micro irrigation with canal irrigation ... (along with) innovative methods of recharging the groundwater"[28] is estimated to have a coverage of 17.38 MH available from surface water and 64.05 MH from groundwater as the source, both together providing 81.43 MH out of which a total of 49.99 MH were utilized, to which surface water contributed 11.44 MH and groundwater 38.55 MH (Table 4.5). However, altogether, including the major and medium projects, a total of 81 MH of potential was utilized. At the same time it may be further interesting how water requirements for different sectors in the country grow through coming years. As show in Table 4.6, the demand for irrigation for agriculture is likely to increase the lowest (156%) between 2010 and 2050, while it increases by 525 per cent for industry against 2600 per cent for energy. Altogether it does not sound to be a promising picture, not reassuring availability of food in step with its increasing demand for a growing population. (According to UN World Urbanization Process 20th Revision, the total population of India increases by 126 per cent, from 1,282 million in 2015 to 1,620 million by 2050 when, as one of the three countries in the world—India, China and Nigeria—recording the largest urban growth in the world between 2014 and 2050, India is going to add 404 million to her urban population against China's 292 million and Nigeria's 212 million).

Table 4.5: Irrigation Potential in India and Utilization (in MH)

Source	*Irrigation Potential*	*Potential Utilized (1997-2001)*
MMI (Major & Medium)	58.47	31.01
Surface Water	17.38	11.44
Ground Water	64.05	38.55
Sub-total	81.43	49.99
Total	**139.90**	**81.00**

Source: Compiled from Government of India, Eleventh Five Year Plan Report.

Table 4.6: Water Requirement for Various Sectors in India, (in Km^3) (Estimates made by the Ministry of Water Resources, Government of India)

Sector	*2010*	*2025*	*2050*
Irrigation	688	910	1072
Drinking Water	56	73	102
Industry	12	23	63
Energy	5	15	130
Others	52	72	80

Source: Compiled from Government of India, Eleventh Five Year Plan Report.

Interestingly, irrigation practices in India, according to literary evidences, go back to early third millennium B.C., referring to the existence of farming communities in Baluchistan and Kutch (India) providing instances of impounding rainwater by way of constructing dams using stone rubble for irrigation. Further evidence of irrigation practices during the period are also available from the Indus Valley Civilization (2600 B.C.-

1500 B.C.) when rainwater used to be collected in reservoirs for irrigation.[29] Besides, flood-irrigation practised by the Harappans in Indus Valley around this time used to be coincidental with the arrival of monsoons.[30] That water harvesting had been a time-old practice in India with regional variations in the manner of practices is evidenced all over India. For example,

> "archaeological and historical records show that Indians were constructing dams, lakes and irrigation systems in the time of Chandragupta Maurya (321-297 B.C.). There was a regular class of officers to superintend the rivers, measure the land and inspect the sluices by which water was let out from the main canals ... the terms used ... relating to water harvesting systems are several—*setu* for embankment or dam for storing water; *parivaha* for channel; *tataka* for tank; *nadyayatana* for water from a river such as a dam; *nadinibandhayatana* for a structure dependent on a river, such as a dam; *nibandhayatana* for canals from a river dam; and *khata* from a well. Kautilya mentions two types of *setu*—the *sahodaka,* where there is a natural spring or flow of water, and the *aharyodaka,* which is a sort of storage tank with water."[31]

Undoubtedly, the great variety of water harvesting systems developed, perfected as well as neglected, in the country through a period stretching from early third millennium B.C. till date, with mining groundwater may be as much as 7000 years old (Agarwal and Narain, 1999) and would perhaps yet be looked upon as a very important tool in resurrecting the future of Indian agriculture, accommodating further expansion forestalling hunger associated with poverty in the prevailing situation of bad management when availability of food for a large section of Indian population makes the most urgent need.

In this context we may refer to the opinion very strongly expressed by Nobel Laureate Amartya Sen, such as

> "India's overall record in eliminating hunger and undernutrition is quite terrible. Not only is there persistent recurrence of severe hunger in particular regions, there is also a dreadful prevalence of endemic

> hunger across much of India. Indeed, India does worse in this respect than even Sub-Saharan Africa. Calculations of general undernourishment—what is sometimes called 'protein-energy malnutrition'—show that it is nearly twice as high as in Sub-Saharan Africa on the average ... the proportion of under-nourished children in Africa is 20 to 40 per cent, whereas the percentage of undernourished children is a gigantic 40 to 60 per cent. About half of all Indian children are, it appears, chronically undernourished, and more than half of all adult women suffer from anaemia ... India's record is among the very worst in the world."[32]

According to Sen (2006), the onus for this lies with the Government of India for its bad policy of building up large stocks of food grain in the Central Government's reserve

> "without finding good use for them. In 1998, the stock was around 18 million tonnes. ... It has climbed and climbed since then, finally surpassing 62 million tonnes (by 2001). To take Jean Dreze's graphic description, if all the sacks of grain were laid up in a row, this would stretch more than a million kilometres, taking us to the moon and back. To see it in another way, the stocks substantially exceeded one ton of food grain for every family below the poverty line."[33]

Sen points out very clearly that though the initial intention behind building up a stock was based on the

> "government's commitment to high minimum support prices for food grains. ... The bonanza for food producers and sellers is matched by the privation of food consumers. Since the biological need for food is not the same thing as the economic entitlement to food (what people can afford to buy given their economic circumstances and the prices), the large stocks procured are hard to get rid of, despite the rampant undernourishment across the country. The very price system that generated a massive supply kept the

> hands—and the mouths—of poorer consumers away from food. ... The overall effect of high food prices is to hit many of the worse-off members of society extremely hard."[34]

Other Limitations

Water being the major limiting factor for agricultural expansion promoting increase in food supply commensurate with growing demand of a world where stabilization of population is yet a far cry, the next best opportunity for enlarging production is not effectively possible without expansion of agricultural land which was the sole factor till mid-twentieth century for increasing grain harvest. Since then, however, the role reversed, land becoming scarce for further expansion, as mentioned earlier in this chapter, took a back-seat while all the credit as the major source of growth in global grain production hinged on the rising yields during the last 60 years of so (Brown, 2012).* As a matter of fact, a very

> "small fraction of the increase in food production since 1950 that is attributable to an expansion of cropland. In 1950, 593 million hectares were in grain; by 1970, that had increased by 21 per cent to 720 million hectares but production has increased by 139 per cent due to more than a doubling of average yield, from about one ton per hectare per year to about 2.3 ton per hectare per year."[35]

Smil (1994), citing the findings of the FAO (1981) points out that 51 of 90 poor countries (excluding China) had 'abundant or moderately abundant reserves of arable land' but together these countries had a very small population, about one-third of the total of all the countries studied, while the 18 countries with half of the total population were already cultivating over nine-tenths of the potentially arable land. The cultivated area increased by 50 per cent during the six decades prior to 1990 but the scope, Smil (1994) believes, is very limited even though an addition of

---

* Brown, Lester R., *Full Planet, Empty Plates: The New Geopolitics of Food Security*, Earth Policy Institute, W.W. Norton & Company, New York, London, 2012: p. 48.

20 per cent by the year 2050, adding about 300 Mha of cropland (the lowest growth rate since 1800) would increase total production by another 400 mt. However, at the same time, Smil (1994) warns that

> "expanding the cultivated area will not suffice to feed an additional 2-2.5 billion people. Intensification of farming rather than extension of cultivated land will have to provide the bulk of new harvests."[36]

Yet, Smil (1994)* points out to the cultivation of abandoned fertile field as a worldwide phenomenon,

> "numerous instances of low intensity use of farmland and a surprisingly common existence of idle fertile land throughout China (estimated to be as high as 5 per cent of all cultivated area) and in such densely settled regions as parts of West Africa, the Caribbean Islands and South-east Asia ... even in central Java, the world's most densely inhabited rural region. If these oddlands were to add just 3 per cent to the 1990 total of arable land, and if the productivity of those lands were no higher than the average 1990 yield, additional harvests from that area would be equivalent to 50-100 mt of unmilled grain."[37]

Taking all these views into account for serious consideration as a means for expansion in the production of grain needed for satisfying the growing demand it gives an unchallengeable idea that land is already a very scarce resource, leaving no scope for augmentation in its supply to the extent required. Instead, we should accept its limitations and look for other avenues to meet our future requirements.

Restoring the earth's health is felt urgent for checking soil erosion resulting from the land surface exposed by removal of forest cover amounting to about 5 billion hectares at the beginning of the twentieth century, which has been reduced to 2.9 billion hectares, an area roughly double the world's cropland

---

* Smil, Vaclav, How many People Can the Earth Feed? in *Population and Development Review*, Vol. 20, No. 2, June 1994.

area. The developing countries have witnessed this major loss, losing 6.5 per cent of their forests per decade, turning the deforested areas into wasteland, finally reducing rainfall runoff and increasing associated flooding. Besides, soils get eroded fast in the absence of forest cover and recharging of aquifers is greatly reduced, cutting on the supply of groundwater for human use.

Opportunities and Possible Means of Escape

Evidently, both water scarcity and land scarcity together have come to almost a threatening level, stalling any further progress in agricultural expansion and, as a result, we have no other option but to depend on other means to get out of this tight situation made by our harmful actions of taming the nature in various ways to suit, quite often, our whimsical requirements having thus arrived today to a very critical stage, posing a gloomy future.

On the whole, the means of escape, taken as opportunities, fall into two categories: such as *restorative* or *preventive* measures, while others include *technological* as well as *improved* methods.

For example, afforestation as a protective or restorative measure saves land from further degradation, along with resuscitating the rate of rainfall runoff and enhancing the role of recharging underground waterbodies which, in the long run, saves the land for more fruitful use on the one hand and protect the land from misuse on the other. One of the very important steps to be taken for an effective reduction in the demand for wood for paper production is suggested to be recycling and if taken seriously by all the large paper consumers in the world. (Germany and South Korea already recycle respectively 72 and 66 per cent) (Brown, 2006),* it will save a considerable portion of forests from getting removed. At the same time, the largest single demand on trees—the need for its use as fuel—accounting for over half of all wood removed from forests may be replaced by highly efficient wood cooking stoves, as is done in Kenya, or

* Lester R. Brown, *Plan B 2.0: Rescuing a Planet Under Stress and Civilisation in Trouble* (New York and London, Earth Policy Institute, W.W. Norton and Company, 2006).

development of alternative cooking fuels based on wind, solar and geothermal energy. Evidently, replacing firewood with solar thermal cookers, with electric hotplates fed by wind-generated electricity or with some other energy source, will lighten the load on forests. The most salutary factor in restoring forests is tree plantation as a restorative measure for recreating the original natural habitat and five countries, including China, which have a very little of original forests left, taking the leading role in replantation followed by Russia, the U.S., India and Japan, while Brazil tracing all of them in expanding the forest areas (Brown, 2006).*

Further, aforestation takes a great role in checking soil erosion, which may otherwise lead to the formation of highly formidable dust bowls. It may be taken seriously as has been done in many countries, including one of the three largest grain producers in the world where it was noticed that by 1982 the United States was losing annually an estimated total of 3.08 billion tons of top soil from its cropland (Brown, 2004, Indian Reprint)† due to overploughing. It was further noticed that about 20 tons of top soil per hectare, each year removed by water erosion, reduced the yield of corn and wheat by almost 6 per cent per hectare in the Corn Belt. The consequences of overploughing in the United States led the government to adopt measures for the conservation of soil launched in 1985 encouraging farmers to take their highly erodible land out of production by providing government payments under 10-year contracts to plant the land in grass or trees (Brown, 2004).‡ The drive for leaving land idle temporarily led to the conversion of nearly 15 million hectares, or roughly 10 per cent, of the national total cropland area to grassland. The erstwhile Soviet Union, as mentioned earlier, had the same experience in its 'Virgin Land Project' ultimately turning into a dust bowl through overploughing, which also happened in China. Brown (2004)

---

* *Ibid.*

† Lester R. Brown, *Eco-Economy: Building an Economy for the Earth,* (Orient Longman, 2004).

‡ Lester R. Brown, *Full Planet, Empty Plates: The New Geopolitics of Food Security* (New York, London, Earth Policy Institute, W.W. Norton & Company, 2012).

draws our attention to the sad experience of Africa, where soil erosion and other forms of land degradation reduced grain harvest by 8 million tons, expected to climb to 16 million tons by 2020 if soil erosion continues unabated, making it incredibly difficult for feeding its population, climbing to 2 billion by 2025. Such losses are quite heavy in countries like Costa Rica, Malawi, Mali and Mexico and taken together soil erosion reduces soil productivity to the extent of 0.5-1.5 per cent of these countries' gross domestic product (Brown, 2004).

In this context, Brown (2012)* further stresses his serious concern about soil erosion and in his view the rate of erosion started exceeding the rate of soil formation some time within the last century, calling soil as 'the skin of earth—the frontier between geology and biology'. The rangelands locates mostly in semi-arid regions of the world supporting the life of 3.4 billion head of cattle, sheep and goat subjected to overgrazing, became very much vulnerable to wind erosion. Notably,

> "the world cattle population increased by 32 per cent between 1970 and 2010, the sheep population stayed static; but goat population more than doubled. This dramatic shift in the composition of the livestock herd, with goats now in such a dominant role, promises continuing grassland deterioration and accelerating soil erosion."[38]

Interestingly, as Brown (2012)† points out, goat population has been increasing in some other developing countries, particularly in Africa and Asia, and Pakistan presents a remarkable case of increase where the cattle population doubled between 1961 and 2010, the sheep population nearly tripled while the goat population multiplied almost sevenfold. Loss of top soil eventually leading to losing the capacity to feed their population has badly affected countries like Lesotho, Mongolia, North Korea, and Haiti. As Brown (2012) observes, the shrinkage

---

* Lester R. Brown, *Full Planet, Empty Plates: The New Geopolitics of Food Security* (New York, London, Earth Policy Institute, W.W. Norton & Company, 2012).

† *Ibid.*

of productive area to match with growing population are on a collision course. For example, for ploughing land with a sloping surface contour strip cropping is a better way of reducing soil erosion during heavy rains. Another very effective way of soil conservation is offered by no-till or minimum till farming which, apart from reducing both wind and water erosion, helps in retaining water, raises soil carbon content and reduces the energy needed for crop cultivation (Brown, 2006). As mentioned earlier, no-till practice is already popular as a means of preserving soil from the actions of nature's elements. Two most important ways of conserving the top soil are—(a) retiring highly erodible land which no longer can sustain cultivation, estimated to be one-tenth of the world's cropland accounting for half of all erosion, and (b) conservation practices, such as contour farming, strip farming, and adoption of minimum or no-till farming practices on a large scale. The highly erodible soil estimated to be roughly 10 per cent of the world's cropland is needed to be planted to grass or trees before it turns completely barren (Brown, 2006).

Another way of meeting the growing food demand is to put greater stress on raising land productivity, for which multiple cropping where soil moisture permits it, as evidenced by tripling of world grain harvest since 1950, resulting partly from impressive increase in multiple cropping in Asia. This happened in different crop-combinations as mentioned earlier, such as wheat and corn (China), wheat and rice (North India), double/triple cropping of rice (China/South India/South-east Asia).[39]

Efforts are also being made in the U.S. to 'breed earlier maturing varieties' along with multiple cropping to raise crop output on a par with Western Europe, with its mild winters. High-yielding winter wheat has the possibilities of developing multiple cropping as a means for larger production, while in Brazil and Argentina the presence of a longer frost-free growing season supports extensive multi-cropping with wheat or corn and soybeans in combination, using chemical fertilizers. Interestingly, however, the use of chemical fertilizers has reached a limit in the U.S., in Western Europe and Japan to derive any more benefit out of it while they still now have an effective role in providing higher production in Africa.

However, the simultaneous planting of grain and leguminous trees in Africa gives a promising return as the slow growth of trees permitting grain crops to mature and be harvested earlier, followed by the quick growth of the trees to several feet in height, with dropping leaves providing nitrogen and organic matter to the soil, adding to its fertility. This makes a simple technology developed by scientists at the International Centre for Research in Agroforestry in Nairobi, having enabled the farmers to double their grain yields (Brown, 2006).[40]

Brown (2006) very strongly advocates that stabilization of population is essential for bringing a balance between food and people, along with cutting down the consumption of high animal-protein food as practised in the developed industrial countries and restricting the conversion of food crops for the production of automobile fuels, such as ethanol. Besides, serious thought needs to be given to increase land productivity.

Raising water productivity provides another sure way to get over the gap between production and demand for food. The practice of irrigation, as pointed out earlier, is far from efficient. According to analysts like Sandra Postel and Amy Vickers, the efficiency of surface water irrigation varies widely between countries, such as between 25 and 40 per cent in India, Mexico, Pakistan, the Philippines and Thailand; between 40 and 45 per cent in Malaysia and Morocco; and between 50-60 per cent in Israel, Japan and Taiwan. The degree of efficiency depends on factors like soil types, temperature, and humidity. Considering their effect, China has decided to raise the level of efficiency of the use of irrigation water from 43 per cent in 2000 to 51 per cent in 2010 and to 55 per cent in 2030 (Brown, 2006).

As a matter of fact, more effective steps already proved useful may be adopted for raising irrigation water efficiency. They are, as mentioned before, shifting from flood or furrow irrigation to overhead low-pressure sprinkler irrigation or drip irrigation considered to be 'the gold standard of irrigation' (Brown, 2006),* reducing water consumption almost from 30 to 50 per cent for raising yields. As a labour-intensive and more

---

* Lester R. Brown, *Plan B 2.0: Rescuing a Planet Under Stress and Civilization in Trouble* (New York and London, Earth Policy Institute, W.W. Norton & Company, 2006).

suitable, particularly for developing countries, water-efficient practices supported by minimum losses of water through evaporation are used by many countries. The water-efficient irrigation system has, of late, further been improved by converting it into the 'tiniest drip irrigation system' using a bucket or drum with 'flexible plastic tubing to distribute water to irrigate small vegetable gardens—25 to 125 metres in size, reducing water costs and increasing yields raising incomes of the small-holders. As mentioned before, according to Sandra Postel, India has a potential of irrigating 10 million hectares, that is almost one-tenth of her total cropland, by drip irrigation technologies, promising a huge return while China too has similar potential which has already been taken up seriously facing scarcity of water (Brown, 2006).*

At the same time, shifting to water-efficient crops, like moving away from rice to wheat, raises water productivity, which is already in practice in some countries, such as China and Egypt. Besides, making change in dietary habit, namely reduction in consumption of meat, makes a considerable reduction in water use, when a small reduction in the consumption of meat, milk and eggs could easily cut grain use per person by 100 grams from an annual consumption of grain as food and feed averaging 800 kilograms (or four-fifths of a ton) for an average American, which for a population of presumably 300 million, makes an appreciable reduction of grain consumption by 30 million tons and use of irrigation water by 30 billion tons (Brown, 2006). An astounding amount, indeed, on both counts.

> "The second way to raise both land and water productivity is to produce animal protein more efficiently. With some 38 per cent (about 730 million tons) of the world grain harvest used to produce animal protein, the potential for more efficient grain use is large. World meat consumption increased from 47 million tons in 1950 to 200 million tons in 2005, more than doubling consumption per person from 17

---

* *Ibid.*

kilograms to 40 kilograms. Consumption of milk and eggs has also risen."[41]

According to the same author providing information in this respect (Brown, 2012), production trends of beef, pork and eggs in recent years suggests the changing demand for each of them. The production of beef rose less than 1 per cent annually, for pork 2 per cent, and for eggs 3 per cent annually but 4 per cent for poultry annually. In comparison, aquacultural products, that is fish etc., expanded by almost 8 per cent per year, rising from 13 million tons in 1990 to 60 million tons in 2010. But what happened in terms of change in the feed for all these protein-yielding lives was a drastic change in the type of feed—incorporation of soybean into the feed system following a ration of about '1 part soybean meal into 4 parts grain', leading to a 'much more efficient conversion of grain into animal protein.' Thus, at present, while 35 per cent of the total 2.3 billion tons of annual grain harvest in the world is used as animal feed, almost the entire production of soymeal is used for feeding animals. However, the preference for both pork and poultry is mostly grain, while beef and milk production is more dependent on a combination of grass and grain. But the three largest meat producers, China, the U.S. and Brazil, rely heavily on soybeans as animal feed (Brown, 2012). In this context, India presents altogether a different picture of saving grains from their use as animal feed, where the milk production has made a magical increase between 1970 and 1997 from 21 million to 117 million tons, a six-fold increase, making the world's largest dairy using almost entirely roughage or crop residues, such as wheat straw, rice straw and corn stocks and grass. The animals are stalk-fed.

Similarly, China has also developed a practice of feeding cattle with roughage available from harvesting wheat, an early summer crop which needed to be cleared quickly for sowing corn. The straw provided by wheat harvest is fed to cattle followed by feeding them with cornstalks later, when corn is harvested. The practice of double cropping pursued in four provinces of central China using roughage as cattle-feed has enabled these four provinces—Hebei, Shangdong, Henan and Anhui—to produce much of the beef for the country.

China also excels in its remarkable achievement in

aquaculture, a source of highly efficient animal protein available from aquaculture evolved through centuries. For example, production of carp has developed a polycultural system involving four different species of carps grown simultaneously, one of them feeding on phytoplankton, another feeding on zooplankton, the third thriving on aquatic grass while the fourth one is a bottom-feeder, and together they form a small ecosystem each filling a particular niche, providing the major part of China's carp harvest amounting to 16 million tons in 2011.[42]

What is really worrying all experts is the changing situation in which a growing section of world population is moving up the food chain, with growing demand for animal-protein, and in consequence is making a greater demand for corn as animal feed besides using it for the production of ethanol as car-feed. Already the production of corn having maintained almost a similar level between 1950 and 2000, surged ahead faster, climbing to 960 million tons in 2011 while wheat fell much behind to 700 million tons (Brown, 2012).[*]

As a result, the emerging global food situation bears the ominous sign of a very grim future. The growing consumption of livestock products, along with increasing pressure on conversion of food grain into fuel, have already escalated the demand from 20 million tons of grain about a decade ago into 40 million tons in recent years, making it very difficult to support human life. In this background of growing uncertainty in the availability of human food it may be noted, as Brown (2012) has pointed out, consumption of grain having more than tripled between 2005 and 2011 for the production of biofuel in the U.S. having increased from 41 mt to 127 mt, had a severe impact on price rise for food crops, such as the prices of wheat, corn and soybean nearly doubling of their historical level by mid-2012, causing severe strain on the purses of the low-income people. The most painful outcome of this policy of unbridled action on the part of the U.S. exposes the fact that

---

* Lester R. Brown, *Full Planet, Empty Plates: The New Geopolitics of Food Security,* Earth Policy Institute, W.W. Norton & Company, New York, London, 2012

> "the appetite for grain to fuel cars is seemingly insatiable. The grain required to fill a 25-gallon fuel tank of a sport utility vehicle with ethanol just once would feed one person for a whole year. The grain turned into ethanol in the United States in 2011 could have fed, at average world consumption levels, some 400 million people. But even if the entire U.S. grain harvest were turned into ethanol, it would only satisfy 18 per cent of current gasoline demand."[43]

The most humanistic issue of mere survival of human community carries no meaning for the U.S. which, in its uncontended avarice for obtaining car-fuel from ethanol, has so far rushed relentlessly for enlarging its production, bringing it to 23 billion gallons in 2011 with Brazil following the lead, with 6 billion gallons, together accounting for 87 per cent of the global production, while among the other producers with very modest shares are China, Canada, France and Germany. However, the policy for replacing natural oil with ethanol sounds very much unrealistic as well as headstrong considering the fact that grain-based ethanol hardly meets 6 per cent of U.S. gasoline requirements. At the same time, biodiesel produced globally from oil-bearing crops like sunflower seed, palm oil and rapeseed, production of which is making dramatic increase from about 3 million gallons in 1991 to a little less than 1 billion gallons in 2005 and jumping to almost 6 billion gallons (Brown, 2012)* does not make itself any important competitor of petroleum.

In this context it is very important to note that biofuels are raising food prices and simultaneously have a deep impact on increasing the number of hungry people. Furthermore, conversion of enormous volumes of grain into fuel means that the price of grain is now more closely tied to the price of oil than ever before.

"One of the consequences of integrating the world food and fuel economies is that the owners of the world's 1 billion motor vehicles are pitted against the world's poorest people in

---

* Lester R. Brown, *Full Planet, Empty Plates: The New Geopolitics of Food Security*, Earth Policy Institute, W.W. Norton & Company, New York, London, 2012.

competition for grain"[44]—one for just to keep cars moving and the other for getting out of hunger. The unmitigated demands threatening untimely death may translate into social unrest, quite often taking a violent turn in the form of food riots, such as resulting from the doubling of food prices from 2007 to mid-2008 and, according to the U.S. State Department reports, there had been food unrest in some 60 countries between 2007 and 2009, involving countries like Afghanistan, Yemen, Ethiopia, Somalia, Sudan, the Democratic Republic of the Congo and Haiti (Brown, 2012).*

Nevertheless, there is an emerging possibility of decline in biofuel production, as already indicated by its projected fall by 2 per cent in 2012, bringing down the use of automotive fuel by 11 per cent by 2012 from its peak in 2007, followed by greater fall in 2013 resulting from rising corn prices caused by heat and drought in the Mid-West of the U.S. The corroborative evidence of reduction in the size of the U.S. vehicle fleet from its peak of 250 million in 2008 afterwards, along with the introduction of rigorous 'auto-fuel efficiency' measures, reduces the use of gasoline by new cars sold in 2025 which will be 'half of required by new cars sold in 2010'. Besides, retiring old, less efficient cars will further add to the decline of grain-based ethanol as car-fuel. The technological advances made in recent years on cars driven by electricity or other means is likely to bring down the use of ethanol to an appreciable extent (Brown, 2012).†

> "All new cars sold in Europe will be electric in less than two decades as a result of government support, falling battery costs and economies of sale, the Dutch bank ING has predicted. ... The bank's forecast for 2035 is much more aggressive than most other projections. National Grid says it expects 90 per cent of new cars in Britain to be electric by 2050. France's commitment last week to banning new petrol and diesel car sales by 2040 suggests it also thinks the rollout of electric vehicles will be

---

* Lester R. Brown, *Full Planet, Empty Plates: The New Geopolitics of Food Security*, Earth Policy Institute, W.W. Norton & Company, New York, London, 2012.

† *Ibid.*

slower than the ING's report expects. ... By 2024 the report's authors forecast that in Germany the cost of owning an electric car will be the same as a conventional petrol or diesel model. ... ING said that European car makers were likely to miss out in the electric revolution to Asian and US competitors." (Adam Vaughan, The Guardian, UK, 14 July 2017).

Food Requirement and Availability in Around 2050

According to Brown (2006), requirement of food for a person is variable measured by different standards such as mentioned earlier, consumed not at the U.S., nor as the Italian but at the Indian level, a consumption of about 200 kilogram of grain annually by a person the available food will support 10 billion people.

Obviously, besides incomes, dietary satisfaction depends on habits created by people guided more by taste than physical requirement. The greater intake of animal-protein is not a healthy practice, as observed from the increasing proportions of cardiac arrests, obesity and other life-threatening diseases. Instead, a mid-way is preferred, such as greater dependence on the products of aquaculture which is also a land-efficient practice and a grain-efficient source of protein. In this context, perhaps, we can emulate the example set by China where the farmed fish harvest exceeds the wild fish catch. As a matter of fact, rising income, especially in densely populated Asia and in other countries, has been instrumental in increasing dependence of people on fish as a source of protein, following China's example. This is also at the root of a project taken up by countries like India, Thailand and Vietnam. Thailand took up in 2001 a project of developing 700,000 ha of land for aquaculture, producing 1.7 mt of fish and shrimps, as mentioned earlier, with a larger target in future.[45]

Food security for over 9 billion people by 2050 is, no doubt, cannot be guaranteed unless sectors apart from agriculture come forward with their own experts making it as a joint responsibility. Newer measures applicable for strengthening as well as improving land and water productivity need to be bolstered further with programmes and their implementation of stabilizing global population, to decide on the implications of introducing viable projects on renewable energy sources to lessen our dependence on fossil fuels. It is felt very urgent that some of the initiatives in these directions need to be considered by all governments treating them as joint ventures since the world cannot be fragmentally considered when the interest of the entire human community is involved. We need to be reminded at the very beginning that it is a finite planet we live on and should not be pushed further to burst around its seams when, as stated by 'The Living Planet Report 2004 of World Wildlife Fund' that if we want to follow the lifestyle of the average West European, we would need three planet Earth's resources to make life sustainable. Already, the human society in its craze for consumerism is using two planets' worth of resources. Further push will be much more disastrous if we are not seriously careful to avoid such a catastrophic situation. For example, land already scarce requires re-planning, the transportation systems relying more on

> "less land-intensive transport forms including light rail, buses and bicycles which also affect world food security. Policies adopted by the ministers of transportation in land-scarce countries like China and India directly affect world food security."[46]
>
> "Vast quantities of fresh produce grown in the US are left in the field to rot, fed to livestock or hauled directly from the field to landfill because of unrealistic and unyielding cosmetic standards, according to official data and interviews with dozens of farmers, packers, truckers, researchers, campaigners and government officials.
>
> From the fields and orchards of California to the population centres of the east coast, farmers and others in the food distribution chain say high-value and nutritious food is being sacrificed to retailers' demand for unattainable perfection.
>
> It is all about blemish-free produce, says Jay Johnson, who ships fresh fruit and vegetables from North Carolina and central Florida. ... Produce is lost in fields,

> warehouse, packaging, distribution, supermarkets, restaurants, and fridges. By one tally, about 60 million tonnes of produce, worth about $ 160 billion (£119 billion), is wasted by retailers and consumers every year—one-third of all foodstuff." (Suzanne Goldenberg, *The Guardian*, 14 July 2016)

At the same time there should be an agreement on saving food loss in various forms including food wastage, the latter presenting a formidable situation at present besides seeking food from other available sources as supplement to at least in dire necessity. Food loss at various stages, mentioned earlier, makes quite a significant part of the total harvest and as reported by Ehrlich *et al.* (1993) and other experts, such loss could amount to as high as 40 per cent of the global harvest which "could be substantially lowered by controlling rodents, insects, fungi and other organisms that attack food in storage."[47] Smil (1994),* however, gives a much lower estimate in this regard and, according to him, the post-harvest losses may be widely variable, from a low of about 10 per cent to a high of as much as half of the total harvest, depending on various stages between harvest and handling, threshing, drying, storage and milling.[48]

Another form of food loss presents a comparatively much more grim picture than conceivable. It is report in *The Guardian* (U.K.), 14 July, 2016, quoting Suzanne Goldenberg from the U.S. that, "Americans throw away almost as much as they eat because of a cult of perfection, deepening hunger and poverty, and inflicting a heavy toll on the environment." The monstrosity of the whole issue of food wastage emerging from the report in '*The Guardian*' is that the amount of wholesome, perfect food wasted by retailers and consumers every year in the U.S. amounts to 60 million tonnes, valued by the government at $ 160 billion. Undoubtedly, it has further to be admitted that 1.6 billion tonnes of food is wasted globally every year, worth about $ 1 trillion, "enough to reach the moon if packed in 80 million skips",[49] when even in the U.S. an estimated 5-10 per cent of the

---

* Vaclav Smil, 1994. "How Many People Can The Earth Feed?" in *Population and Development Review*, Vol. 20, No. 2 (June 1994).

population go hungry. (See Note F)

The first country to ban food wastage by law and compelling supermarkets to donate excess to charities, Italy, wasting about 5.1 million tonnes of food a year has made a law asking companies and farmers to donate food to charities, encouraging greater use of doggy bags at restaurants,[50] as is the practice prevalent in the U.K. as well.

There are several sources providing great scopes for augmentation of food supplies which, available as the by-products of nature, ensures not only a free gift but also adding to a healthy food-system. One of such sources is, as mentioned earlier, the de-forested land after afforestation—planted with genetically improved trillions of trees providing nuts—may be a permanent source of high-quality protein.[51] On the other hand, according to Smil (1994), poor countries quite often under-estimate 'some qualitatively essential food supplies', such as wild meat, an 'important source of high quality protein'. Further,

> "edible wild plants may also be sources of high-quality nutrients. In West Africa, parts of 24 out of 165 studied plant species are regularly eaten, and in the whole continent more than 500 wild plants are consumed as food."[52]

Indeed, the most important as well as emulating example in this context is provided by Mazhar *et al.* (2007)*, exploring the meaning of Agriculture. As mentioned in Chapter 2, referring to two contrasting environments, one in the plains of Bangladesh and the other in the dry Deccan Plateau in India. According to them,

> "when women do weeding work or return home from grazing animals they routinely gather these items ... done

* Farhad Mazhar, Daniel Buckles, P.V. Satheesh and Farida Akhtar, *Food Sovereignty and Unchallenged Biodiversity in South Asia: Essays on the Poverty of Food Policy and the Wealth of the Social Landscape* (International Development Research Centre, Academia Foundation, New Delhi, 2007).

> in a way that does not interfere with cultivated crops. From their point of view, the uncultivated plants and animals constitute a prominent place in the local food system. ... A large number of studies show that uncultivated plants and animals are critical to survival during times of extreme hardship ... The value of these foods in meeting the more regular nutritional needs of vulnerable groups such as young children is also well documented."[53]

It is further pointed out by these authors (Mazhar *et al.*, 2007) that there are about 102 species of uncultivated species used as food, consisting of herbs, creepers, aquatic plants, shrubs and trees most abundant during the monsoon season when planted crops are not ready for harvest. Besides, plants cultivated widely for seeds providing oil, such as mustard, and jute for its fibre, also make an important source of food with their leaves plucked.[54]

NOTES

Note A

As reported in *The Statesman,* 2 January 2018, Kolkata (India) issue, "Zero tillage farming is fast becoming popular among farmers in Alipurduar district (West Bengal, India). ... It is learnt that there are 1,30,000 ha of land on which farming can be done in the district, and out of this 500 ha have been used for zero-tillage farming system ... Maize, paddy and wheat are cultivated in the zero-tillage farming system ... We (Dy. Director of the Alipurduar District Agriculture Department Harish Chandra Roy) have targeted more agricultural land for this system of farming in the coming years in the district."

Note B

"China may face the biggest challenges for all. After the economic reforms in 1978 that shifted the responsibility for farming from large state-organized production teams to individual farm families, China's cattle, sheep and goat numbers spiralled upward. A classic tragedy of the commons was unfolding. The United States, with comparable grazing capacity, has 94 million cattle, a somewhat larger herd than China's 84 million. But when it comes to sheep and goats, the United

States has a combined population of only 9 million, whereas China has 285 million. Concentrated in China's western and northern provinces, these animals are stripping the land of its protective vegetation. The wind then does the rest.

Wang Tao, one of the world's leading desert scholars, reports that from 1950 to 1975 an average of 600 square miles of land turned to desert each year. Between 1975 and 1987, this climbed to 810 square miles a year. From then until the century's end, it jumped to 1,390 square miles of land going to desert annually.

A U.S. Embassy report, entitled 'Desert Merger and Acquisitions', describing satellite images showing two of China's largest deserts, the Badain Jaran and Tengger, expanding and merging to form a single, larger desert overlapping Inner Mongolia and Gansu Provinces. To the west in Xinjiang Province, two even larger deserts—the Taklimakan and Kumtag—are also heading for a merger. Highways running through the shrinking region between them are regularly inundated by sand dunes."

Source: Brown, Lester R., *Full Planet, Empty Plates: The New Geopolitics of Food Security,* Earth Policy Institute, W.W. Norton & Company, New York, London, 2012: pp. 48-49.

Note C

"India's rivers, especially the smaller ones, have all turned into toxic streams. And even the big ones like the Ganga are far from pure. The assault on India's rivers—from population growth, agricultural and modernization, urbanization and industrialization—is enormous and growing by the day. ... Most Indian cities get a large part of the drinking water from rivers. This entire life stands threatened (CSE, 1999, p. 58)."

Source: United Nations, *Water Development Report: World Water Assessment Programme, Water for People, Water for Life* (UNESCO Publishing, Bergham Books, 2003).

Note D

Human Activity	*Impact on Ecosystems*	*Benefits/Services at Risk*
Dam Construction	Alters timing and quantity of river flows, water temperature, nutrient and sediment transport, delta replenishment, blocks fish migrations	Provision of habitat for native species, recreational and commercial fisheries, maintenance of deltas and their economies, productivity of estuarine fisheries.

(*Contd.*)

Note D: (*Contd.*)

Dike and Levee Construction	Destroys hydrologic connection between river and flood-plain habitat	Habitat, sport and commercial fisheries, natural flood plain fertility, natural food control.
Excessive River Diversions	Depletes stream flows to damaging levels	Habitat, sport and commercial fisheries, recreation, pollution dilution, hydropower, transportation.
Draining of wetlands	Eliminates Key Component of aquatic environment	Natural flood control habitat for fish and water fowl, recreation, natural water purification.
Deforestation/poor land use	Alters run-off patterns, inhibits natural discharge, fills water bodies with silt	Water supply quantity and quality, fish and wildlife habitat, transportation, flood control.
Uncontrolled Pollution	Diminishes water quality	Water supply, habitat, commercial fisheries, recreation
Overharvesting	Depletes Species Populations	Sport and commercial fisheries, waterfowl, other biotic populations.
Introduction of Exotic Species	Eliminates native species, alters production and nutrient cycling	Sport and commercial fisheries, waterfowl, water quality, fish and wildlife habitat, transportation.
Releases of metals and acid-forming pollutants to air and water	Alters chemistry of rivers and lakes	Habitats, fisheries, recreation, human health.
Emissions of climate-altering air pollutants	Potential for dramatic changes in run-off patterns from increases in temperature and changes in rainfall	Water supply, hydropower, transportation, fish and wildlife habitat, pollution dilution, recreation, fisheries, flood control.

(*Contd.*)

Note D: (*Contd.*)

Population and consumption growth	Increases pressures to dam and divert more water, to drain more wetlands, etc.; increases water pollution, acid rain, and potential for climate change	Places virtually all aquatic ecosystem services at risk.

Source: Postel, Sandra and Brian Richter (2003). *Rivers for Life: Managing Water for People and Nature,* Island Press, Washington, Cavelo, London: pp. 14-15.

Note E

"All new cars sold in Europe will be electric in less than two decades as a result of government support, falling battery costs and economies of sale, the Dutch bank ING has predicted ... The bank's forecast for 2035 is much more aggressive than most other projections. National Grid says it expects 90% of new cars in Britain to be electric by 2050. France's commitment last week to banning new petrol and diesel car sales by 2040 suggests it also thinks the rollout of electric vehicles will be slower than the ING's report expects ... By 2024 the reports authors forecast that in Germany the cost of owning an electric car will be the same as a conventional petrol or diesel model ... ING said that European car makers were likely to miss out in the electric revolution to Asian and US competitors." (Adam Vaughan, *The Guardian,* UK, 14 July 2017).

Note F

"Vast quantities of fresh produce grown in the US are left in the field to rot, fed to livestock or hauled directly from the field to landfill because of unrealistic and unyielding cosmetic standards, according to official data and interviews with dozens of farmers, packers, truckers, researchers, campaigners and government officials.

From the fields and orchards of California to the population centres of the east coast, farmers and others in the food distribution chain say high-value and nutritious food is being sacrificed to retailers' demand for unattainable perfection.

It is all about blemish-free produce, says Jay Johnson, who ships fresh fruit and vegetables from North Carolina and central Florida ...

Produce is lost in fields, warehouse, packaging, distribution, supermarkets, restaurants, and fridges. By one tally, about 60 million tonnes of produce, worth about $ 160 billion (£119 billion), is wasted by retailers and consumers every year – one-third of all foodstuff." (*Source*: Suzanne Goldenberg, *The Guardian*, 14 July 2016)

REFERENCES

1. Brown, Lester R., *Plan B 2.0: Rescuing a Planet Under Stress and Civilization in Trouble,* Earth Policy Institute, 2006: p. 143.
2. Brown, Lester R., *Full Planet, Empty Plates: The New Geopolitics of Food Security,* Earth Policy Institute, W.W. Norton & Company, New York, London, 2012: p. 48.
3. Brown, Lester R., *Plan B 2.0: Rescuing a Planet Under Stress and Civilization in Trouble,* Earth Policy Institute, 2006: p. 150.
4. Brown, Lester R., *Full Planet, Empty Plates: The New Geopolitics of Food Security,* Earth Policy Institute, W. W. Norton & Company, New York, London, 2012: p. 50.
5. *Ibid.*
6. Postel, Sandra and Brian Richts (2003). *Rivers for Life: Managing Water for People and Nature,* Island Press, Washington, Cavelo, London: pp. 13-15.
7. McCully, Patrick, 1998 (Indian Ed.)., *Silenced Rivers: The Ecology and Policies of Large Dams,* Orient Longman: p. 7.
8. *Op. cit.*
9. UN: *World Water Development Report: World Water Assessment Programme.* Water for People Water for Life, 2003, UNESCO Publishing: Berghahn Books: p. 10.
10. *Ibid.*, p. 13.
11. *Ibid.*, p. 11.
12. Brown, Lester R., *Full Planet, Empty Plates: The New Geopolitics of Food Security,* Earth Policy Institute, W.W. Norton & Company, New York, London, 2012: pp. 63-64.
13. *Ibid.*, p. 70.
14. United Nations, *World Water Development Report: World Water Assessment Programme, Water for People, Water for Life* UNESCO Publishing, Bergham Books, 2003: p. 121.
15. *Ibid.*, p. 131.
16. Postel, Sandra and Brian Richter, 2003, *Rivers for Life: Managing Water for People and Nature,* Island Press, Washington, Cavelo, London: p. 26.
17. *Ibid.*, p. 27.

18. *Ibid.*, p. 31.
19. *Ibid.*, p. 7.
20. Andrew Balmford, Aaron Bruner, Philip Cooper, Robert Constanza, Stephen Farbes, Rhys E. Green, Martin Jenkins, Paul Jeffriss, Valma Jessamy, Joan Madden, Kat Munro, Norman Myers, Shahid Naeem, J. Paavola, Mathew Rayment, Sergio Rosendo, Joan Roughgarden, Kate Trumper, and Karry Tarner, Economic Reasons for Conserving Wild Nature in *Science Magazine,* American Association for the Advancement of Science, 2002.
21. Postel, Sandra and Brian Richts, 2003, *Rivers for Life: Managing Water For People and Nature,* Island Press, Washington, Cavelo, London: p. 37.
22. *Ibid.*, pp. 37-38.
23. *Ibid.*, pp. 202-204.
24. United Nations, *World Water Development Report: World Water Assessment Programme, Water for People, Water for Life* (UNESCO Publishing, Bergham Books, 2003).
25. *Ibid.*, pp. 204-209.
26. *Ibid.*, p. 10.
27. *Ibid.*, p. 217.
28. Planning Commission, Government of India, *Eleventh Five Year Plan, 2007-2012, Vol III,* 2008, Oxford University Press: p. 44.
29. Agarwal, Anil and Sunita Narain, *Dying Wisdom: Rise, Fall and Potential of India's Traditional Harvesting Systems,* Centre for Science and Development, New Delhi, 1999: p. 10.
30. Bhattacharya, Bimalendu (2006). *Urban Development in India Since Pre-Historic Times,* Concept Publishing Company, New Delhi, (Revised Edition): pp. 25 and 48.
31. Agarwal, Anil and Sunita Narain, *Dying Wisdom: Rise, Fall and Potential of India's Traditional Harvesting Systems,* Centre for Science and Development, New Delhi, 1999: pp. 10, 11.
32. Sen, Amartya (2000). *The Argumentative Indian: Writings on Indian Culture, History and Identity,* Penguin Books, p. 212.
33. *Ibid.*, p. 213.
34. *Ibid.*, pp. 213-215.
35. Ehrlich, Paul R., Anne H. Ehrlick and Gretchen C. Daily (1993). "Food Security, Population and Environment", in *Population and Development Review, 19, No. 1 (March)*: p. 7.
36. Smil, Vaclav, How many People Can the Earth Feed? in *Population and Development Review,* Vol. 20, No. 2, 1993: p. 275.
37. *Ibid.*, pp. 276-277.
38. Brown, Lester R., (2012). *Full Planet, Empty Plates: The New Geopolitics of Food,* Earth Policy Institute, W.W. Norton & Company, New York, London, pp. 52-53.

39. Brown, Lester R. (2012). *Plan 2.0: Rescuing a Planet Under Stress and a Civilization in Trouble,* Earth Policy Institute, W.W. Norton & Company, New York, London, pp. 164-165.
40. *Ibid.,* p. 166.
41. *Ibid.,* pp. 170-171.
42. Brown, Lester R. (2012). *Full Planet, Empty Plates: The New Geopolitics of Food,* Earth Policy Institute, W.W. Norton & Company, New York, London, pp. 33-36.
43. *Ibid.,* pp. 37-38.
44. *Ibid.,* p. 40.
45. Brown, Lester R. (2012). *Plan 2.0: Rescuing a Planet Under Stress and a Civilization in Trouble,* Earth Policy Institute, W. W. Norton & Company, New York, London, p. 179.
46. *Ibid.,* p. 180.
47. Ehrlich, Paul R., Anne H. Ehrlich and Gretchen C. Daily, Food Security, Population and Environment, in *Population and Development Review, 19, No. 1 (March 1993)*: 16.
48. Smil,Vaclav, (1994). How Many People Can The Earth Feed? in *Population and Development Review Vol. 20, No.2* (June 1994): p. 259.
49. *The Guardian,* UK, 14 July 2016.
50. *The Guardian,* UK, 4 August 2016.
51. Brown, Lester R. (2006). *Plan B 2.0: Rescuing a Planet Under Stress and Civilization in Trouble,* Earth Policy Institute, p. 145.
52. Smil, Vaclav (1994). How Many People Can the Earth Feed? in *Population and Development Review Vol. 20, No.2* (June 1994): p. 259.
53. Mazhar, Farhad,, Daniel Buckles, P.V. Satheeh and Farida Akhtar, (2007). *Food Sovereignty and Unchallenged Biodiversity in South Asia: Essays on the Poverty of Food Policy and the Wealth of the Social Landscape* International Development Research Centre, Academia Foundation, new Delhi: p. 2.
54. *Ibid.,* p. 10.

5
Climate Change and Mitigating Strategies

Donella Meadows, the lead author of the 'Club of Rome's' 1972 Report, *The Limits to Growth,* has cautioned us about nature's limitations in helping man, reminding in very firm words, "Just so much, and no more", by which she meant,

> "Just so much soil. Just so much water. Just so much sunshine. Everything born of the Earth grows to its appropriate size and then stops. The Planet does not get bigger: it gets better. Its creatures learn, mature, diversify, evolve, create amazing beauty and novelty and complexity, but live within absolute limits."[1]

She wants human society not to go on putting increasing pressure on earth's resources which are finite and might react violently, as it is doing already in many forms for man having crossed limits in its consumerist life style which, if continued unchecked, will require three planets' worth of natural resources, mentioned earlier. The main problem is that the finite Earth is faced with the infinite greed of mankind, which is an unmanageable approach to the fulfilment of human requirements.

This uneven competition is already on a collision course much more disastrous for meeting human requirements for food at the global level, and needs to be avoided at all cost when the goal is achievable adopting a more reasonable course. As Smil (1994) observed some time back, it does not appear realistic to assume Earth's capacity to support a population of 10-11 billion in the next century (21st), but it does not give any reason for complacency and transformations suggested at different stages need not falter for lack of natural resources or ecosystem services. At the same time we should remain very much conscious about the fact that there is nothing dramatic about such achievements emphasizing rational use of energy. This should be followed by agronomic measures mentioned by Smil (1994) required for achieving additional harvests to meet global demand for food for a larger population by 2050, or around that time (Table 5.1) and this is based on appropriate measures to be taken in the intervening period. It is further pointed out by Smil (1994) that,

> "global grain output being about 2 billion tons in 1990. If this total were to grow annually by almost 2 per cent (the mean rate during the past decade), the yearly harvest of cereals would surpass the Earth's mass in less that 1500 years, roughly an equivalent of the time elapsed since the dissolution of the Western Roman Empire."[2]

But, however, we may try, all our efforts at feeding the burgeoning global population may not be fruitful as opposed by forces beyond our control even though in many cases humanity

Table 5.1: Conservative Estimates of Additional Harvests Achievable by the Year 2050

Agronomic Measures	*Harvest Equivalents (Mt. unmilled Grain/Year)*
Intensification of existing Cropping Practices raise yields by 35 per cent	700
Extension of Cultivated Land (20 per cent increase compared to 1990)	500
Cultivation of the Idle Land	75
High-efficiency irrigation	100
No beef production with intensively grown feed	50
Irrigation with saline water	25
Agrisilviculture, aquaculture and new crops	50
Total	**1500**

Source: Smil Vaclav, 1994.

itself is to be blamed for such a changing situation. It is comprehensible that hunger and malnutrition gripping a considerable section of the global population—923 million in 2007 (FAO, 2008)—results not from inadequate quantity of food since, according to the same source, there had been record grain harvest in 2007 with excess food in the world to feed at least 1.5 of the global demand, accompanied by global food production increasing by 2 per cent a year over a period of two decades prior to 2010 when population growth fell to 1.14 per cent a year. Non-availability of food for those people—hungry and malnourished—was largely due to inability of these people to buy food. According to Holt-Giménez (2010), as mentioned in Chapter 2, the world's hungry are simply too poor to buy enough food because of prohibitive prices. Many of these people are subsistence farmers with very small amount of land in possession and without access to other inputs like water, fertilizers, are far from a position to compete in the world market where factors like more and more agricultural land getting converted to the production of crops used for producing biofuel were instrumental in raising food prices, ultimately further reducing the purchasing power at the lowest rung of the economic ladder.[3]

In this context, the overall situation is not expected to improve further in the coming years as prices of food commodities are likely to remain above those of the previous ten years, prior to 2008 (FAO, 2008). Mechanism of three major factors are operating behind keeping prices high: the first of which is growing purchasing power generated by dietary changes with increasing preference for animal-protein for hundreds of millions of people in emerging economies of the developing world; second, growing demand for biofuel resulting from high oil prices, may gobble up more arable land, to the tune of three times in the next twenty years; and, third, higher fertilizer prices and higher costs of transportation resulting from high petroleum prices are going to restrict food production and, coupled with limited access to water and land, is going to affect food production very hard making the situation harder (FAO 2008) for economically marginalised people all over the world.

The growing inequality in this regard between people who can afford and those who cannot afford to feed themselves has, perhaps, come to a head, as Oxfam reports. The widening chasm between rich and poor has a direct relevance to our promise to bring people out of poverty so that they could acquire purchasing power to feed themselves. In order to have a clear view of this inequality we may refer to the observations made by Oxfam that three years ago, such as prior to 2016,

> "world's richest 85 people had the same wealth as the poorest half of the planet combined. The next year, it was found that the world's top 1 per cent own more wealth than everyone else combined. And now, in 2016, the number of billionaires who share the wealth of the poorest half of the world is just 62."[4]

While in India, according to the same source (Oxfam, 2016) 1 per cent of the people in India have 73 per cent of its total wealth.

Putting differently, this extreme inequality means that the poorest people of the world are destined to live a life 'shorter, harder and unhappier, having quite different experiences born as human being.' This automatically brings us to another very hard truth: that while the "poorest half of the global population—3.6 billion—are responsible for the generation of nearly 10 per cent of carbon emissions, the world's richest 10 per cent produce around half. Further, interesting to know that in Sub-Saharan Africa an average person would take 180 years to register the same emissions as the average American does in one year" (Goldring, 2016).

In this context, what is really worrying is our future in realising the close link between growing inequality and climate change. In this economy of the 1 per cent, as Goldring (2016) calls it, we have been oblivious of the dire consequences that leaving the poorest behind, welcoming rise in GDP, relentless consumption of natural resources beyond their limit by way of burning, chopping and extraction, we have already created a situation where many of the natural elements have changed for the worse as manifested in changing temperature, changing rainfall patterns, changing flood and drought occurrences and their growing virulence, consequential forest fires, dissolution of ice covers, melting of permafrost, rise of sea level and in circulation in ocean waters around the world, to name a few. The cumulative effect of these in various forms leading to colossal harvest failures, leaving poor people to starvation as well as untimely death. But none of these individually compares with *El Nino* weather system in its virulence.

Climate Change and Its Overall Impact on Food Situation

Ehrlich *et al.* (1993)* warned at the end of the last century that rapid climate change presents a greater threat to food production than ozone depletion when climatic zones will be shifting as much as 50 times faster than they have done in the previous 11,000 years, since the beginning of agriculture developed over a period of remarkable climatic stability. But now, whenever a violent drought or flood occurs fed by incessant rains beating all previous records in concentration or distribution, upsetting the agricultural system, there is no immediate relief that the situation will come back to its normal state. It always remaining uncertain in the face of global warming becomes instrumental to such uncertainties which are going to disrupt human activities, sometimes severely imperilling to the extent of threatening human existence in many areas. It is described as one of the defining forces shaping human prospects in the Twenty first century through its impact on the environment. The reasons for these growing uncertainties in climate behaviour may easily be traced to factors known to us.

For example,

> "since 1970, the earth's average temperature has risen more than 1 degree Fahrenheit. If we continue with business as usual, burning even more oil, coal and natural gas, it is projected to rise by 11 degrees Fahrenheit (6 degrees Celsius) by the end of this century. The rise will be uneven. It will be much greater in the high latitudes than in the equatorial regions, greater

---

* Ehrlich, Paul R., Anne H. Ehrlich and Gretchen C. Daily, "Food Security, Population and Environment," in *Population and Development Review 19, No. 1 (March 1993).*

over land than over oceans, and greater in continental interiors than in coastal regions."[5]

Brown (2012)* further points out that rising temperature will interfere with pollination and reduce photosynthesis of basic food crops and among them corn is particularly vulnerable. In the case of rice, the fall in pollination with high temperature from 100 per cent at 93 degrees Fahrenheit (34 degrees Celsius) to near zero at 104 degrees, destroys the crop. Further, citing the results of another group of experts, Brown (2012) maintains further that photosynthetic activity in plants increases until temperature reaches 60 degrees Fahrenheit, plateaus at 95 degrees Fahrenheit, beyond which it starts declining, ceasing altogether at 104 degrees Fahrenheit.

All these changes naturally affect crop-yields and, in general, it has been found that 1 degree Celsius rise in temperature reduces yields of corn, wheat and rice by 10 per cent, but the result has been disputed by some other experts, putting the decline at 17 per cent for corn and soybeans, which seems to be more convincing. Ultimately, the result is that, with such declining yield of major staples, it becomes increasingly difficult to feed the growing global population.

Simultaneously, as defined by experts, rising temperature has also an indirect effect on crop-yields, with very severe impact on food production. For example, mountain glaciers melting at a faster rate, twice the rate a decade ago, with small ones already disappearing, diminishes the supply of water for irrigation by rivers, themselves affected by depleting supply from receding glaciers—as it is happening in the Andes, the Rocky Mountains and the Alps.

The world food security is worst hit by melting glaciers originating in the Himalayas and the Tibetan Plateau which feed rivers like the Indus, Ganges, Yellow and Yangtze rivers and will bring disaster to food production in Pakistan, India and China, with greatly reduced summer flow creating an 'ecological catastrophe'. Equally, food production system is imperilled by

---

* Brown, Lester R., *Full Planet, Empty Plates: The New Geopolitics of Food Security*, Earth Policy Institute, W.W. Norton and Company, New York and London, 2012.

loss of snowmelt in Central Asian countries, including Afghanistan, Kazakhstan, Kyrgyzstan, Tajikistan, Turkmenistan and Uzbekistan, depending on Hindu Kush, Pamir and Tien Shan mountains as their source of life-giving support. The severity of high temperature has another cataclysmic, life-threatening effect in the melting of Greenland and Antarctic ice-sheets and consequent rise in sea-level, jeopardising rice-growing river deltas in Asia, including lands in Bangladesh and a large part of Vietnam, in the last of which reduction in rice harvest will displace millions of people. On the other hand, complete melting of Greenland—though may take a millennium—would raise sea level by 23 feet, with a rise of 6 feet within this century, as predicted. Besides, scientists are also expecting increase in drought resulting from reduced precipitation and it was predicted by the US National Academy of Sciences that the rise of atmospheric CO_2 from the then current level of 391 parts per million (ppm) to above 450 ppm in 2009 was going to cause irreversible dry-season rainfall reductions in several regions of the world (Brown, 2012). Rising temperatures as a principal manifestation of climate change fuels extensive wild fires of virulent nature, and as evidenced—'a 2.9 degree Fahrenheit rise in summer temperature could double the area of wild fires in the western states of the United States' (already one of the devastating wild fires making havoc in California in 2017) caused by rising temperatures causing disastrous effects on crop production, as witnessed in US Mid-West in 1988, bringing down US grain harvest from an annual average of 324 million tons to 204 million tons. Another heat wave hitting Western Europe in 2003 claimed 52,000 lives. Similar incomparable instances of death and destruction caused by severe heat waves took place in Russia in 2010, when high temperatures igniting wild fires destroyed $300 billion worth of the country's forests, claimed almost 56,000 lives and brought down annual harvest from about 100 million tons to 60 million tons. Almost an equally severe heat wave struck Texas, in the US, next year, in 2011, the average temperature reaching 100 degree Fahrenheit, continued without break for 40 consecutive days, causing loss of agricultural output exceeding worth $7 billion when farmers, getting bereft of any forage and water, were forced to sell their herds, the only means of living (Brown, 2012).

All these are instances of a grave situation from which there is no easy escape unless we accept our responsibility of controlling factors responsible for giving rise to these unwelcome events. We know, for certain, that temperature has already increased by 0.7°C (1.3°F) since the beginning of industrial era, leading to global warming, and the rate is accelerated by a rise of 0.2°C every decade. According to the opinion of climate scientists, the threshold for marking as dangerous is 2°C (3.6°F). Crossing this 2°C threshold makes a significant risk of catastrophic outcomes for future generations (UNDP, 2007/2008).

Crossing the 2°C threshold would accelerate the action of various climatic elements with greater impact on human activities, such as prolonged drought and rainfall variation reducing crop harvest, endangering food security; indirectly, rising temperature accelerating glacial melt would threaten water supply for urban populations, agriculture, hydroelectricity worldwide, and by 2080 climate change will affect 1.8 billion people who will face water scarcity. According to IPCC, droughts and floods becoming more frequent due to temperature-rise have already turned out to be the major drivers in climate-related disasters, such as drought, violent cyclones and floods, affecting about 262 million people between 2000 and 2004, over 98 per cent of them living in developing countries. The intensity of violent cyclones will increase further with rise in temperature beyond 2°C threshold, inundating low-lying areas in Bangladesh, Egypt and Vietnam while rising sea-level holds more frightening prospect of inundating coastal areas besides drowning island countries like Maldives and many more. Furthermore, the rate of extinction of marine species, such as corals, as mentioned earlier, accelerated beyond 2°C rise in temperature, affecting 20-30 per cent of species, turning it into a high-risk level with temperature rising by 3°C. It is at the same time predicted that globally human health will be at greater risk with temperature rise, affecting an additional 220-400 million people with malaria (UNDP 2007/2008).

Human Role in Inducing Climate Change

There cannot be any denying of the fact that human activities over time have been directly instrumental in bringing sweeping changes in climate endangering human life.

Temperature is the key or most fundamental measure of climate change. Rise in temperature recorded probably the highest of 'any 50-year period for the past 1,300 years' is accelerating of late, as evidenced by 11 of the 12 warmest years since 1850 occurring between 1995 and 2006. The temperature of the Earth has increased by 0.7°C over the past 100 years.

Atmospheric concentration of CO_2 and other greenhouse gases is directly linked to rising temperature, which is quite different from the system where the concentration of these gases to some level is harmless as they block outward passage of heat from the Earth and thus keep Earth's temperature at a level making it habitable. This is known as 'greenhouse effect', without which the earth would be 30°C colder, or uninhabitable in other words.

In contrast, the current warming cycle results from the concentrations of CO_2, at a much faster rate, its total stock in the atmosphere having increased by one-third, exceeding the natural range of the last 650,000 years, accompanied by increasing concentrations of other greenhouse gases (UNDP, 2007/2008).

Climatic experts take two phases of transformation in energy use directly responsible for greater concentration of CO_2 in atmosphere as inducement to climate change. The first transformation took place when water power was replaced by coal as a source of energy, removing all obstacles to unprecedented increase in productivity.

The second phase of transformation, happening 150 years later, was harnessing of oil to the internal combustion engine in the early twentieth century and the combined action of burning coal, oil and natural gas led to vast increase in 'wealth and productivity'. But, looking from another angle, the entire socalled economic achievement was made at the cost of increasing emission of CO_2, responsible for 90 per cent increase in global warming effect, when emissions have been 'at least six times faster' than at any time before the industrial revolution. Concentration of CO_2 in 2005 was about 375 ppm.

The oceans acting as the largest carbon sinks of the world, absorbing about 0.1 Gt more carbon per year than they release, have reversed their role, soaking up an extra 2 Gt a year—more than 20 times the natural rate, with consequential serious ecological damage. Warmer oceans becoming increasingly acidic attacks 'carbonate, one of the essential building blocks for corals' and others in marine food chain. According to an observation, extremely alarming for the oceans for playing their part in human survival is that,

> "based on current trends, future carbon dioxide release could produce chemical conditions in the oceans that have not been witnessed in the past 300 million years, except during brief catastrophic events."[6]

Changing Scenarios Due to Climate Change

The total emissions of greenhouse gases from all sources recorded one-fifth increase between 1990 and 2004, the rising increases mean rise in temperatures which might exceed the threshold limit of 2°C. Following the trend, the atmospheric stock of greenhouse gases will be increasing at 4-5 ppm a year by 2035, nearly double the current rate, with the accumulated stock of greenhouse gases rising to 550 ppm and, even without further addition to emission, the accumulated stock is predicted to reach over 600 ppm by 2050 and 800 ppm by the end of the twenty first century (UNDP, 2007/2008). In this context, it is quite relevant to identify the role of Asia in global warming. As Amitav Ghosh (2016) observes,

> "The vulnerability of Asia's population is only one aspect of their centrality to global warming. The reality is that the continent has also played a pivotal role in setting in motion the chain of consequences that is driving the present cycle of climatic change ... numbers are critical, for it was the rapid and expanding industrialization of Asia's most populous nations, beginning in the 1980s, that brought the climate crisis to a head."[7]

As emphasized by Ghosh (2016) 'Asia's centrality to global warming' rests upon the numbers of people making them at the same time as the potential victims, for the density of population has given rise to some of the worst disasters in the Bengal Delta, like Bhola cyclone in 1971 killed some 300,000 people; another in

Bangladesh in 1991 killed 138,000, majority of whom were women. Ghosh (2016) warns about sea-level rise and the great intensity of storms giving rise to larger inundations all along the coast line. At the same time, subsidence of the delta regions across Asia, as elsewhere in the world, causes faster rise of sea level, the cause of subsidence resting largely on faulty human action like dam building, extraction of groundwater and oil. The rivers in the southern parts of Asia are particularly vulnerable and among them Indus no longer reaches the sea, while 'salt water has pushed inland by forty miles swallowing up over a million acres of agricultural land' (Ghosh, 2016).

In this respect, India seems to be much more vulnerable with a likely loss of about 60,000 square kilometres of land, some of it most fertile, due to rise of sea level, drowning the Lakshadweep chain of islands forcing migration of about 50 million people in India and 75 million in Bangladesh.

The continuing changes in climate in the form of droughts, periodic flooding and extreme weather events have jeopardized the lives of people in the interior of the continent and almost 24 per cent of India's arable land is slowly being converted into desert and a rise in temperature by 2°C would 'reduce country's food supply by a quarter'. Similar grain situation is faced by Pakistan where '100,000 acres of salt encrusted land are being abandoned each year', while a fifth of the remaining land is badly waterlogged and a quarter of it produces 'only meagre crops'. China faces an annual loss amounting to $65 billion due to the ongoing process of desertification (Ghosh, 2016).

According to Ghosh (2016), compared to the situation depicted above, Asia's accelerating water crisis is much more frightening where rivers sustaining China, South and Southeast Asia originating in Tibet and the Himalayas, get their supplies of water stored in the form of accumulated ice, support the lives of '47 per cent of the global population'. But,

> "this region is warming twice as fast as the average global rate, and in 2008 it was found that the Himalayan glaciers had already lost all the ice formed since the mid-1940s; by some reckonings one-third of them will disappear by 2050."[8]

It is not at all difficult to imagine the inescapable consequences, such as the accelerated rates of melting will increase river flows succeeded by unprecedented low in the dry season giving rise to disastrous floods, reminding us of the flood in the Koshi river in India in 2008, the Indus floods in 2010, while shrinkage of glaciers will lead to catastrophic water shortages in their basin area, reminding again the fact that a quarter of the world's rivers are already running dry, many of them, if not most, are in Asia, making the livelihood of half a billion people at risk. Added to this is the problem of depletion of underground water resources, subjecting 214 million people to their peril in the 12,500 square miles of North China (Ghosh, 2016).

According to the Fifth Assessment Report of the IPCC 2014,

> "changes in precipitation in a warming world will not be uniform. The high latitudes and Equatorial Pacific are likely to experience an increase in annual mean precipitation by the end of this century. ... In many mid-latitude and sub-tropical dry regions, mean precipitation will likely increase. ... Extreme precipitation events over most mid-latitude land masses and over wet tropical regions will very likely become more intense and more frequent as global mean surface temperature increases. It is likely that the area encompassed by monsoon systems will increase and monsoon is likely to intensify and El Nino-South Oscillation (ENSO) related precipitation variability on regional scales will likely intensify."[9]

The same report (IPCC, 2014) warns about the continuation of global warming during the twenty first century and weakening of the Atlantic Meridional Overturring Circulation over the twenty first Century, which is very likely to make a quite uncomfortable winter as this vast conveyor belt of warm water in the Atlantic Ocean keeps Europe 8°C warmer in winter, making it less stressful. However, according to this report, there is no possibility of any abrupt transition or collapse of this circulation during the twenty first century. On the other hand, the sea-level rise will continue during the twenty first century worldwide, though it will not be uniform, but by the end of the century sea-level is very likely to rise in more than 95 per cent of the ocean area. Global warming, as reported, will cause reductions in Arctic Sea ice, resulting in almost an ice-free Arctic Ocean in September in certain areas before mid-century. Besides, there is prediction of a decrease in sea-ice extent and volume in the Arctic. At the same time, it is virtually certain that mean surface temperature increases will reduce the near-surface permafrost extent at high northern latitudes, the area of permafrost getting reduced in upper – 3.5m—surface by 37 per cent to 81 per cent (IPCC, 2014).

Sea-level rise as a consequence of temperature rise perhaps nowhere proves more threatening than linked to the accelerated disintegration and eventual disappearance of Greenland and West Antarctica Ice Sheets, the last one is getting thinner by several metres a year. According to one of the world's top climatic scientists, the sea-level would rise by 5 metres this century at the present rate of melting but complete melting of Greenland ice-sheet would give rise to about 7 metres to sea-levels (UNDP 2007/2008).

Carbon Footprints in Global Perspective: El Niño: Droughts and Famines

Undoubtedly, there is wide difference in carbon footprints between rich and poor countries, depending on the origin of CO_2 from different sources as defined by economic progress. For example, in 2000 over half of all emissions was from burning of fossil fuels, power generation accounting for about one-quarter of the total followed by transport as the second largest source of energy-related CO_2. These two together increased their greenhouse gas emission 140 and 120 per cent respectively over the past three decades. Change in land use as well plays an important role, such as deforestation, as the largest source in this connection, sharing, according to best calculations, between 11 and 28 per cent of total emissions.

Interestingly, though the responsibility of increasing carbon footprint lies with the developing world, the 'historic responsibility of carbon emissions rests heavily with the developed world' (UNDP 2007/2008). It has been pointed out in this report that if every person living in the developing world had the same carbon footprint as the average person of the industrial world, the global carbon emissions would rise to a total requiring six planets.

"Rich countries dominate the overall emissions account (Fig. 5.1). Collectively, they account for 7 out of every 10 tonnes of CO_2 that have been emitted since the start of the industrial era. Historic emissions amount to around 1,100 tonnes of CO_2 per capita for Britain and America, compared with 66 tonnes per capita for China and 23 tonnes per capita for India. These historic emissions matter on two counts. First,... cumulative past emissions drive today's climate change. Second, the envelope for absorbing future emissions is a residual function of past emissions. In effect, the ecological space available for future emissions is determined by past action."[10]

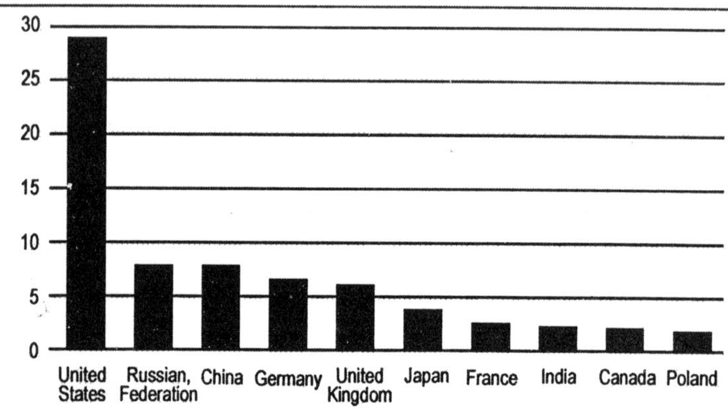

a. Includes a share of USSR emissions proportional to the Russian Federations current share of CIS emissions.

Fig. 5.1: Share of Global CO_2 Emissions by Rich Countries 1840-2004 (%)
Source: CDIAC 2007: UNDP 2007/2008.

In this context it is important to note that the overall domination in CO_2 emissions lies with a small group of countries and among them the United States is the largest emitter, accounting for about one-fifth of the total, while collectively China, India, Japan, the Russian Federation and the United States—the top five—together account for over half of the emission, while the top 10 account for over 60 per cent (Fig. 5.2). Significantly, the share of global emissions is rising with the developing world accounting for 42 per cent in 1990, which is likely to increase to over half of the total by 2030, but while China is going to overtake the United States as the largest emitter, India will follow as the fourth largest emitter.

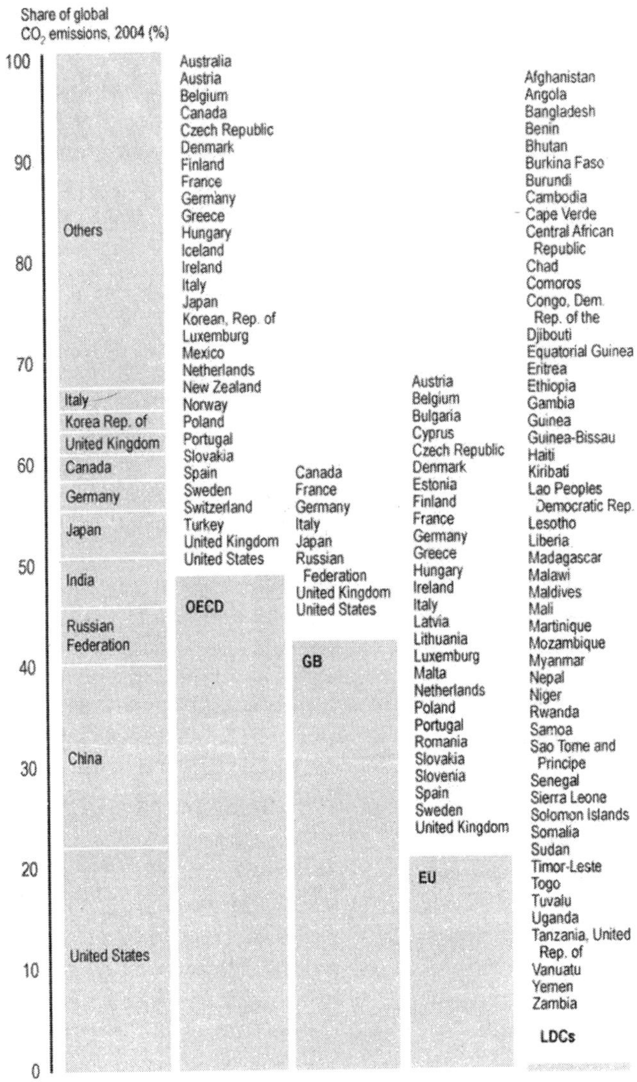

Fig. 5.2: CO_2 Emissions with its Countrywise Share (%) 2004
Source: CDIAC 2007.

El Niño: Droughts and Famines

However, any investigation on climate change cannot escape the role of El Niño as the worst manifestation of climate change, responsible for the largest toll of human life all through the last few centuries. El Niño represents a climatic condition when

> "the equatorial Pacific Ocean, acting as a planetary heat engine coupled to the trade winds (is) able to affect rainfall patterns throughout the tropics and even in temperate latitude. Rapid warmings of the eastern tropical Pacific (called El Niño events), for example, are associated with weak monsoons and synchronous drought throughout vast parts of Asia, Africa and north-eastern South America. When the eastern Pacific is unusually cool, on the other hand, the pattern reverses (called a La Niña event), and abnormal precipitation and flooding occur. ... The entire vast see-saw of air mass and ocean temperature, which extends into the Indian Ocean as well, is formally known as El Niño-Southern oscillation (or ENSO, for short)."[11]

Interestingly, there have been eight or nine very strong El Niños since 1728, once every 12 years on an average but three of the very strongest (1882-82 and 1997-1998) have occurred recently, at 14 years interval between each. A global assessment of El Niño's effect on different regions gives a clear idea about the devastating role. Starting our investigation from South-East Asia in this regard, according to the reports of experts in the field, 93 per cent of droughts in Java during the colonial period were caused by El Niños, going back as far as 1514 (Davis, 2014), and considering the 1902 El Niño in this regard, made a 'much bigger rainfall deficit' in both Indonesia and the Philippines than was done by 1899—El Niño. The El Niño droughts were found to be closely associated with increased frequency of uncontrolled forest fires in many of these regions. There is found to be a close similarity in the prevalence of droughts in India and Australia which leave no doubt that severe droughts occur as a rule 'simultaneously over the two countries' resulting from the effects of El Niño and

> "correlation of droughts with ENSO (El Niño Southern Oscillation) is strongest in New South Wales and northern Victoria, when tremendous losses were sustained by agriculture and the wool industry during the El Niño events of 1877, 1884, 1888, 1897, 1899, 1902, 1915, 1918 and 1958. At such times, vast areas become an antipodean Dust Bowl."[12]

Incidentally, in South America, the droughts of 1877-79 and 1888-91, associated with El Niño were the most severe ones and the 1896-97 drought was exceptionally severe, occurring again in 1915 and 1918. El Niño droughts have played particularly destructive roles in the history of Andean and Amazonian cultures. The role of ENSO as the chief 'climatic regulator of Amazonian Basin ecology producing periodic droughts and accompanying wild fires (as in 1998)' may turn Amazonian Basin temporarily from a major net CO_2 source to a net sink of comparable magnitude (Davis, 2014).

The warm water piling up against the equatorial coastline of South America driven far northward, leading to warming up and rise in sea-level, has profound meteorological effects, giving rise to severe droughts, one of them in 1997-98 producing one of the severest droughts in the western part of Mexico, causing hundreds of forest fires producing a thick layer of smoke reaching as far as some parts of the United States. As a matter of fact, devastating droughts happening between 1907 and 1911 coincided with political unrest in the country, leading to the downfall of the government. Similarly, southern Africa has been the scene of catastrophic droughts, worst of which in this century happening in 1991-92 reducing the production of maize by 82 per cent. Taking a final look into the major events of El Niño visits, with the time of appearance spread over a period from 1782-83 to 1997-98 (Table 5.2), some very interesting facts may be gathered from Table 5.2, showing China very closely followed by India as the most popular playground for El Niño, visiting frequently, as per records available from 1782-83 to 1997-98. The next important victims are Brazil and South Africa, having suffered from intense droughts accompanied by famines, probably killing people in millions, for which detailed accounts are not available. It only gives us an idea about the frequency of major events of El Niño onslaughts, leaving one to their guesses about the minor ones which may not have also been infrequent.

Surprisingly, the distinct link between El Niño and the emergence of a poor economy in countries, bunched together known as the **Third World, can no longer be brushed aside**. True that El Niño as a manifestation of climate change induced by human action happening in greater frequency since the industrial revolution had been instrumental in destroying the economy of those countries, like India and others already colonised by powers in Europe. Lamentably, though, at the time of colonisation these countries had, in many cases, such as India, a better economy than the powers which colonised them. Mike Davis (2014 Reprint) quoting Bairoch and Maddison shows this difference in income and wealth in the eighteenth century.

Table 5.2: Major ENSO (El Nino-Southern Oscillation Events since 1780)

El Nino	*Strength*	*Regions affected by Drought/Famine*
1782-83	S	China, India
1790-93	Vs	India
1803-04	S+	India/South Africa
1824-25	M+	China/India/South Africa
1828	Vs	South Africa
1837	M+	China/India
1844-46	S	China/Brazil
1867-70	M+	China/India
1873-74	M	India
1876-78	Vs	China/India/South Africa/ Egypt/Java/Brazil
1887-89	M+	China/Ethiopia/Sudan/Sahel
1891	Vs	China/India/Brazil
1896-97	M+	India/Brazil
1899-1900	Vs	China/India/South Africa
1901-02	M+	China/South Africa
1911-13	S	China/India/Brazil
1917-19	S	China/India/Brazil/Morocco
1925-26	Vs	China (floods)/India
1957-58	S	China/Brazil
1965-66	S	China/India
1972-73	S	China/India/ Ethiopia/Sahel/Brazil
1982-83	Vs	China/India/Indonesia/South Africa
1991-95	S	South Africa/ East Africa/Mexico
1997-98	Vs	China (floods)/Indonesia/Brazil

Source: Mike Davis, 20th Reprint.
Key: M=Moderate; S = Strong; Vs = Very Strong

> "It is very likely that, in the middle of the eighteenth century, the average standard of living in Europe was a little bit lower than that of the rest of the world. When *sans culottes* stormed the Bastille, the largest manufacturing districts in the world were the Yangzi Delta and Bengal, with Lingan (modern Guangdong and Guangxi) and coastal Madras not far behind. India alone produced one-quarter of the world, manufactures and while its pre-capitalist agrarian labour productivity was probably less than the Japanese-Chinese level, its commercial capital surpassed that of the Chinese. ... Indeed, there is compelling evidence that South Indian labourers had higher earnings than their British counterparts in the eighteenth century and lived lives of far greater financial security."[13]

It is further noted that the productivity of land in South India, being higher than in Europe, provided its weavers and other artisans with better diets than average Europeans, earning higher incomes than their British counterparts in the eighteenth century, enjoying greater financial security. It as well applies to China. Mike Davis (2014 Reprint) quotes another author, Kenneth Pomeranz, stating that 'ordinary Chinese enjoyed a higher standard of consumption than eighteenth century Europeans' and goes on to say that

> "the Lower Yangzi appears to have produced roughly as much cotton cloth per capita in 1750 as the UK did cotton, wool, linen and silk cloth combined in 1800—plus an enormous quantity of silk. In addition, as Maddison demonstrates, the Chinese GDP in absolute terms grew faster than that of Europe throughout the eighteenth century, dramatically enlarging its share of world income by 1820."[14] (See Note A)

Sadly, the overall situation changed slowly, the colonising countries pursuing a systematic, planned course of destroying the manufactural base of the colonised countries, making their grip firmer, converting the entire economy of the colonised country. India, for an instance, into a veritable source of raw materials needed by the growing industries of the coloniser countries, such as the UK, and making it the major market of the industrial products of the coloniser. The slow death of the local economy, growing impoverishment of the local people in the absence of work for making a living, gave rise to hunger, poverty and malnourishment and the tragedy fuelled further by severe droughts and accompanying famines brought on by frequent visits of El Niños. The colonisers, using these as weapons in all the countries, stretching from Indian sub-continent to Africa and South America, made their grip firmer with time, making full use of locally available resources as well as labour (slave labour at many places) of the colonies, ultimately giving rise to a set of subdued economies, taken together came to be known as the 'Third World' countries. We need to be aware of the strange coincidence of the formation of colonies at a time very much prone to the appearance of El Niños, a human-induced natural phenomenon developed from the greed of a section of people bent on consumerism fuelling the atmosphere with larger carbon emissions. It is a vicious cycle: rising temperature bringing drought and famines to destroy economy, pushing countries under the grip of colonisers into a much lower level of existence than what they had been before getting subjected to foreign rule. Thus, El Niño is indirectly the product of human action, of the most greedy section deciding the fate of people who are the victims of climate change. The role of El Niño domination cannot be ruled out.

Climate Change and Mitigating Strategies in Geographical Perspective

Exploring the future of food security in the perspective of climate change and associated factors leaves no scope for going into further details about the association of El Niños or such climatic behaviour with politico-historical changes in the world. It is, rather, more justifiable to look for possibilities of escape routes out of this highly worrying and consistently worsening situation created by man's unintentional urge for improving his life and living standard.

Arguably, we cannot tame climate but what can be done is to check its further deterioration. The major issue at the root of climate change, with its various manifestations and their effects on human life and activities, is carbon emission, which needs to be checked without further delay and the challenge was taken up by countries assembled in 1997 at Kyoto to bring down carbon emission from its 1990 level in industrial countries, and the resolution made on this came to be known as 'Kyoto Protocol'. Incidentally, climate change if not checked will have the most harmful effect on agriculture and, as predicted, there is increasing possibility of bringing down agricultural production alarmingly decreasing 9 per cent in the developing countries, while boosting production in developed countries by 8 per cent through longer growing seasons, thus making the former dependent on imports of food grains from the latter with greatest losses in Sub-Saharan Africa and Latin America, resulting from prolonged droughts (UNDP, 2007-2008) (Fig. 5.3).

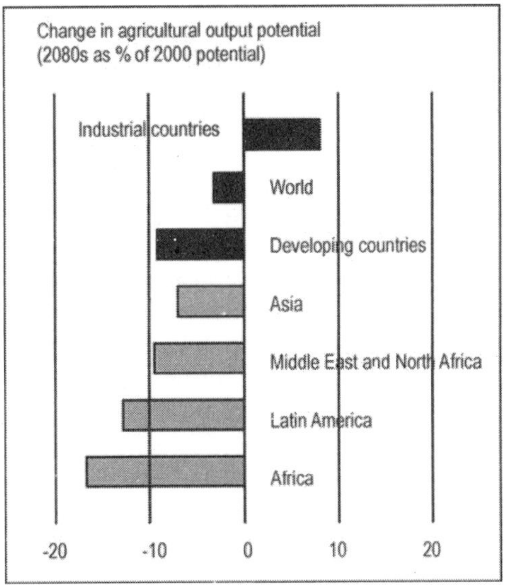

Fig. 5.3: Effect of Climate Change on Agriculture in Developing Countries

Source: Cline 2007/UNDP 2007-2008.

Incidentally, the effect of climate change will be of a contrasting nature in India, as predicted, since there are large uncertainties in the actions of El Niño Southern Oscillation (ENSO), the ocean-atmosphere cycle spanning a third of the globe spreading drought across South Africa, and parts of South and East Asia, deciding largely the agricultural future of the country, as a result of which there will be more rain in already rain-abundant parts of the country creating risks of flooding in large drought-prone areas comprising Andhra Pradesh, Gujarat, Madhya Pradesh and Rajasthan, where temperature rising by 3.5°C by 2050 will bring down agricultural production by 8-9 per cent, rice becoming the most affected crop (UNDP, 2007/2008).

The 'Kyoto Protocol' itself was an exercise in setting down the targets for bringing down emissions by every country within a stipulated period. Such as

> "most OECD countries—Australia and the United States are the major exceptions—are committed to achieving reductions by 2008-2012 against a 1990 base year. ... Under the Kyoto Protocol the European Union is required to achieve an 8 per cent reduction in emission. However, in 2007 it committed itself to cutting greenhouse gas emissions by at least 20 per cent by 2020 and by 2030 if an international agreement is reached, with a reduction of 60-80 per cent by 2050."[15]

Setting targets for carbon emissions is preceded by carbon budgeting as the most necessary step, putting a limit on the total quantity of CO_2 emissions over a specified period of time, making governments answerable to the citizens in case of failure in keeping the promise. In the opinion of scientists, a 70 per cent reduction in carbon emission at 1999 level is needed to stabilize climate. As mentioned earlier, the Earth's average temperature rising by 1 degree Fahrenheit since 1970, if continues uninterrupted, will rise by some 11 degrees Fahrenheit by the end of the twenty first century. It will have disastrous effect on food production. This is explained very succinctly by Brown (2012) in the following words:

> "High temperature interferes with pollination and reduces photosynthesis of basic food crops. The most vulnerable part of a plant's life cycle is the pollination period. Of the world's three food staples—corn, wheat and rice—corn is particularly vulnerable. In order for corn to reproduce, pollen must fall from the tassel to the strands of silk that emerge from the end of each ear. Each of these six strands is attached to a kernel site on

> the cob. If the kernel is to develop, a grain of pollen must fall on the silk strand and then journey to the kernel site, where fertilization takes place. When temperatures are uncommonly high, the silk strands quickly dry out and turn brown, unable to play their role in the fertilization process. When it comes to rice ... the pollination of rice falls from 100 per cent at 93 degrees Fahrenheit (34°C) to near zero at 104 degrees, heading to crop failure."[16]

Scientific studies have proved that 1° Celsius rise in temperature reduces yield by 17 per cent.

Two major ways of dealing with reduction of carbon emissions are—greater dependence on renewable energy sources replacing fossil fuels and increasing energy efficiency, together they are expected to reduce Europe's carbon emission by almost one-third. Most effective but quite easy measures for increasing energy-efficiency include replacement of 'old, inefficient refrigerators, switching to high-efficiency light-bulbs, and insulation of roofs.' The European Commission proposed a plan in 2005. For an addition of 15,000 megawatts of wind power, a five-fold expansion of ethanol production and a three-fold in biodiesel production is necessary to tackle, with energy generated by using fossil fuels. At the same time people were urged to use hybrid cars and dispose of their old cars using fossil fuel (See Note B). The plan was likely to save 60 billion Euros by 2020, stimulating 'economic growth and create new jobs' (Brown, 2006).

Efficient use of energy is another very effective way of raising energy productivity. Bill Prindle of the Washington-based 'Alliance to Save Energy' pointed out in 2001 different ways of reducing the demand for electricity. Such as (a) 'more stringent residential air conditioner efficiency'; (b) 'raising commercial air conditioner standards'; (c) 'using tax credits and energy codes to improve the efficiency of new buildings and raise energy efficiency of new buildings. Measures like using more energy-efficient household appliances, elimination of incandescent light bulbs, shifting to gas-electric hybrid cars, as mentioned before, and re-designing urban transport system, giving stress on public transport, such as bus and cycles will raise efficiency to a large degree (Brown, 2006).

It has already been pointed out that power generation is one of the most potent sources of CO_2 emission, with four out of every ten tonnes contributed by it, and among the fossil fuels coal takes the lead, strengthening the position further in future with greater investment between 2005 and 2030, with over half of this investment in the developing countries (Fig. 5.4). Substituting fossil fuel by power generated from renewable sources like sun, wind, sea tides and geothermal sources, could prove to be the most important way of reducing carbon emission but till now they could not take a competitive role because of technological drawback (if not for fossil fuel lobby-pressure). On the other hand, nuclear power with almost zero carbon footprint could have been a great choice but policy makers in different countries have not taken a positive, encouraging, role in this regard.

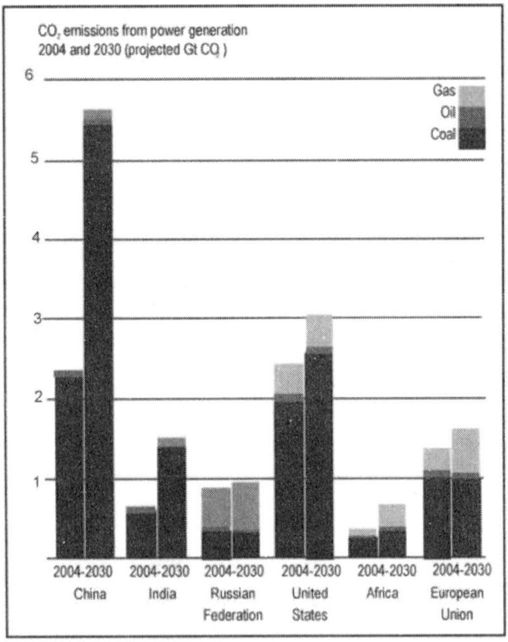

Fig. 5.4: Share of CO_2 emissions in power generation by sector Coal, Oil and Gas between 2004 and 2030.

Note: 2030 emissions refer to the IEA Reference Scenario as defined in IEA 2006c.

Source: IEA 2006c CADP 2007-2008.

Nevertheless, the potential for rapid growth in renewable energy from various sources is gaining ground, expanding with remarkable efficiency. It is reported that modern wind turbines produce 180 times more energy at less than half the cost per unit than turbines 20 years ago (UNDP, 2007/2008). Brown (2006)* reports that generation of electricity using wind power in the world having increased at 29 per cent per year has jumped from less than 5,000 megawatt in 1995 to 47,000 megawatt in 2004, over nine-fold increase, in comparison with 1.7 per cent for oil, 2.5 per cent for natural gas, 2.3 per cent for coal and 1.9 per cent for nuclear power. Brown (2006) mentions six of its wind power properties making much more acceptable than any other source of energy, such as 'it is abundant, cheap, inexhaustible, widely distributed, clean and climate-benign'. Europe leads the world in using wind energy, with Germany beating the United States with the highest generating capacity and in Denmark over 20 per cent of electricity is provided by wind power. The total generation from wind as the source of power for Europe is planned to reach 230,000 megawatt by 2020, satisfying residential needs of 195 million consumers, or half of Europe's population (Brown, 2006).† One of the major advantages of wind power is that it

> "can be used to electrolyze water to produce hydrogen, which provides a way of both storing and transporting wind energy. At night, when the demand for electricity drops, the hydrogen generators can be turned on to build up reserves. Once in storage, hydrogen can be used to fuel power plants. ... (and) can thus become a back up for wind power ... The principal cost for wind-generated electricity is the upfront capital outlay for initial construction. Since wind is a free fuel, the only ongoing cost is for turbine maintenance."[17] (See Notes C and D)

There has been a phenomenal 57 per cent increase in the sales of solar cells in 2004, pushing the production of solar

* Brown, Lester R., *Plan B 2.0: Rescuing a Planet Under Stress and Civilization in Trouble,* Earth Policy Institute, 2006

† *Ibid.*

energy to a global total of 4,300 megawatt, doubled in two years, almost equivalent of 13 coal-fired power plants. The residential use of solar cells has been increasing at a 'breakneck' pace in some countries, one of them being Japan, planning to get 10 per cent of its total requirement of electricity from solar cells by 2030, making it the global leader in this respect, followed by Germany, reaching a goal of 100,000 solar roofs in 2003. China, by far the 'world leader in this technology' is planning to quadruple its current 52 million square metres of collectors by 2015. The global installations of 150 million square metres, excluding the one-fourth that is used for swimming pools, supplies water or space heating for 32 million households. It needs to be mentioned in this respect, that 'a single family residence can reduce water-heating bills by 70 per cent' (Brown, 2006).

Another quite inexhaustive source of renewable energy is geothermal energy with great potential, pioneered by Italy in 1904 in its production. The generation of power from this source spread fast, the global capacity increasing from 5,800 megawatt in 1990 to 8,400 megawatt in 2003, a 44 per cent growth. Two countries—the United States, with 2000 megawatt, and the Philippines, with 1900 megawatt, holding second place, gets 27 per cent of its total supply of electricity from this source. Apart from these two countries, its production is largely concentrated in Italy, Mexico, Indonesia, Japan and New Zealand. On the other hand, direct use of geothermal power for various heating purposes, such as for heating pump, is even larger, equivalent to 12,000 megawatt, globally over 30 countries using geothermal energy for heating. In this respect, Iceland and France give leadership, with 93 per cent of the country's homes in Iceland heated with geothermal energy, saving $100 million per year in avoiding oil-imports, with over one-third of total energy used in Iceland. In France, it is used for heating and providing hot water to about 200,000 homes. Geothermal energy has proved to be an ideal source for heating greenhouses to produce fresh vegetables in winter in countries like Russia, Hungary, Iceland and the United States, while it is used for aquaculture in some 16 countries, like China, Israel and the United States.

It leaves to no guessing that use of renewable energy on a large scale would undoubtedly be the easiest, most useful, much less expensive as well as least complex way of cutting down carbon emission. Among them, abundance and the low cost of production of wind energy make it more preferable. Among many of its advantages, the frugal use of land is one which makes it more acceptable.

> "Within the United States, a quarter-acre of land in the Corn Belt can be used to site an advanced designed wind turbine that will produce $100,000 worth of electricity per year or it can be used to produce 40 bushels of corn that will yield 100 gallons of ethanol worth perhaps $200. If the goal is to minimise competitive from the automobile fuel economy for food resources, wind generated electricity is the obvious choice."[18]

However, every country needs to adopt a strategy for carbon reduction and make its own choice of renewable energy, such as Iceland depends on geothermal energy, 82 per cent of its electricity comes from hydropower which is further used for electrolyzing water, to produce hydrogen. In the United States wind power is likely to emerge as the most important power generator meeting most of its requirements, even for production of steel, while 7 per cent of its electricity comes from hydropower, endowed further with substantial provision of geothermal power, particularly in western states besides enormous solar cell potential throughout the country. In Germany greater emphasis is being laid on wind energy, followed by generating electricity from solar cells, and planning to reduce its overall energy use by 37 per cent using improved technology raising energy efficiency. Of the remaining 67 per cent 45 per cent will come from renewable energy sources making an overall cut of carbon emission amounting to 65 per cent by 2050 (Brown, 2006). The UK is another country having an enormous potential in wind power generated from off-shore wind farms and much of the country's requirement of power may be met from wind power, abundant wave power as well as solar panels. India, however, presents a very dismal picture in this regard where it is reported by Sayesha Bhattacharya in *The Statesman*, Kolkata edition, dated 3 May, 2018, citing government sources, reported that total contribution of all renewable sources taken together to gross electricity generation in the country stands at 15.75 per cent, while coal as yet is at the top of the chart with a 76.71 per cent contribution followed by crude oil. Nevertheless, the likely prospect of increasing contribution from renewable sources to 40 per cent by 2030 is encouraging.

As reported further by Brown (2006), renewable energy in its different forms is gradually going to take a very important role in the economy of various countries, particularly in the developing world, with significant impact on reducing carbon emission, such as Indonesia is richly endowed with geothermal energy besides having abundant potential for solar and wind resources. In Spain, the year-round availability of energy from solar cells may meet all its requirements of electricity and it can also use wind as a major source of energy. On the other hand, Brazil is in a position to give up use of petroleum as an automotive fuel by ethanol, produced in the country, along with a generous supply of hydropower, wind and solar cells. China has big potential in wind power with a capability of doubling its supply, largely replacing coal and oil as sources of power when 15 per cent of electricity used in the country comes from hydropower. Similarly, Argentina getting 42 per cent of its electricity from hydropower is highly endowed with wind power potential, along with solar power potential (Brown, 2006).

At the same time, use of nuclear power endowed with lower carbon footprint is an extremely debatable choice for carbon mitigation in view of environmental and military risks involved. Currently accounting for about 17 per cent of the world's electricity generation, four-fifths of which is concentrated in the OECD countries, its share in the energy-mix for the production of electricity varies widely from over 20 per cent for the UK and the US to 80 per cent in France. However, two major handicaps are—it is prohibitively capital intensive, and disposal of nuclear waste is one of the biggest problems very difficult to solve (UNDP, 2007/2008).*

---

* United Nations Development Programme (UNDP), *Human Development Report 2007-2008, Fighting Climate Change: Human Solidarity in a Divided World.*

Some other mitigating measures are likely to have a greater bearing on cutting carbon emission with effect than may be done by substituting energy derived from fossil fuels by renewable energy sources, obviously taking longer time. Quite significantly,

> "energy use patterns in the residential sector have an important bearing on global carbon footprint. In the OECD countries, around one-third of the electricity produced ends up in heating and cooking systems, domestic refrigerators, ovens, lamps and other household devices. The residential sector accounts for around 35-40 per cent of national CO_2 emissions from all fossil fuels, with appliances alone producing roughly 12 per cent."[19]

It has been estimated that application of energy-efficient measures would give rise to a 29 per cent saving in emissions by 2020 in these countries or three times current emissions from India alone. In North America, where households consume 2.4 times more electricity per household than do households in Europe, reduction at that rate through energy-efficiency would save US $65 for each household for each tonne of CO_2 emission avoided, which is equivalent to 169 Euro for each household in Europe.

Another example is provided by lighting, which accounts for about 10 per cent of global electricity demand generating 7 per cent of CO_2 emissions which, with the installation of low-cost sources, such as fluorescent lamps could reduce energy use by 38 per cent. At the same time, 'building standard regulations' can generate very large savings in CO_2 emissions, gains in energy consumption 'could be increased by one-fifth', equivalent to 60 billion Euros for the European Union. The importance of best energy-efficiency in operating all electrical appliances in the OECD countries was claimed as having a capability of saving 322 million tons of CO_2 by 2010, equivalent to the withdrawal of all the cars off the roads in Canada, France and Germany combined. On the other hand, personal transportation as the largest consumer of oil contributes a lot to growing carbon emission, growing fast in the developing countries which, in

OECD countries alone, accounted for two-thirds of global carbon emission by 2004. However, though higher fuel efficiency has been attained in the European Union than in the United States, emissions from road transport has increased by 26 per cent since 1990, its share in overall emission from transport climbing from about one-sixth to one-fifth over a decade, and it is predicted that if greenhouse gas emissions continue to rise with economic growth, this could be 50 per cent by 2050 above 1990 levels (UNDP 2007/2008). (See Note E)

There is a growing interest among different countries in replacing use of oil/petroleum by ethanol for reducing carbon emission. It acts as a double-edged weapon, reducing carbon emission on the one hand while, on the other, cutting down on oil-imports. In this respect, one of the most impressive instances of judicious mix of incentives and regulation in the transport sector is provided by Brazil, where biofuels account for one-third of the total use of transport fuel and thus reducing dependence on imported oil as well as reduction in carbon emission. Another way of dealing with carbon emission is changing the fuel-mix comprising compressed natural gas (CNG) already by both India and Pakistan, taking prohibitive measures for a range of vehicles from using non-CNG fuels, such as in Delhi it is mandatory for all public vehicles to use CNG. Pakistan, on the other hand, plays a different card, such as price of CNG is kept 50-60 per cent lower than petroleum, converting almost 0.8 million vehicles to the use of CNG and the share is fast rising. (UNDP 2007/2008) (See Note F).

However, greater dependence on ethanol encouraging greater conversion of food (like maize), oil crops etc. directly hits on the availability of food for human consumption and, as it is already proved, corporate houses are more interested in the production of ethanol, remaining wilfully oblivious to the increasing demand for food in step with growing population. The fact remains uncontested that stabilizing population will take a longer time than we believe it could be achieved, while economic growth changing the nature of food in greater demand makes the situation more complex and critical.

Low carbon technologies developed through further research, as already being done in many countries—like the European Union and the United States—may take a decisive role in carbon mitigation. One of the major agents of carbon emission is coal, with the generation of coal-fired power accounts for 40 per cent of the world electricity and CO_2 emissions. Generation of more power with less coal, hence less emission, has been achieved using 'super-critical technologies', attaining efficiency levels of around 45 per cent. This was followed by the development of new **Integrated Gasification Combined Cycle** (IGCC) technologies and five such plants established in the 1990s, as the joint efforts of the European Union and the United States, used for burning synthetic gas produced from coal or another fuel and to clean emission. This was followed by another path-breaking development, a highly potential breakthrough technology for coal known as **Carbon Capture and Storage** (CCS), involving separating the gas emitted from burning fossil fuels, process it into liquified or solid form, transport it by ship or pipeline to a location, preferably sea-bed, disused coal mines, depleted oil wells or other location, where it can be stored. In effect, applications of CCS process has a potential for near-zero CO_2 emissions. Though there is no other better way of mitigating climate change, CCS process may prove highly effective, yet faced with obstacles of international agreements connected with storage of CO_2 beneath sea beds.

As the lowest-cost option, CCS stands out as the key technology in fighting carbon emission and rescue the world from dangerous climate change. The European Technology Platform for Zero Emission Fossil Fuel provided a framework that brings together the governments, industry, research institutes and the European Commission, aiming at the construction and operation of 12 demonstration plants by 2015, with all coal-fired power-plants built after 2020 fitted with CCS (UNDP 2007/2008). Undoubtedly, it requires much more effort to make this achievable with greater stress on making the technology available to all countries using coal as source of power which needs international co-operation to build up an accord in finding financial resources and locating places for safe storage of carbons (UNDP 2007/2008).

A very important step involves transfer of technology from developed to developing countries, which takes a crucial role since 'low levels of energy efficiency hold back human development and economic growth in many countries'. Use of coal for power generation provides an important case in this respect. For example,

> "the average thermal efficiency for coal plants in developing countries is around 30 per cent, compared with 36 per cent in OECD countries. This means that one unit of electricity produced in a developing country emits 20 per cent more CO_2 than an average unit in developed countries."[20]

Hence, transfer of technology makes a very important issue for fighting carbon emissions. Failure to develop meaningful co-operation in the development of CCS technology is very disheartening as it seems to be the best way of keeping carbon emission under control. However formidable a task it may be, to build up international co-operation in this respect, the Kyoto Protocol provided the platform for addressing global co-operation. The post-2012 Kyoto Protocol made further progress in proposing the creation of an integrated Climate Change mitigation Facility (CCMF) 'to facilitate the development of low-carbon energy system' in developing countries, providing support in 'financing technology transfer and capacity-building'.

One of the most handy, effective ways of mitigating climate change requiring no technological efficiency at all, is banning deforestation by every government in all countries, particularly in the developing world. Apart from treating forests as one of the most invaluable natural resources supporting human life and economy, they are 'vast repositories for carbon, their removal accounting to about one-fifth of the global carbon footprint'. It may be observed that the rate of deforestation is quite alarming, as between 2000 and 2005 the net forest loss worldwide average 73,000 square kilometres a year, and rainforests are getting removed at about 5 per cent a year, while it is worthy of noting that pristine rainforests can store about 500 tonnes of CO_2 per hectare.

Deforestation results from various requirements, such as poverty inducing poor people to use trees as fuel-wood or expansion for subsistence agriculture. In contrast, the pressure is much larger from corporate farming for products like beef, soybeans, palm and cocoa besides commercial logging, which is mostly illegal. Apart from forests [illegible] itories of carbon, they need to be treated for their dive[illegible] ctions, as ecological resources generating wide-ranging benefits for society, providing home and basis of livelihoods for many poor people. Besides being productive assets, providing human food in the form of nuts, berries, tubers etc., they are a source of biodiversity. International co-operation in slowing the pace of deforestation, coupled with an agenda for finance and technology transfer to developing countries, together claim urgent attention as two very positive steps towards a meaningful reduction in carbon emission and mitigating climate change.

At the same time we should take a serious view of Nobel Laureate Amartya Sen's observation in this context of mitigating climate crisis:

> "In thinking about the steps that may be taken to halt environmental destruction we have to search for constructive human intervention. For example, greater levels of female education and women's employment can help to reduce fertility rates, which in the long run can reduce pressure on global warming and the increasing destruction of natural habitats. Similarly, the spread of school education and improvements in its quality can make us more environmentally conscious. Better communication and a rather richer media can make us more aware of the need for environment-oriented thinking."[21]

Contextually one feels tempted to take a stock of the situation referring to some instances showing the effect of climate change in its stark reality. They are as follows, citing instances drawn from Paul Brown's (2007)* work:

(i) Climate change is very clearly manifest in melting Arctic Sea ice at an alarming rate, with serious implications like imperilling the people and wildlife, such as polar bears in search of food are drowning in the lack of ice cover.

---

* Brown, Paul, Global Warming; The last Chance for Change, *Readers' Digest*, Readers' Digest Association Inc., 2007, New York.

(ii) The Arctic is warming twice as fast as the rest of the planet, bringing it to its lowest cover over a century in 2005, faster than predicted by scientists, as an effect of warmer globe resulting in climate change.

(iii) Forest fires resulting from drought ravaged over 8.6 million acres in 2005 in the United States alone.

(iv) The Gulf of Mexico experienced the worst hurricane in 2005, 'Hurricane Katrina', causing $26 billion damage and taking over 1000 lives. The latest in the series is Hurricane 'Irma', hitting Florida on 10 September, 2017, lashing low-lying western regions with winds up to 130 mph rising to 185 mph in Caribbean hitting hardest and threatening record storm surges (up to 4.5 metres) and flooding in cities, from which over 6.5 million people fled.

"The most powerful storm ever recorded in the Atlantic Ocean, killing at least 22 people in Florida alone, more than 7 million people without power, though Florida was not in the eye of the storm. Its major havoc lay elsewhere. Hurricane Irma tore across the Caribbean in an arc of horror and destruction yesterday, killing at least 10 people and leaving near-total destruction with the storm's winds 185 mph. The Caribbean Islands hit hardest by Irma, causing widespread damage to Barbuda (90% of the buildings destroyed, half of the population left homeless), Anguilla, St. Kitts and Nevis, the Virgin Islands, Puerto Rico, the Dominican Republic, Haiti and Turks and Caicos. The most powerful storm ever recorded in the Atlantic ocean making its first landfall at 1.45 am on 6 September, 2017, with sustained winds of 185 mph, rising to over 225 mph, tearing through islands mentioned above, struck South Florida as its last target on the 11th, home to 7 million people. On its destructive path it hit Cuba on Saturday, 9 September, 2017, arriving at midnight in Havana with its waters rising neck high in no time, killing at least 10 people. Another climatic disaster quick to follow Hurricane Irma was Hurricane 'Harvey' this week, dumping 17 trillion US gallons of rain on Texas."

Source: The Guardian, UK, 31 August, 2017.

(v) A heat wave in 2003 was responsible for over 49,000 deaths in Europe, further causing forest fires and flood due to intense thunderstorms. It is reported in *The Guardian*, the U.K., 5 August, 2017, that many of the southern and central European countries, like Italy, Switzerland, Hungary, Poland, Romania, Bosnia, Croatia, Serbia, Southern Spain and France were put on red alert while an amber warning concerning an extreme heat wave nicknamed 'Lucifer', with temperatures in many places exceeding 40°C, visiting as the most sustained heatwave since 2003. The highest temperature on 3 August, 2017 was 42°C in Cordoba in Spain and Catania in Sicily while Split in Croatia recorded 42.3°C on the previous day and it was predicted to exceed 46°C or higher in Italy and parts of Balkans.

"Authorities in Italy, which is suffering its worst drought in 60 years, have placed 26 cities on the maximum heat alert, including Venice and Rome. ... The current extreme temperatures (coupled with strong winds, have fanned wildfires that have caused more than 60 deaths this summer in Portugal and caused widespread damage in Southern France, Greece and Italy. About 300 firefighters and military personnel were fighting 75 wildfires yesterday in Albania, with firefighters also busy in Serbia, Macedonia, Croatia, Greece and the French island of Corsica). The heatwave is likely to cost Italy's agricultural sector billions of Euros, with as many as 11 regions facing critical water shortages. Olive yields in certain areas are forecast to be down 50 per cent and some milk production has fallen by up to 30 per cent."

Agricultural output has nearly halved by drought in Bosnia, representing 10 per cent of the country's economic output while corn production in Servia is likely to be cut by a third.[22]

(vi) The Antarctic ice core shows the evidences of increase in atmospheric greenhouse gases by an unprecedented rate and volume. The glaciers are in retreat due to climate change, seriously affecting the habitat of unique species.

(vii) The Danube floods in 2006 saw record levels of flood

waters dangerously affecting Balkan countries. Melting snow combined with heavy rain causing devastating floods, the waters reaching the level of 26 ft., the highest for over a century.

(viii) The permafrost in Siberia, existing since the last Ice Age, is melting, transforming an area of about a million square kilometres into shallow lakes, releasing up to 70 billion tons of methane into the atmosphere.

(ix) Land lost to deserts in China has increased from 602 square miles between 1950-1975, to 1,389 square miles by the end of the twentieth century, bringing Gobi Desert within 93 miles of Beijing.

(x) According to the United Nations, about 11 million people were in serious danger of drought in East Africa by 2006 and climate change is likely to cause death of 184 million people in Africa in years to come.

(xi) Climate change causing rise in sea level may totally inundate the Maldives in the Indian Ocean in near future, while Bangladesh ravaged by devastating floods of increasing intensity is threatened further with complete inundation of one-third of her landmass due to sea level rise resulting from climate change.

(xii) Rising sea temperatures and changes to the chemistry of the ocean giving rise to coral bleaching have already caused the death of coral life worldwide and, according to experts, there will be no living coral on the Great Barrier Reef by 2050, causing an unaccountable loss both economic and social to humanity.

All these instances are drawn from Paul Brown's (2007) Global Warming; The Last Chance for Change.[23] According to him everybody of us responsible for killing the climate, bringing it to its present phase, has to bear the responsibility in clearing the mess and it may be in the form of not adding even one more plastic bag when we can afford to meet it. One of the most pernicious products of human action polluting the environment to no end, creating a situation already beyond redemption gauged from the fact that we have already produced some 8.3 billion tonnes of plastic so far since its production began in the 1950s, which was 2 billion tons in 1950, rising to 8.3 billion tons by now (2017), projected to reach 34 billion tons by 2050. According to *The Guardian*, U.K., 20 July, 2017, 'a million plastic bottles are bought around the world every minute', which is likely to increase another 20 per cent by 2021. They are overrunning some of the most beautiful beaches of the U.K. and remote countries, endangering wild life. According to experts,

> "some of it is already finding its way into the human food chain. ... Found in a third of U.K.-caught fish, including cod, haddock, mackerel and shellfish."[24]

Of the 300 million tons of plastic produced globally each year, 'roughly equivalent to the entire weight of human kind', 5 million tons of this ends up in the oceans, making the total weight of plastic greater than the total of fish in the oceans by 2050 (See Note G). It is believed plastic takes at least 500 years to decompose. It has been estimated by the UN this year that there were 'some 51 billion microplastic particles in the ocean today, and according to another estimate, if the 8.3 billion tons of plastic produced by us are spread out as ankle-deep waste—about 10 inches high—it could cover an area of the size of Argentina, the world's eighth largest country. Much more horrific is its presence everywhere on the globe, taken by five circulating ocean currents across the globe, recently detected by scientists even in remotest islands, nearly 18 tons of plastic in one of the world's most remote islands, an uninhabited coral atoll in the South Pacific. A recent study, made in 2015, found

> "of the nearly seven billion tons of plastic waste generated, only 9 per cent was recycled, 12 per cent incinerated and 79 per cent accumulated in landfills or the environment."[25]

Reverting back to the situation created by rising temperature, Europe's battle with Lucifer draws our attention to similar climatic irregularities, in many cases making us increasingly more concerned about the growing manifestations of changing climate resulting from human frivolities. For instance, the Middle East, accustomed to hot summer, is experiencing something much more horrific now when birds drop from the sky in heat, with temperature soaring to 51°C, one of its capitals recording 48°C for a whole month barring one day.

Noticeably, close relationship between the death of human beings and rise in temperature is highly significant. Extreme heat waves kill even healthy people within hours in areas like the Indian subcontinent, exposing almost 1.7 billion population in the Ganges and Indus valleys to extreme danger towards the end of this century resulting from a deadly combination of heat and humidity, as assessed by analysis.

It is claimed that climate change is directly related to the suicide of 60,000 Indian farmers over the past three decades and, according to a study published in the *journal PNAS,* it is claimed that

> "an increase of 5°C on any one day was associated with an additional 335 deaths. ... It estimates 59,300 agricultural sector suicides over the past 30 years could be attributed to warming. Rainfall increases of as little as 1 cm each year were associated with an average 7 per cent drop in the suicide rate. ... More than 300,000 farms and farm workers in India have killed themselves since 1995 ... in 2015, one of the worst years on record, about 12,600 farmers killed themselves across India."[26]

As reported by Oliver Milman (*The Guardian,* U.K., 1 August, 2017), there is hardly a 5 per cent chance that the earth will avoid warming by at least 2°C by the end of this century since emission and population are two of the greatest hurdles to the path of keeping it below the 2°C threshold, set out in the Paris Agreement, signed by 195 countries. A recent study made by the North Carolina University asserts that rising temperature increasing air pollutants, or climate change in other words, would cause 60,000 deaths globally in 2030, and 260,000 by 2100 when, as observed by the Washington University, 'there is 90 per cent likelihood that temperatures will rise between 2°C and 4.9°C by 2100, obviously making situation more critical to handle. A careful analysis of the emerging situation appears almost beyond redemption.

> "For each of the past three years temperatures have hit peaks not seen the birth of meteorology and probably not for more than 110,000 years. The amount of carbon dioxide in the air is at its highest level in 4 million years... For every half a degree Celsius in warming, there is about 3 per cent increase in atmospheric moisture content.... This means the sky is full more quickly and has more water to dump.... Human impact on the climate has added to the tendency for more severe droughts and fiercer storms. The city of Mumbai and some other cities in India present a grim reminder of worst flood in century."

Haroon Siddique and agencies (*The Guardian*, U.K., 31 August, 2017) report that "heavy monsoon rains brought Mumbai to a halt for a second day ... as the worst floods to strike South Asia in years continued to exact a deadly toll, killing over 1200 people across India and flooding across the Himalayan foothills in Bangladesh, India and Nepal caused landslides, damaged road networks and powerlines, washing tens of thousands of homes and swaths of croplands. While in the State of Bihar alone, in India, 17.1 million people have been affected, in Bangladesh the fourth significant floods this year has affected over 7.4 million people, damaging more than 697,000 houses."

Stray instances like these, out of thousands more happening all around us, disturbing life and economy irrespective of the developed and developing countries, leave not an iota of doubt about their connection with climate change. As observed in the Editorial of *The Guardian* (U.K., 11 August, 2017), this should be taken as a wake-up call for us to finally decide about 'making a shift in the way we produce, distribute and consume energy' and we should come out of control still exercised by fossil-fuel companies, hydrogen carbon billionaires and their policies, particularly in the West, who have made handsome profits while making the globe further warmer. They are the actual polluters, enjoying fossil-fuel benefits at the cost of world's poor, destroying any scope for future generations to live a healthy life. People all over the world should join their hands in making an all-round effort at taking up the fight against climate change as a challenge to make this Earth a liveable place for its inhabitants.

NOTES

Note A

"Chinese life expectancy (and thus nutrition) was at roughly English levels (and so above Continental ones) even in the late 1700s. (Chinese fertility was actually lower than Europe's between 1550 and 1850, while its population grew faster, thus mortality must have been low.) Moreover, my estimates of non-essential consumption come out surprisingly high. Sugar consumption works out to between 4.3 and 5.0 pounds per capita ca. 1750—and much higher in some regions—compared with barely 2 pounds per capita for Europe. China circa 1750 seems to have produced 6-8 lbs of cotton cloth per capita; its richest area, Yangzi Delta (population roughly 31 million), probably produced between 12 and 15 lbs per capita. The U.S., even in 1800, produced roughly 13 lbs of cotton, linen and wool cloth combined per resident, and Continental output was probably below China's."

Source: Mike Davis (2014 Reprint), quoting Kenneth Pomeranz.

Note B

++Experts claim that "U.K. energy had reached a tipping point after two wind farms secured a state-backed price for their output that was nearly half the level awarded last year to Britain's first nuclear power site in a generation, Hinckley Pointe, thus heralding the 'epoch of renewables as the most cost-competitive technology' providing off-shore wind power at £ 62.14 per megawatt against £ 92.50 for nuclear power, guaranteeing a low carbon future."

Source: The Guardian, U.K., 12 September, 2017.

Note C

In another attempt at reducing carbon emission, the top adviser in Britain suggests that replacing petroleum/diesel driven cars by electric ones is not solution as the latter though do not emit exhaust fumes, "they still produce large amounts of tiny pollution particles without limit." According to him, to tackle air pollution crisis, "cars must be forced out of cities, as "toxic air causes 40,000 early deaths a year in Britain", from where, as announced by the Government, the "sale of new diesel and petrol cars will be banned from 2040."

Source: The Guardian, U.K., 5 August, 2017.

Such measures, mentioned, will prove highly beneficial in two ways, like reduction in carbon emissions and bring down oil imports by 51 per cent in 2035.

Source: The Guardian, U.K., 25 August, 2017.

Note D

I. As reported in *The Independent*, London, 30 October, 2017,

"There is a catastrophic gap between what needs to be done on climate change and what governments and companies are actually doing, the UN has warned. Despite pledges to work to mitigate and deal with climate change, current plans still lead to a 3-degree Celsius rise in temperature by the end of the decade, a major news report warns ... UN officials are making renewed push to maintain momentum generated by the Paris Climate Accord of 2015. It aims to cap global temperature increases to 2 degrees Celsius by the year 2100 compared to average world temperatures at the start of the industrial era. But that agreement has come under threat after Donald Trump suggested he might opt to pull out of it."

Source: *The Statesman*, Kolkata Issue (India), 1 November, 2017.

II. As reported by Indo Asia News Service, "Driven by China's greater use of coal, global emissions of carbon dioxide from burning fossil fuels are projected to rise again in 2017, after a three year hiatus ... Global emissions from all human activities will reach 41 billion tonnes in 2017, following a projected two per cent rise in burning fossil fuels ... the figures point to China as the main cause of the renewed growth in fossil emissions—with a projected growth of 3.5 per cent.

Source: The Statesman, Kolkata Issue (India), 15 November, 2017.

III. It is reported by Dataleads/Asia News Network, Philippines on 15 November, 2017 that "The Global Climate Risk Index for 1996-2015 reveals that China has suffered the most financial loss. The losses amount to US $32,847 million since 1996 ... due to climate change as per the ranking released by the German Watch, a Berlin-based development and environmental organization in its latest Global Climate Risk Index (CRI). India has suffered a loss of US $11,385 million to the impact of climate change, such as stark weather events, sea-level rise or desertification. Asian, countries in particular may prove to be the most acutely affected by soaring temperatures, or extreme weather attributed to climate change, a 2017 study by the Asian Development Bank has warned.

Source: The Statesman, Kolkata Issue (India), *16 November, 2017*.

IV. Parthasarathi Chakraborty, formerly associated with the UNICEF, mentions in his article published in the Editorial page, that "the air that Indians breathe is turning more toxic by the day and an average of two deaths occur due to air pollution, according to the noted medical journal, *The Lancet*. This also substantiates the fact that over a million Indians die or are at the point of death due to air pollution and some of the worst polluted cities of the world are in India, including the capital. Delhi bears witness to a collective and colossal failure of the elected government technocrats and bureaucrats. ... *The Lancet* has contradicted some Indian reports and has pointed out that coal-fired power plants contribute to 50 per cent of the external pollution."

Source: The Statesman, Kolkata Issue (India), 17 November, 2017.

Note E

"The United States accounts for around 40 per cent of oil-based CO_2 emissions from transport.... The fuel efficiency standard divide between the United States and the rest of the world has widened. Today the United States' standard is just one half of the level in Japan. The 136 million passenger cars on United States' roads contribute 35 per cent of national transport-based greenhouse gas emissions, and 87 million light trucks another 27 per cent."

Source: United Nations Development Programme (UNDP), *Human Development Report 2007-2008, Fighting Climate Change: Human Solidarity in a Divided World*, p. 139.

Note F

The President of the Federative Republic of Brazil is of the opinion that, "The Human Development Report 2007/2008 should be mandatory reading for all governments, especially those in the world's richest nations. It reminds us that historic responsibility for the rapid build-up of greenhouse gases in the Earth's atmosphere rests not with the world's poor but with the developed world. It is people in the richest countries that leave the deepest footprint. The average Brazilian has a CO_2 footprint of 1.8 tonnes a year compared with an average for developed countries of 13.2 tonnes a year. As the Report reminds us, if every person in the developing world left the same carbon footprint as the average North American we would need the atmospheres of nine planets to deal with the consequences. ... One of the reasons that Brazil has such a low per capita footprint is that we have developed our renewable energy resources and now have one of the world's cleanest energy systems. Hydropower accounts for 92 per cent of our electricity generation, for example the upshot is that Brazil not only has a lighter carbon footprint than rich nations, but that we generate less than half as much CO_2 for every dollar in wealth that we generate. Put it differently, we have lowered our emissions by reducing the carbon intensity and the energy intensity of our country."

Source: United Nations Development Programme (UNDP), *Human Development Report 2007-2008, Fighting Climate Change: Human Solidarity in a Divided World*, p. 141.

Note G

According to the predictions of Ellen MacArthur Foundation, there will be more plastic than fish in the oceans by 2050 unless we are adequately conscious about this highly forbidding prospect, when one single company, Coca-Cola, generates more than 100 billion plastic bottles a year and 'just 5 per cent of plastics' generated from all sources are effectively recycled, 40 per cent end up in landfill and a third in fragile ecosystems, such as oceans. John Sauven, UK Executive Director, Greenpeace, is of the opinion that "we need to make sure this does not just replace sustainably. ... The end objective is we have to keep plastic out of the natural environment, particularly stop it going into the oceans."

An encouraging example in this respect is cited as practised in Estonia since 2005, when customers were encouraged to deposit on a bottle of cola, for example, reclaiming it as a discount on the next purchase on returning the empty bottle to the shop received back 75 per cent of cans and 87 per cent of recyclable bottles. In making similar attempts the relevant governments need to take the initiative.

Source: *The Guardian*, U.K., 2 August, 2017.

REFERENCES

1. Meadows, Donella (2002). *Resurgence and Ecologist*, September-October 2016: p. 33.
2. Smil, Vaclav (1994). "How Many People Can the Earth Feed?" in *Population and Development Review*, Vol. 2, No. 2, June: p. 283.
3. Holt-Giménez, Eric (2010). "From Food Crisis to Food Sovereignty: the Challenge of Social Movements," in *Agriculture and Food Crisis: Conflict, Resistance and Renewal*. Edited by Fred Magdoff and Brian Tokar, Monthly Review Press, New York, p. 209.
4. Goldring, Mark (2016). "We are Sleepwalking into Catastrophe Unless We Tackle Inequality", in *Resurgence and Ecologist*, September/October, p. 14.
5. Brown, Lester R. (2012). *Full Planet, Empty Plates: The New Geopolitics of Food Security*, Earth Policy Institute, W. W. Norton and Company, New York and London, p. 83.
6. United Nations Development Programme (UNDP), *Human Development Report 2007-2008, Fighting Climate Change: Human*

Solidarity in a Divided World: p. 33.

7. Ghosh, Amitav (2016). *The Great Derangement; Climate Change and The Unthinkable,* The University Press of Chicago, Chicago and London, p. 91.
8. *Ibid.*, p. 90.
9. *IPCC Fifth Assessment Synthesis Report, 2014*: pp. 64-65.
10. United Nations Development Programme (UNDP), *Human Development Report 2007-2008, Fighting Climate Change: Human Solidarity in a Divided World*: p. 41.
11. Davis, Mike (2014). *Late Victorian Holocausts: El Niño Famines and Making the Third World.* Verso, London, New York, p. 13.
12. *Ibid.*, p. 255.
13. *Ibid.*, p. 292.
14. *Ibid*; p. 293.
15. United Nations Development Programme (UNDP), Human Development Report 2007-2008, Fighting Climate Change: Human Solidarity in a Divided World: p. 113.
16. Brown, Lester R. (2012). *Full Planet, Empty Plates: The New Geopolitics of Food Security,* Earth Policy Institute, W. W. Norton and Company, New York and London, p. 84.
17. Brown, Lester R. (2006). *Plan B 2.0: Rescuing a Planet Under Stress and Civilization in Trouble,* Earth Policy Institute, p. 189.
18. *Ibid.*, p. 200.
19. United Nations Development Programme (UNDP), *Human Development Report 2007-2008, Fighting Climate Change: Human Solidarity in a Divided World*: p. 136.
20. *Ibid.*, p. 140.
21. Sen, Amartya, quoted from United Nations Development Programme (UNDP), Human Development Report 2007-2008, Fighting Climate Change: Human Solidarity in a Divided World, p. 29.
22. *The Guardian,* U.K., 5 August, 2017.
23. Brown, Paul, (2007), "Global Warming: The Last Chance for Change," *Readers' Digest,* Readers Digest Association Inc., Pheasant Hill, New York, Montreal/Singapore: pp. 36-37.
24. *The Guardian,* U.K., 20 July, 2017.
25. *Ibid.*, 2 August, 2017.
26. *PNAS* (Proceedings of the National Academy of Sciences of the United States of America), Vol. 100, No. 50, 2011.

6
Food Scarcity and Human Survival

Paradoxically, food sustaining human and animal life is one of the greatest atmospheric polluter, adding over 25 per cent of total greenhouse gases (GHG) to the atmosphere through use of nutrients in the form of fertilizers containing nitrogen and phosphorous in ever larger quantities than required in many cases, much of which not required by the crops produced leaching out pollute aquifers, lakes and rivers in a process called **eutrophication**. Ultimately, the excess nutrients entering the oceans create low oxygen 'dead zones', destroying the local aquatic ecosystems and fisheries (Tilman and Clark, 2015).*

There is about 9 billion hectares of land suitable for human use, of which five billion are already used 'as cropland and pasture lands' which, apart from feeding men and animals, are at the root of destruction and extinction of many plant and animal species and are also responsible for the heavy loss of biodiversity, or, in other words, the 'natural capital', thus depriving the future generations of their multifarious benefits. On the other hand, the highly depressing side of the prospective role of feeding human population, the production of food, is expected to be double in another forty to fifty years, the human population peaking to 9.6 billion by 2050 and 10.9 billion by 2100, require agricultural production to increase by 30 per cent by 2050 and 50 per cent by 2100. According to Tilman and Clark

---

* Tilman, David and Michael Clark, "Food, Agriculture and the Environment: Can We Feed the World and Save the Earth?" in *The American Academy of Arts and Sciences, Vol. 144* Issue 4, Fall 2015.

(2015), the changing dietary habits of a growing number of people around the globe commensurate with rising income is going to put a great pressure on future agriculture, with greater preference for animal-protein and thus causing shifts in emphasis on the nature of products accounting, according to them, for about 70 per cent of this increase. To be more specific, the diet-shifts associated with larger income has a greater preference for animal products such as meat, dairy and eggs, along with more sugars, oils, fats and alcohols, the latter commonly referred to as 'empty calories'.

Quite interestingly, for a person in one of the fifteen 'richest' countries the amount of daily food consumed measured as 3500 calories, but 25 per cent of this is wasted after reaching the household; about 20 per cent of the daily food consumed in the household of wealthy nations come from meat, milk and eggs while 38 per cent of the calories are from 'empty calories'. In contrast, the average person's daily food in twenty or so poorest economies amount to about 2000 calories, very little of which is wasted, 3 per cent of which comes from meat, milk and eggs while 12 per cent is from 'empty calories'. The net result of these dietary habits has already turned 2.1 billion people worldwide overweight or obese, resulting from excess food while, as mentioned before, another 800 million suffer from malnutrition or are undernourished from lack of adequate food (Tilman and Clark, 2015).[1] (See Note A)

Putting in this light we can firmly conclude that the world with an additional load of 80 per cent more people in 2050 makes it necessary to double the production of agricultural crops as animal-feed to meet the growing demand of animal-protein by one billion people with rising income in the developing countries. A situation like this is called the global nutrition transition marked by income rise and resulting change in dietary habits on one side supplemented by obesity, diabetes, higher rate of heart diseases as instanced by China, where the rate of diabetes has already increased from 1 per cent to over 10 per cent without any pause, while globally the record is more alarming, diabetes increasing 45 per cent between 1990 and 2013 (Tilman and Clark, 2015).

As mentioned earlier, the next very pertinent question is how far a green revolution, induced by Nobel Laureate Norman

Borland in the 1960s with new strains of wheat 'capable of much greater yields' with a greater input of fertilizers and water doubling cereal production worldwide between 1965 and 1995, is relevant to the changing situation. It has already been pointed out that the said 'revolution' necessarily came at a great cost-increasing 'nitrogen application seven-fold (from 10 m tons to 70 m tons), tripled phosphorous application and doubled irrigation-making rivers in many cases (such as Colorado) failing to reach the sea. Alongside global use of herbicides, insecticides and other pesticides increasing almost six-fold—from one-half million metric tons in 1960 to over 3 million metric tons by 1996—made hazardous effects on human healthy, fish, birds and mammals. But what is more alarming in its environmental costs came in the form of clearance of 150 mha of forestland for crop production and another 300 mha of pastureland for animal rearing.

> "The conversion of forests, savannas and grasslands to agriculture destroyed high-diversity native ecosystems and replaced them with frequently disturbed systems planted with one or a few crops or pasture species. Such habitat destruction is a major threat to global biodiversity with risk of extinctions escalating as more land is cleared."[2]

Major Impediments to Global Food Security

If food for all has to be considered as a fundamental, irrevocable, right irrespective of economic status, we need to be much more conscious about the real evils responsible for negating this right to a very large section—800 million people as FAO thinks—at this moment, perhaps a gross understatement from the actual number (923 million or 1 billion, to be more honest?) when almost every government hides the fact, to save its pride (See Note B).

According to Collins, Murduch, Rutherford and Ruthven,

> "a daily income of less than two dollars per person has become a widely recognized benchmark for defining the

> world's poor. The World Bank counted 2.5 billion people in this in 2005—two-fifths of humanity. Among them ... the poorest 1.1 billion were scraping by on less than one dollar a day."[3]

Fighting poverty altogether from a different perspective had, perhaps, shown for the first time that initiative may be taken without doling out money as charity and the feasibility of deriving real benefit from such a project was established beyond any doubt by Muhammad Yunus, a Professor of Economics by profession, in Bangladesh. He initiated a project for lending out money to people in Bangladesh, women in particular, on easy terms, taking the role of a bank but making no profits. His organisation, called 'Grameen Bank'

> "focused on the poorest households—those owning less than half an acre of cultivable land. Representatives from households that met this criterion were invited to form groups of five, each from a different household (and) ... by the 1990s nearly all were women"[4]

a member of which met a Grameen worker each week, contributing a small compulsory deposit into a jointly owned fund refunding loans taken by each member for using in a new or existing small business and as much each member could monitor loans repaid in time was entitled to a far bigger loan in future. This simple but quite ingenious system of micro-credit became highly effective in to time to improve the economic status of the poor families, enabling better food, chance of educating children and taking healthcare facilities. The main idea of micro-credit was placing greater trust on women in taking care of the family more than men do, which is a universal truth. In this context, one may feel interested to hear directly from Professor Yunus about the idea that motivated him for this novel idea of credit system. In his words,

> "Traditional banks in Bangladesh are gender biased and do not want to lend money to women. ... If the goals of economic development include improved standards of living—removal of poverty, access to dignified

> employment and reduction in inequality—then it is quite natural to start with women. They constitute the majority of the poor, the underemployed and the economically and socially disadvantaged. And since they are closer to the children, women were also our key to the future of Bangladesh. So gradually we focused almost exclusively to women,"[5]

which, undoubtedly, faced a stiff opposition from various quarters including the government officials.

The tremendous success of the project was proved in the fact that the number of Grameen Bank's clients reached a million in 1991 and between 1990 and 2000 there were more than two million active Grameen 'members', as the clients were called.

> "Muhammad Yunus' original vision for Grameen Bank helped the world see the power that access to simple loans can have in helping villagers build small businesses"[6]

that ultimately reduce the number of hungry people in the world and thus add to food security for many.

Nevertheless, the respite confined to a small section of people in one of the poorest countries in the world—Bangladesh—cannot meet with the existing enormous challenge of keeping a huge population away from hunger, as Collier (2007) observes, concentrated mainly in

> "Africa and Central Asia with a scattering elsewhere of one billion people who are living and dying in fourth-century conditions ... as of 2006 there are around 980 million people living in these trapped countries (increasing to one billion). Seventy per cent of these people are in Africa ... Countries of the bottom billion do not form a group with a convenient geographic label ... I describe them as "Africa +" with the + being places such as Haiti, Bolivia, the Central Asian countries, Laos, Cambodia, Yemen, Burma and North Korea. ... In the bottom billion average life expectancy is fifty years, whereas in other developing countries it is sixty-seven

> years. Infant mortality—the proportion of children who die before their first birthday—is 14 per cent in the bottom billion, whereas in other developing countries it is 4 per cent. The proportion of children with symptoms of long-term malnutrition is 36 per cent in the bottom billion as against 20 per cent for the other developing countries."[7]

All these undeniably lead us to our primary, final conclusion that feeding all the people on this planet is still largely subjected to food insecurity for many in the backdrop of wide disparity in consumption between rich and the poorest nations.

> "In 2000, for example, per capita use of calories and protein by the richest nations (Group A) were 256 per cent and 430 per cent greater respectively than used by the poorest nations (Groups F and G). These large differences in crop demand partially result from greater dietary meat consumption at higher income (6, 7) and low efficiency with which some types of livestock convert crop calories and protein into edible foods."[8]

Meeting future growing needs estimated by these authors of 100-110 per cent increase in crop production by 2050 is a complex process, involving

> "agricultural extensification (that is clearance of additional land for crop production) or intensification (that is achieving higher yields through increased inputs, improved agronomic practices, improved crop varieties and other innovations) ... In particular ... the combinations of current or improved agricultural technologies, enhancement to soil fertility and land clearing that could meet our projected 2050 global calorific demand ... soil fertility can also be enhanced by legumes, cover crops and other means and that yields could increase with less Nitrogen fertilizer than in the past if Nitrogen efficiency increases."[9]

However, on the negative side, the enhanced crop

production will entail greenhouse gas emission, rising at present from all forms of transportation which is 14 per cent of the total global emission, while the current level of emissions from agriculture is 25 per cent of present total global emission. As pointed out by Tilman and Clark (2015), the contributors to agricultural emissions are beef and lamb production, application of nitrogen fertilizers and land clearing. As such, reduction in meat consumption replaced by low-fat animal products, eating crops with moderate fertilization and minimizing food waste can make a remarkable reduction in greenhouse gas emissions along with ensuring food security to a great extent.

According to these authors, global agriculture is capable of feeding 10 billion people by 2050 and holds greater prospect if existing **yield gaps** could be property dealt with. Yield gap means

> "the difference between crop yields that could be obtained on a piece of land by using current technology and management techniques and the yields that are actually obtained."[10]

Nations with lower per capita incomes tend to have larger yield gaps, such as in much of Sub-Saharan Africa crops like maize, wheat and rice yields are about 20-25 per cent of their actual potential, making a yield gap of 75 to 80. In other words, use of better technologies could enable these countries using the same amount of cropland as they do now to produce 300-400 per cent more food. The reasons behind such low returns (yields) are not difficult to find. They use less than five kilograms of nitrogen fertilizer per hectare and other inputs when the rich nations use thirty times the amount. Reduction in yield gaps is much more preferable than increasing production by clearing more land, leading to greater emission.

As such, experts recommend giving emphasis on closing global yield gap to increase food supply to malnourished people. As found by a new study, an achievement of 95 per cent yield of attainable level (still leaving a 5 per cent yield gap), no new land is needed to meet global food demand in 2050. At the same time, reducing the yield gap by using fertilizers at 'rates of about 80 per cent of those in the richest nations and thus decreasing environmental harm from overfertilization', the poor countries 'could increase global crop production by 70 per cent' (Tilman and Clark, 2015).

It may be pointed out that the doubling of crop yield made in the 1960s and 1970s by Green Revolution was primarily based on crop breeding, fertilization and irrigation, and the trend of getting higher yield continued later on based on crop breeding and agronomic techniques but it is highly interesting to note that the yield-rate increases have shrunk, having been only 0.8 per cent for major crops like soybeans, rice and wheat, making a strong indication of approaching biophysical yield ceilings, or an upper limit already having been experienced by leading producers of wheat, like the U.K., the Netherlands and France without any further increase over the past 10 to 15 years, while yield plateaus have already been experienced by Korea, Indonesia and California in rice, though some other crops, such as roots, vegetables, fruits, minor cereals, seed and oil crops so far not having experienced intensive breeding programme hold much greater prospect of raising their yield-rate using advanced agronomic techniques (Tilman and Clark, 2015).

Changing Character of Food and Human Health

We need to be reminded that croplands comprise one of the most extensive ecosystems on Earth, stretching across almost 12 per cent of the planet's ice-free land surface, representing almost 10-15 per cent of the total biological productivity of our planet. It may be pointed out that changes in life style, with decreasing dependence on diets heavy in animal-protein derived from grain-fed meat, holds great promise for relieving pressure on grain crops, releasing the same for direct human consumption. Further, growing transition towards diets high in processed foods, refined sugar, refined fats, oils and meats has contributed to 2.1 billion people becoming overweight or obese. These dietary shifts and resulting increases in body mass indices (BMI) are associated with increased global incidences of chronic non-communicable diseases, especially Type II diabetes, coronary heart disease and some cancers, which are predicted to become two-thirds of the global burden of disease if dietary trend continues.[11] Incidentally, China, as mentioned before, is a very strong case of dietary victim, the occurrence of Type II diabetes having increased from 1 per cent of its population in 1980 to 10 per cent in 2000, providing one of the most alarming instances of dietary changes with greater preference for animal-protein.

Looking back, it can be said that consistent rise in income, especially in developing countries, and urbanization have jointly brought an effective change in the dietary composition during the past five decades. As observed by Tilman and Clark (2014), annual increase in income (1961-2009) was followed by a concomitant increase in per capita daily consumption of meat-protein among all economic groups of people. For example,

> "In 2009, the richest 15 nations (Group A) had a 750 per cent greater per capita demand for meat-protein from ruminants, seafood, poultry and pork than the 24 poorest nations (Group F). Total protein demand also increased with income but legume protein demand decreased as an animal protein demand increased. India, a nation with low rates of meat consumption, is the major exception to an otherwise global trend in the income-dependence of demand for meat protein. China initially had meat demand increase more rapidly with income than Groups A-F, but was similar to them by 2009."[12]

Surprisingly, the unavoidable link between diet as the determinant of human health has not yet been taken very seriously even when rich animal-protein diet is at the root of affecting over 2 billion people among the richest nations, with incurable deadly diseases. On the contrary it is regrettable to note that a considerable reduction in the proportion of animal protein consumed by the rich would have done a world of good if it was available at even a much lower proportion in the diets of the highly ill-nourished millions at an affordable price. The initiative for this should come from the governments of the respective countries.

As reported recently, rapid urbanization accelerates nutrition transition or, in other words, diet change.

> "Urban as opposed to rural diets are characterized by the consumption of superior and polished grains (rice or wheat rather than corn or millet), more fats and animal products, more sugar, more processed foods, and more food consumed away from home."[13]

The impact of economic factors on nutrition transition makes a very important case for study. The traditional Asian diet, high in carbohydrates and low in fat, is undergoing profound change with a decline in the proportion of energy from carbohydrates replaced by a corresponding increase in the proportion of energy from fats. As a matter of eating, pleasure is giving way to the introduction of new food items in the diets of people who could not afford the price before, a fact that remains unaltered even now. Obviously,

> "as incomes grow diets become more diverse and more people incorporate meat and fish, milk, eggs and cheese, as well as vegetables and fresh fruit, into their habitual diets. In so far as new foods are being introduced into the diet, they invariably include meat, eggs and sweets, previously inaccessible to more low-income people. Some of those new foods are high in fats, simple sugars or both. As a result dietary diversity and the proportion of fats in the diet are sometimes directly linked."[14]

Patterns of Food Consumption and Dietary Transition

There has already been a significant improvement in global food consumption per person per day from 2411 Kcal to 2789 Kcal between 1969/1971 and 1999/2001, thus reducing under-nutrition in general, barring in some developing countries, such as Somalia, Burundi, Rwanda and Kenya in Sub-Saharan Africa (Drewnowski, 1997). However, between 1963 and 2003 large differences in calories remained between developed and developing countries, as characterised by large increases in calories from meat (119%), sugar (127%), and vegetable oils (199%) in developing countries and only an appreciable increase in the consumption of vegetable oil (105%) took place in the industrial countries.

However, the picture becomes clearer with a close look at the position of different food items in this respect. For example, cereals retained their position as the most important source of food, providing 50 per cent of calories, rising to 54 per cent in developing countries, making up as much as 70 per cent in Africa and parts of Asia, which is likely to decline in the developing countries slowly to 46 per cent in 2050. Among the cereals, rice-based diet is likely to go down 16 g per capita per day in Europe against 253 g in Asia by 2050. In contrast, consumption of wheat increased faster than all other cereals (Kearney, 2010).

Meat, on the other hand, has always made itself the centrepiece of meals in developed countries: pigs, sheep and cattle making the major sources, and products like sausages, burger, pork pies etc. comprising almost half of all meat in these countries. Use of meat in different forms has increased 62 per cent worldwide, with the biggest increase, three-fold since 1963, having taken place in developing countries, particularly in China with nine-fold increase, followed by Brazil, with a three-fold rise in consumption. Contrarily, however, the lowest intake of meat is in the U.K. with consumption decreasing over the past three decades. Interestingly, worldwide increase in meat consumption is contributed by poultry which, along with pork, will take the major part while the consumption of beef having already stagnated and slightly fell in North America, Oceania and Europe but shows some increase in Brazil and China.

While the levels of egg consumption (grams per capita per day) have doubled worldwide since 1963, more in developing than developed countries, milk intake has increased in a number of developing countries, especially in Asia, but has fallen in the US and it is predicted that consumption of eggs will continue to rise but, in the case of milk, it is likely to decline particularly in developed countries though the consumption of butter and cheese will remain unaffected (Kearney, 2010).

The consumption of fish increasing worldwide, over-fishing is fast depleting its stock. As an important source of good quality protein and low fat, they may also be a major source of iodine. In comparison to many European countries like Portugal and Spain, consumption of fish in the U.K. is rather low: 22 g per capita per day. However, there has been a remarkable pattern of change in the consumption pattern, which involves growing popularity of seafood and freshwater fish, both of which have made a remarkable progress since the early 1960s. Both Oceania and China recorded the highest increase in the latter, from about 11 g per capita per head in 1963 to about 69 g per capita per head in 2003, and China recording almost a ten-fold increase (Kearney, 2010).

In comparison, edible plants, including root crops, tubers, leaves, stems, buds, flowers and fruits, show a contrasting nature of consumption. Overall consumption of roots, tubers, comprising cassava, sweet potatoes, potatoes, yams, taro and plantain is slowly declining all over the globe, particularly in China and Sub-Saharan Africa, while a contrasting relationship may be observed in the consumption pattern of sweet potatoes registering a sharp fall in many developing countries, with a parallel rise in the consumption of potatoes in a number of developing countries. At the same time, consumption of pulses has declined globally, in particular among developing countries, recording a ten-fold fall in China alone between 1963 and 2003, going down respectively from 30 g to 3 g (Kearney, 2010).

On the contrary, however, consumption of vegetable oils has increased in developed as well as developing countries, two-fold and three-fold respectively, most specifically in China, Brazil and India. It is highly significant to note reverse trends in the consumption of animal fats which, unlike in the early 1960s, is on decline in parallel with rise in vegetable oils, and the trend is likely to continue in future.[15]

In general, an overall increase in the consumption of vegetable oil, sugar, salt, sweeteners and meat involving nutrition transition play a threatening role in human life. The dietary behaviour, particularly in highly urbanized societies the world over has encouraged

> "an unwholesome growth of fast-food industry dominating urban life providing quick access to cheap take-away meals. These meals also satisfy the consumers' demand for food high in salt, fat and sugar. Indeed, the most popular fast-food items, including hamburgers, pizzas and fried chicken, have 30 per cent

> of their food energy in fat. Thus, the major consequences from a nutrition perspective of urbanization are a profound shift towards higher food energy, more fats and oils and more animal protein from meat and dairy foods. This results in a diet that is lower in fibre, vitamins and minerals and higher in energy, total and saturated fat."[16]

In this respect, it may be highly interesting as well as very significant to note that there has been quite a slow but revolutionary change in food consumption in recent times when

> "the task of cooking has vanished from many households and food consumed in much of the world is shifting from purchases made at local fresh markets to packaged and processed ready-to-eat or ready-to-heat food."[17]

Maybe it happens in general in the urban areas of the world but the world is going to be dominated by urban population, comprising almost 67 per cent of the total global population by 2050.

Some experts speaking in the same vein mention two major shifts in diet, one of which consists of an acceleration in the consumption of animal-source food, particularly in low-and-middle-income countries (LMIC) while there has been no reduction in the consumption of these products in the higher income countries and, besides, there has been an increase in the consumption of 'ultra-processed' food. The intimate relationship between diet transition has a positive relationship with people who are called overweight or obese. At the same time

> "Hispanics, Asians and many subpopulations across the globe have very different distributions of fat, different genetic predispositions to disease, and face many nutrition and health conditions going back to pregnancy and infancy. ... In general, in all LMICs the proportion of deaths, disabilities and years lived with disability have increased. NCOs (non-communicable diseases) have risen generally over the last several decades but

> particularly in LMICs. Diabetes and hypertension seem to be the first diseases to emerge in most of the Asian, African and Latin American countries."[18]

Regrettably, this life-threatening role of food transition has not, however, been taken as seriously as expected though it has to be admitted that many governments have taken some form of direct measures in the following four categories such as (a) implementing sugar-sweetened beverages (SSB), promulgated in California as well as on junk-food keeping check on the sale of products particularly to children; (b) labelling profiles with positive or negative logo on the front of the package; and (c) implementing 'special regulations related to schools and/or other government facilities.' (d) 'Marketting Control' with greater emphasis on marketing to children. Countries showing signs of real concern in fighting the self-inflicted harm is Mexico becoming the first country among the LMICs to put a tax of about 10 per cent on the sales of SSB and 8 per cent on junk food, recording significant decline in their purchases. Chile put a 5 per cent tax on SSB sales, though brought down to 3 per cent later. Both Colombia and South Africa seriously intended to tax 18 per cent and 20 per cent respectively on the sales of SSBs as a

> "critical step towards addressing obesity, diabetes and other cardio-metabolic problems linked with excessive SSB consumption. Both measures face strong industrial opposition but, thus far, the governments remain supportive of implementing the taxes."[19]

Among other countries is Thailand having adopted front-of-package label which also is a practice in Singapore for decades, and there are thirteen Pacific Islands where implementation of taxes on SSBs is in operation over a decade. Apart from this, many countries keep a vigilant eye on school food programmes and, among them, Brazil takes lead in watching food consumed by school children.

In spite of the serious concerns, particularly about the consumption, Kearney (2010) observed that the Americans drank more than four times milk than carbonated soft drinks 50 years ago but 50 years later the consumption of the latter increased two-and-a-half times more than milk, as induced by advertising (particularly by TV) and heavy subsidies to the products of corn sugar, having surpassed cane and beet sugar by 1985, making it 'responsible for the epidemic of obesity among children in the USA'. This equally applies to countries like China, India, Brazil and Mexico, where consumers spend more on processed and unhealthy food.

Loss of foresight, along with unfathomable greed of a part of the society mostly represented by corporate house, has brought the status of food to such a miserable state that the closely intertwined relationship between agriculture, healthy food and environment has become severely affected, with grave consequences. Before the entire situation gets out of control and food security becomes thoroughly jeopardized, we need to devise a food policy which circumvents all odds or obstacles on its path and conforms to a model system based on certain rules and principles, with strict adherence. As observed by Kearney (2010),

> "food systems that diversify beyond subsistence farming, and include fruits, vegetables, legumes and animal products result in improved nutritional status. Healthy agriculture must be the goal whereby nutritional considerations become part of multinational agricultural policy-making and, at the same time, agricultural considerations must be incorporated into the improvement of nutrition and health. As Feenstra (2002) aptly put it—we should endeavour towards. 'A collaborative effort to build more locally-based self-reliant food economies—one in which sustainable' food production, processing, distribution, and consumption are integrated to enhance economic, environmental and social health. Thus, food policies will only be effective if they are developed with input from both agricultural and health sectors, thereby enabling the development of coherent policies that will ultimately be beneficial to agriculture, human health and the environment."[20]

Ensuring Food Security for Future

Reduction of yield-gaps, and thus realise the growth potential of agricultural land in different climatic situations, is one of the most effective ways of increasing crop production to meet growing global demands for food.[21] An analysis of global patterns of crop yields for 18 different crops estimating the differences between actual yield and the climatic potential using prevailing technology, along with best management practices and high-yielding crop varieties for each climatic zone, reveals the prospect of a better future. The results in the form of rate of yields are likely to change further with the application of more advanced technology and genetics and agricultural technology. Raising yield rates, in other words realising greater returns of crops per unit of land, can provide a much larger harvest than we get today.

Better management undoubtedly holds greater prospect of obtaining more out of the same amount of land, though the result in the form of potential for each climatic zone and each variety and scope for it is not possible to predict in the face of climate changes resulting from global warming. A volatile situation like this leads to the most important question of

> "the nutritional needs that a food meets and how much is consumed to do so. Fruits and vegetables are important sources of micro-nutrients, anti-oxidants and fibre. Unlike root crops and legumes, which are calorie-dense or protein-dense, most vegetables are not primarily consumed for calories or protein and should be evaluated by emissions per serving. For instance, 20 servings of vegetables have less GHG emissions than one serving of beef. However, fish and meats, which are high in protein, are also nutritionally dense foods that provide essential fatty acids, minerals and vitamins, and can have relatively low GHG emissions if eaten in moderation. Finally, the nutritional value of some foods can depend on how they are produced. For instance, in comparison to grain-fed cattle, grass-fed beef and dairy have nutritionally superior fatty acid and vitamin content."[22]

Nature of food and its availability determine human health. Diets taken by people worldwide are not the same in composition and the variation makes four major types: Omnivorous, Mediterranean, Pescetarian and Vegetarian. Composition-wise, a vegetarian diet consists of cereals, vegetables, fruits, sugars, oils, eggs and dairy with meat or sea-food served once in a month. In contrast, a Pescetarian diet is a vegetarian diet along with sea-food. On the other hand, a Mediterranean diet is rich in vegetables, fruit and seafood besides including grains, sugars, oils, eggs, dairy and a moderate amount of poultry, pork, lamb and beef. Omnivorous diet includes all food groups (Tilman and Clark, 2014).

Studies made on the effects of different types of diet on human health show that reduction in health risk involving diseases like Type II diabetes, cancer, coronary mortality and all-cause mortality rates vary widely (Fig. 6.1). As shown in Fig. 6.1, vegetarian diet is much more safe in view of the risk of Type II diabetes and coronary mortality, as well as all-cause mortality. Among the three types of other diets, Mediterranean diet is more exposed to coronary mortality, as well as all-cause mortality, than any other diet (Tilman and Clark, 2014). On the whole, vegetarian diet appears to be the safest of all diets in regard to human health.

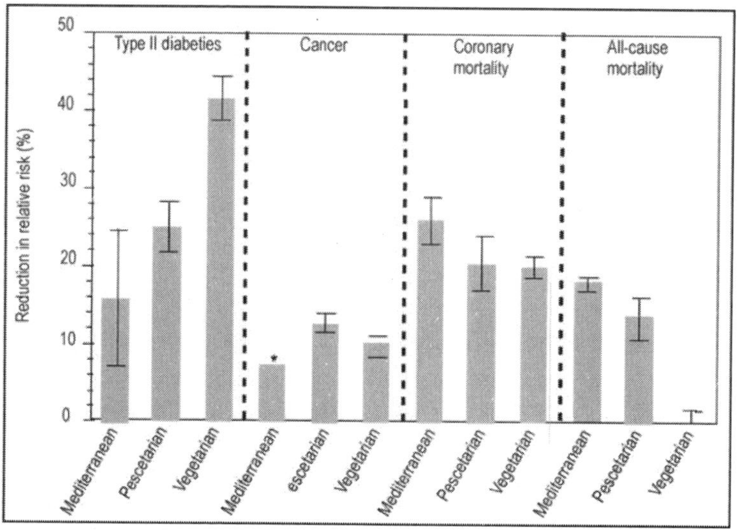

Fig. 6.1: Diet-Dependent Reduction in Health-Risking Diseases
Source: Tilman and Clark, 2014, Nature, vol. 515, 27 November, 2014.

Apart from the impact of diet, or rather food on human health in general, it has a very important role affecting environment as well, which ultimately determines agricultural health ensuring food security. We cannot feed the world with its growing population unless environmental health is congenial for food production. In this perspective, we have to take a serious view of keeping environment less polluted than we do today (See Note C).

> "Global average per capita dietary GHG (Greenhouse Gas) emissions from crop and livestock production would increase 32 per cent from 2009 to 2050 if global diets changed in present income-dependent ways. All three alternative diets could reduce emission from food production below those of the projected 2050 income-dependent diet, with per capita reductions being 30 per cent, 45 per cent and 55 per cent for the Mediterranean, Pescetarian and Vegetarian diets respectively.... Solutions to the diet-environment-health trilemma should seek healthier diets that have low GHG emissions rather than diets that might maximise GHG emissions."[23]

It is highly important to note that emission of GHG cannot be decreased without pursuing a middle course in diet intake, which should be an average of the Mediterranean, Pescetarian and Vegetarian diets. Failing to make this as the ultimate solution in combating environmental pollution, GHG emissions may increase ty 80 per cent by 2050. Major stress in this regard needs to be on income-dependent diet which requires to accommodate changes in composition with shifts from dependence on high-animal protein as far as practicable, keeping tastes of food undisturbed. Further, another great requirement, to make agriculture environmentally sustainable, can be accomplished if all forms of crop and food waste could be reduced globally by 50 per cent by 2050 while, at the same time, it will decrease land clearing by nearly 500 mha by that time. One of the stray instances, besides some others mentioned before, is presented by barbecue food waste-bill worth £428 million in Britain when, as reported by Rebecca Smitherns in *The*

Guardian, U.K., dated 17 August, 2017, with an average of £36.47 food mostly consisting of 'salad leaves, burger rolls, hot dog buns and potato salad are thrown away at each event', the number of which held being 12 million in the month of August 2017 in this country.

In fact, the threatening scale of food wastage at the global level amounting to an astounding one-third of the total agricultural production which, unfortunately, includes food thrown away as excess in the households of high income groups. According to Tilman and Clark (2015), if food waste could be cut in half by 2050 the land required for agricultural production would be saved by 300 mha and reduce GHG emissions by one-fifth. Undoubtedly, reduction in food wastage would require better crop harvesting as well as better storage facilities, refrigeration (cold storage), better and easy transport facilities for carrying crops from the fields to storage sites, with safety from rodents eating away the crops, improved grain-threshing facilities along with proper marketing facilities free of any interference from intermediaries, as it always happens in poor countries, pressurising poor farmers to sell their harvest often at throw-away prices (not even covering the cost of production, sometimes) provided with such facilities as availability of loans on easy/hassle-free terms for the ignorant, often illiterate, farmers, with provisions for crop-insurance facilities guarding against climate vagaries, leading to the loss in many cases of the total harvest.

Post-harvest losses of food is also taken seriously by Smil (2000). According to him,

> "A recent five-year survey of grain losses in leading cereal producing provinces found that about 15 per cent of grain crops are lost during harvesting, threshing, drying, storage, transport and processing. For rice, China's detailed multi-provincial survey came up with losses of 7 per cent in harvesting, 2.5 per cent in threshing and drying, 2 per cent in transport and 5-11 per cent in storage (four-fifths of all grain is stored by peasant households)."[24]

Even he does not find a very reassuring solution in this regard in an advanced country like Canada where, after the crop is harvested,

> "in every subsequent stage—handling, threshing, drying, storage and milling—the losses may be as low as one and as high as 10 per cent for the cumulative totals ranging from well below 10 per cent to as much as 40 per cent (and even higher figures were reported for some African crops). Moreover, year to year fluctuations may be quite considerable."[25]

Smil (2000)* further points out a different type of post-harvest loss following storage of crops. He observes that there are chemical changes sometimes affecting the quality of available nutrients in cereals, pulses, tubers, fruits and vegetables. According to him, although the total protein content remains unchanged, individual amino acids, particularly Lysine, may 'decline quite substantially such as wheat loses about 8 per cent of available Lysine within six weeks of storage and the loss may increase to over 40 per cent over a period of two years.

> "Disparities between apparent food availability and actual intakes diminish as one descends the developmental ladder: the gap is no larger than 15 per cent in China, is well below 10 per cent in India, and apparently non-existent in the poorest African countries. Food losses equivalent to 10-15 per cent of total supply may be unavoidable, but there is no excuse for the enormous losses in affluent countries. If the rich world's food losses could be held to 20 per cent of the overall supply, the annual savings (assuming that the animal foods provide about 25 per cent of all food energy) would be equivalent to at least 100 metric tonnes of grain, or nearly half of all cereals on the world market."[26]

---

* Vaclav Smil, *Feeding the World: A Challenge For the Twenty-First Century,* The MIT Press, Cambridge, Massachusetts, London, England, 2000.

Taking all these factors into consideration, what really is of great concern is the transition in the nature of diet which has remained almost undisturbed in its composition for a long time, thus making a revolutionary change, almost shaking the foundation of the society to its roots, with intense effect on human life, environment as well as adopting a defining role in future agricultural prospects affecting the state of global food security. As pointed out by Drewnowski (1997), there has been a fundamental change in the composition of diet to contain high fat content mostly in the form of meat and milk products. Consumption of this high-fat food originally linked to high-income groups in the urban areas of the industrial countries gradually made way into the food-habits of the people living in the fast urbanizing areas of the low- and middle-income countries of the developing world, particularly in East Asia, and this came to be more practicable with the introduction of cheap vegetable oils, making an ever-increasing proportion of energy in the global diet. Gradual cut in meat consumption in rich nations in response to nutrition policies did not, however, make any change in the fat content in the diet, remaining largely stable with vegetable fats replacing animal fat.

As a result, the original concept of the inevitable link between high income and growing high animal-protein content in diet has come to be replaced by the development of transition of food habits, with greater dependence on junk food in fast urbanizing countries in the developing world where change in life-style, particularly in the urban areas, is de-linked from income-dependence. What we see in these urban settings where both husband and wife/partner having been working outside home for living (earning more than working single) prefers food in restaurants/hotels/eateries offering prepared food made tastier with liberal addition of both sweetness and vegetable fats. Even people of this category take it as an enjoyment on non-working days in the week to eat and stay away from home as far as practicable, often leaving children in charge of carers.

> "Higher individual incomes in the lower-income societies are invariably associated with greater consumption of dietary fats ... (It) points to global convergence toward a diet deriving higher proportion of

> energy from fat. That diet more closely approximates the diets of the United States and Western Europe than any traditional diet of Asia or Africa ... Diets richer in fat also tend to be more varied."[27]

It is true that once such dietary changes giving tastier food becomes a habit of the people even in poorer circumstances such as in low- and middle-income countries, those who can afford luxury like this tend not to go back to traditional root vegetables and coarse grains and, instead, prefer that to be replaced by rice and wheat which also in turn are slowly replaced by high-protein, high-fat and sweeteners at accelerated rates.

Such dietary variety associated with increased proportion of sugar and fat may only be changed with the adoption of appropriate nutrition policies and programmes. But it has come to be one of the greatest challenges to overcome its popularity, particularly with the younger generation, irrespective of the industrialized or industrializing countries of the developing world where conscious approach to the overall situation is not largely appreciated.

The overall outcome of this animal-protein-rich food containing high fat and sugar contents is slowly going to create a situation of no-return in consideration of the associated epidemiologic transition on the one hand and environmental and other costs on the other, hitting hard on the agricultural future of the globe, impacting food security for a growing population. To be more specific, one can no longer ignore concern about global sustainability so far as availability of food for all living on this planet is an unavoidable responsibility. But the current trend of rising consumption of animal-source food in low- and medium-income countries and no relaxation in the consumption of such food in high-income countries, along with the ultra-processed food on an increasingly larger scale, present a very threatening future in particular when conscious efforts at checking the impending danger of different dimensions are far from adequate. As a matter of fact, 'there are now more overweight and obese people than underweight or malnourished in the world' (Kearney, 2010). Interestingly, as observed by Kearney (2010), in some of the upper- to middle-income developing countries, such as in Mexico, Brazil and South Africa, higher obesity is occurring amount people of lower socio-economic status with excessive consumption of energy-dense and nutrition-poor foods.

The pandemic of obesity, Type II diabetes and heart diseases affecting the quality of life and increasing mortality rates in the world as a whole is resulting from this food transition. Changing this situation with strong determination/perseverance lies in consumption patterns with greater dependence on alternative diets 'high in vegetables and fruits, nuts and seeds, whole grains and fish' which is a Mediterranean diet (Tilman and Clark, 2015). Both Mediterranean and Vegetarian diets offer a solution in improving health conditions providing

> "a much greater portion of their calories and protein coming from plant rather than animal sources. ... People who consume a Mediterranean or Vegetarian diet have between 15-40 per cent lower incidence of diabetes and 20-25 per cent lower mortality from coronary heart disease. Pescetarian diets, which basically are Vegetarian diets that include sea-food in place of some of the dairy and eggs, have similar health benefits."[28]

In fact, consumption of all three alternative diets will have a great impact on the reduction of GHG emissions, amounting to 30 per cent, 45 per cent and 55 per cent respectively for Mediterranean, Pescetarian and Vegetarian diets.

Two very revolutionary impacts likely to be derived from the consumption of alternative diets are—there will be less global emissions and it will besides appreciably decrease the necessity of global land clearing between now and 2050 by about 500 mha. At the same time, if food wasted on various counts could be cut in half by 2050, thereby reducing GHG emissions from crop production by one-fifth, the amount of land used for agriculture could be reduced by about 300 mha. Further, cutting down the consumption of animal-protein, along with sweeteners and fats, will reduce the demand for land appreciably for the production of crops like maize, soybeans etc. used as animal-feed, with simultaneous reduction in land clearing, the opposite of what is happening in Brazil for maintaining an increasing supply of beef. Thus, quadruple environmental benefits could be derived from reduction in the consumption of animal-protein, such as (a) reduction in land clearing, resulting in (b) remarkable lessening in GHG emissions; (c) assuring a better prospect for health of the human beings, and (d) saving biodiversity and saving ecosystems.

Viewed from another angle, the prospect of larger food production derived from closing yield gaps, as mentioned earlier, one of the most important steps among many others, such as change in irrigation methods making water always available, coupled with better conservation, application of improved seeds, fertilizers etc., promises better impact on food security.

> "Globally, about 60 per cent of grain production is used as human food, 35 per cent as animal feed, and 5 per cent as biofuels. Greater direct consumption of plant-based foods, preferential consumption of low feed-input animal based foods such as eggs, milk and poultry meat, and elimination of food-based biofuels, would allow current production to feed approximately an additional one billion people without increasing agricultural land requirements and would reduce agricultural gas emissions."[29]

Undeniably, the role of alternative diets is very important in strengthening food security along with providing greater assurance for better human health. A secure food supply increases the stability of the government, making it imperative that this increases access to education for creating better human capital and opening scopes for a better, more creative life for the people, particularly in developing countries. This all-round improvement is possible with increasing agricultural yields as the only means.

NOTES

Note A

"In richer nations, about 8000 calories per day of agricultural crop production are required to produce 3,500 calories of food brought into household by the average person. The 4,500 calorie difference between the calorie content of the crops that must be grown and the calorie content of food brought into the household mainly represents the calories fed to the animals used to produce animal-based food. The reason that increased demand for meat, milk and eggs results in large increases in agricultural production is directly related to the inefficiency with which various animals convert feed crops into edible animal-based foods. For example, for cattle to create one kilogram of edible beef protein it must eat twenty kilograms of plant protein, for a ratio of 1:20. The ratio is 1:5.7 for pork; 1:4.7 for poultry; 1:4.4 to 1:4.8 for aquaculture production of halibut, salmon, cod and Arctic char; 1:3.9 for milk and 1:2.6 for eggs. In total, more than half of all agricultural crop production and land use in richer nations feeds livestock rather than producing crops for direct human consumption. Animal production is not only calorie-intensive, but it is also land-intensive; approximately 80 per cent of global agricultural land is used to graze livestock and a significant proportion of cropland is used for animal feeds."

Source: Tilman, David and Michael Clark, 2015, Food, Agriculture and the Environment: Can We Feed the World and Save the Earth? in *Daedalus, Journal of The American Academy of Arts and Sciences,* Vol. 144, Issue 4, Fall 2015: pp. 8-10.

Note B

As mentioned earlier,

(a) High food prices are a problem because nearly 3 billion people—half of the world's population—are poor and near poor. Around half of the people in the developing world earn less than two dollars (US) a day. Nearly 20 per cent are extremely poor, earning less than one dollar (US) a day.

Source: Eric Holt-Giménez, From Food Crisis to Food Sovereignty: The Challenge to Social Movements, in *Agriculture and Food in Crisis: Conflict Resistance and Renewals,* Edited by Magdoff and Tokar, Monthly Review Press, New York. 2010.

(b) "Nearly half of children in the US live dangerously close to the poverty line and more kids today are likely to live in families barely able to afford their most basic needs. According to researches, the number of poor children in the US grew by 18 per cent from 2008 to 2014 (as reported by the National Center for Children in Poverty—NCCP—at Columbia University)."

Source: The Statesman, Kolkata Issue, India, 4 March 2016.

(c) "Statistics show 30 per cent of children in the UK live in poverty, and more than 188,000 children are homeless or living in temporary accommodation."

Source: Sarah Marsh, *The Guardian,* U.K., 14 August, 2017.

This is in sharp contrast to the fact that, "Three-quarters (74.2%) of the families—who had an average fortune of $1.45 billion (£1.1 billion)—increased their wealth."

Source: Rupert Neale, Wealth Correspondent, *The Guardian,* U.K., 12 August, 2017.

(d) According to the report of Welthungerhilfe, International Food Policy Research Institute and Concern Worldwide, "one in three children under the age of five are too short for their age and can be termed 'stunted'. India ranks 100 in the Global Hunger Index (GHI) out of 119, lagging behind North Korea, Bangladesh and Nigeria and Iraq with a high proportion of undernourished children. ... Only three other countries in this year's GHI—Djibouti, Sri Lanka and South Sudan—show child wasting about 20 per cent, it stated. India's child wasting rate has not shown any substantial improvement over the past 25 years, the study said."

Source: The Statesman, Kolkata Issue, India, 14 October, 2017.

Note C

As the Press Trust of India reports,

"India had the world's highest number of deaths due to air, water and other forms of pollution in 2015, according to a study published in the Lancet journal today (20 October, 2017) which showed that pollution killed as many as 2.5 million people in the country. Most of these deaths are due to non-communicable diseases caused by pollution, such as heart disease, stroke, lung cancer and chronic obstructive pulmonary disease (COPD), researchers said.

According to the study, air pollution is the biggest contributor, linked to 6.5 million deaths in 2015 in the world, while water pollution (1.8 million deaths) and work-place-related pollution (0.8 million deaths) pose the next largest risks.

Researchers ... pointed out that almost 92 per cent pollution-related deaths occur in low- and middle-income countries. In rapidly industrializing countries, such as India, Pakistan, China, Bangladesh, Madagascar and Kenya, deaths due to pollution can account for up to one in four deaths. In 2015, the greatest numbers of deaths due to pollution occurred in India (2.5 million) and China (1.8 million)."

Source: The Statesman, Kolkata Issue, India, 21 October, 2017.

REFERENCES

1. Tilman, David and Michael Clark, 2015, Food, Agriculture and the

Environment: Can We Feed the World and Save the Earth? in *Daedalus, The Journal of The American Academy of Arts and Sciences,* Vol. 144, Issue 4, Fall 2015: pp. 8-23.

2. *Ibid.*, pp. 12-13.
3. Collins, Darryl, Jonathan Morduch (2009), Stuart Rutherford and Orlando Ruthven (2009), *Portfolios of the Poor: How the World's Poor Live on $2 a day,* Permanent Black, p. 1.
4. *Ibid.*, p. 156.
5. Yunus, Muhammad with Alan Jolis (1998), *Banker to the Poor,* The University Press Limited, Dhaka, Bangladesh: pp. 67 and 89.
6. Collins, Darryl, Jonathan Morduch, Stuart Rutherford and Orlando Ruthven (2009). *Portfolios of the Poor: How the World's Poor Live on $2 a day,* Permanent Black, p. 171.
7. Collier, Paul (2008). *The Bottom Billion: Why the Poorest Countries are Failing and What Can be Done About It,* Oxford University Press, pp. 3, 6, 7 and 8.
8. Tilman, David, Christian Balzer, Jason Hill and Belinda L. Befort (2011), "Global Food Demand and the Sustainable Intensification of Agriculture", in *PNAS (Proceedings of the National Academy of Sciences of the United States of America),* Vol. 108, No. 50, p. 20260.
9. *Ibid.*, p. 20261.
10. Tilman, David and Michael Clark, (2015). "Food, Agriculture and the Environment: Can We Feed the World and Save the Earth?" in *Daedalus, Journal of The American Academy of Arts and Sciences,* Vol. 144, Issue 4, Fall 2015: p. 14.
11. Kearney, John (2010), "Food Consumption Trends and Drivers," in *Philosophical Transactions: Biological Sciences,* Vol. 365, No. 1554.
12. Tilman, David and Michael Clark (2014), "Global Diets Link Environmental Sustainability and Human Health," in *Nature,* Vol. 515, 27 September, p. 519.
13. Drewnowski, Adam (1997), The nutrition Transition: New Trends in the Global Diet, in *Nutrition Reviews* Vol. 55, No. 2, p. 34.
14. *Ibid.*, p. 37.
15. Kearney, John (2010), "Food Consumption Trends and Drivers," in *Philosophical Transactions: Biological Sciences,* Vol. 365, No. 1554, pp. 2794-2799.
16. *Ibid.*, p. 2803.
17. Popkin, Barry M. (2017), "Relationship between Shifts in Food System Dynamics and Acceleration of the Global Nutrition Transition," in *Nutrition Reviews,* Vol. 75, p. 73.
18. *Ibid.*, p. 78.
19. *Ibid.*, p. 79.
20. Kearney, John (2010), "Food Consumption Trends and Drivers", in *Philosophical Transactions: Biological Sciences,* Vol. 365, No. 1554, p. 2805.

21. Licker, Rachel, Matt Johnston, Jonathan A. Foley, Carol Barford, Christopher J. Kucharik, Chad Monfreda and Navin Ramankutty, "Mind the Gap: How do Climate and Agricultural Management explain the 'Yield Gap' of Croplands around the world?" in *Global Ecology and Biogeography,* Vol. 9, No. 6.
22. Tilman, David and Michael Clark (2015), "Food, Agriculture and the Environment: Can We Feed the World and Save the Earth?" in *Daedalus, Journal of The American Academy of Arts and Sciences,* Vol. 144, Issue 4, Fall 2015: p. 519.
23. *Ibid.,* p. 520.
24. Smil, Vaclav (2000). *Feeding the World: A Challenge for the Twenty-First Century,* The MIT Press, Cambridge, Massachusetts, p. 185.
25. *Ibid.,* p. 186.
26. *Ibid.,* pp. 209-210.
27. Drewnowski, Adam (1997), "The Nutrition Transition: New Trends in the Global Diet," in *Nutrition Reviews* Vol. 55, No. 2, p. 41.
28. Licker, Rachel, Matt Johnston, Jonathan A. Foley, Carol Barford, Christopher J. Kucharik, Chad Monfreda and Navin Ramankutty, (2010), "Mind the Gap: How do Climate and Agricultural Management explain the 'Yield Gap' of Croplands around the world?" in *Global Ecology and Biogeography,* Vol. 9, No. 6, November.
29. Tilman, David and Michael Clark (2015). "Food, Agriculture and the Environment: Can We Feed the World and Save the Earth?" in *Daedalus, Journal of The American Academy of Arts and Sciences,* Vol. 144, Issue 4, Fall, pp. 17-18.

7
Feeding the Growing Global Population

Growth of population is the primary factor determining whether the food produced under the present system is adequate or not to meet the increasing demand of food. It may be observed that growth of population, as mentioned before, shows an interesting pattern. For instance, while the first billion was attained in 1804, it took about 123 years to reach the second billion (1927), while the third took only another 33 years, the fourth only 15 years and the fifth and sixth only 12 years each.

> "Looking at it in another way, the first millennium saw virtually no net increase from the 300 million people estimated to have been alive around the time of Christ's birth, whereas the second millennium has witnessed a 20-fold growth of population. Perhaps, most dramatically, while the first 1900 years from Christ's birth added 1.3 billion, the last 100 years have added 4.4 billion."[1]

According to UN forecasts, global population will increase from 7.3 billion in 2015 to 9.6 billion by 2050, reaching 10.6 billion by 2100.[2]

Undoubtedly, this makes a challenging situation since population expansion alone makes a higher demand for food, to the tune of 30 per cent by 2050 and 50 per cent by 2100, provided the practice of agriculture remains as it is now and per capita demand for food also remains unaltered. But, as has been discussed in preceding chapters, agricultural practices are already in the process of changing significantly with the application of new technology involving the use of improved varieties of seeds, fertilizers, newly devised irrigation practices, planting methods, lessening yield-gaps and cutting down wastage on various fronts. All these measures, no doubt, open up immense possibilities for a much larger production. On the other hand, percapita consumption is going to increase in step with economic development along with trends in nutrition transition. For example, global consumption per person per day is going to rise by 378 Kcal, from 2411 to 2789 Kcal, between 1969/1971 and 2015 (Table 7.1), making quite an impressive improvement in reducing undernutrition, though this is widely variable, ranging from the highest improvement of 1089 Kcal in East Asia to the lowest of 320 Kcal in Sub-Saharan Africa during the same period. But, what is highly interesting is that, on the whole, improvement in per capita per day consumption of food by 749 Kcal in developing countries indeed shows a great improvement though still remaining at a much lower level—2860 Kcal in 2015 against 3480 Kcal in industrial countries. However, the rise in food consumption in parallel to rise in income remains below the global average all through in the developing countries. But the effect of rising income and growing urbanization in East Asia pushes the level of food consumption exceeding it in all other regions of the developing

Table 7.1: Per Capita Food Consumption (Kcal per capita per day) (Following Alexandratos 2006)

	1969/ 1971	*1979/ 1981*	*1989/ 1991*	*1999/ 2001*	*2015*	*2030*	*2050*
World	2411	2549	2704	2789	2950	3040	3130
Developing Countries	2111	2308	2520	2654	2860	2960	3070
Sub-Saharan Africa	2100	2078	2106	2194	2420	2600	2830
Near-East/ North Africa	2382	2834	3011	2974	3080	3130	3190
Latin America and Caribbean	2465	2698	2689	2836	2990	3120	3200
South Asia	2066	2084	2329	2392	2660	2790	2980
East Asia	2012	2317	2625	2872	3110	3190	3230
Industrial Countries	3046	3133	3292	3446	3480	3520	3540
Transition Countries	3323	3389	3280	2900	3030	3150	3270

Source: Kearney, John (2010), *Food Consumption Trends and Drivers in Philosophical Transactions: Biological Sciences,* Vol. 365, No. 1554: Table 1.

world, including Latin America and the Caribbean in 2015, maintaining the lead thereafter. In contrast, Sub-Saharan Africa presents a dismal picture, keeping the lowest profile during this entire period of almost eight decades (1969/1971-2050), remaining far below the global average.

Kearney (2010) further observes that there has been a remarkable increase in the consumption of meat in the developing world per head per day (in calories) from 147 in 1963 to 369 in 2003, sugar from 75 to 170, vegetable oils from 80 to 239, with reductions in the consumption of pulses from 167 to 99 and roots and tubers from 178 to 154 calories during the same period—1963 to 2003—sufficiently indicating greater preference for meat, sugar and oils, creating health hazards. At the same time, it may be pointed out that developing countries, particularly those fast urbanizing like East Asia and Latin America, closely following the example of industrial countries in food habits yet remain at a far lower level in the consumption of meat, sugar and vegetable oils than the industrial countries where calories obtained from meat has increased from 833 in 1963 to 958 in 2003, sugar from 349 to 328 and vegetable oils from 241 to 494 per person, thus recording a substantial increase though recording a slight decline in the consumption of sugar. In contrast, China, a part of the developing world, however, shows a formidable change on all counts, with steep rise in the consumption of meat, increasing from 90 calories in 1963, to 644 calories in 2003—a 349 per cent increase, sugar from 18 to 73, and vegetable fats from 35 in 1963 to 273 in 2003, making a 680 per cent increase (Kearney, 2010).[3]

All these estimates provide a definite indication of the growing demand for food going to determine the nature as well as quantity of food in demand in future to ensure global food security. The massive preference for food high in meat content, dairy products and vegetable fat have made at the same time food processing a key factor in the transformation of food systems, bring in its wake standardization of agricultural output as dictated by supermarket demands clearly dominated by their specifications almost formulating production policies for exporting countries. On the other hand, processed, semi-processed food, as mentioned earlier, dominates food market so much that

> "between 2001 and 2014, the share of processed food distributed through supermarkets significantly increased in upper middle-income countries, from less than 40 per cent to 50 per cent. In the same period, it grew around 72 per cent to 75 per cent in high-income countries. In lower middle-income countries, it grew from 22 to 27 per cent between 2007 and 2008, with no further change between 2008 and 2014."[4]

While the production of agricultural crops, particularly for the exporting countries, is largely influenced by the demand of the supermarkets, we have to remember in this context that the supermarkets mostly cater to the urban dwellers in larger towns and cities, whereas people living in rural areas generally have a different consumption pattern, with preferences for foodstuff in many ways different from the demands of the urban population.

The growing demand for high-calorie food by urban population, particularly in the high-income countries, shows less preference for fresh food, distribution of which through supermarkets has remained 'below 50 per cent in high-income countries, below 30 per cent in upper-middle-income countries and around 10 per cent in low-middle-income countries' (FAO, 2017).

Interestingly, the role of indigenous food system as highlighted earlier, citing two contrasting situations from two countries, such as Bangladesh and India, give the idea that indigenous foods, growing wild and consisting of several hundred edible and nutritious plants and animals, can contribute substantially to the global food supply.

"First, indigenous superfoods could address some of the nutritional deficiencies that currently affect more than 2 billion people. Second, the production of local plants that are usually consumed in the wild or with minimum domestication in some case, can be scaled up using advanced technologies. This is already done in the biocosmetic and pharmaceutical industries, which rely heavily on the indigenous knowledge of plants and the medicinal properties of forest products. Similar alliances, if developed for food production, might expand the present, narrow food base."[5]

Incidentally, the role of wild date palms and toddy palms in this respect is noteworthy in the rural economy of West Bengal and elsewhere in India.

Actual Requirement of Food

Having considered the changing nature of demand for food containing high animal protein, high vegetable and sugar content, we have to be careful in making a final estimate of the total need of food, keeping in view that such changes in the nature of food mentioned above is precisely confined to the urban areas of the world, representing about 54 per cent of total world population in 2015, increasing to a little over 66 per cent by 2050, leaving out 3,367 million in 2015 and 3,212 million people in 2050 in the rural areas (UN, 2014 Revised Ed.) who, even though rural people are used to a very low protein diet and remaining unaffected by diet transition, together makes quite a large demand for food in absolute quantities. In this respect we may refer to the observation made by Smil (2002)*:

> "In traditional societies that enjoy basically adequate nutrition (average per capita supply of 2,400 Kcal/day) but derive less than 10 per cent of food energy from animal foods, such relatively small amounts of meat, eggs, and milk require little concentrated feed. In contrast, the same society with per capita food energy at 3000 Kcal/day deriving 25 per cent of all food energy from animals will have to resort to large-scale feeding of grain. Even when it is done fairly efficiently, supply of 750 Kcal of animal food would require at least four or five times that amount of plant feed. This would call for additional output of 3000-3700 Kcal of crops, or more than doubling the net crop harvests used directly for human consumption (2250 Kcal/day)."[6]

This naturally leads to the question if harvests could be increased from available agricultural land, which has stabilized

---

* Vaclav Smil, *Feeding the World: A Challenge for the Twenty-First Century*, The M & T Press, Cambridge, Massachusetts, London, 2002 (Paperbook).

at around 4.9 billion hectares when 33 per cent of which is 'moderately to highly degraded' (WHO, 2017), proving to be a great impediment to realizing food security and thereby reducing hunger. According to Alexandratos and Bruinsma (2012),

> "for the world as a whole, net-land under crops may have to increase by some 70 million ha by 2050 (increase in developing countries, decline in developed). The area harvested may increase by almost twice that amount as a result of increased multiple cropping and reduced fallows. The projected 70 million ha increase is the result of 132 million ha expansion in the countries that are projected to increase land under crops (most of it is in countries in Sub-Saharan Africa and Latin America), and a 63 million ha decline in the countries that are projected to reduce it (most of it in the developed countries but some also in developing ones)."[7]

Elaborating on this point of global availability of land for crop production the same authors are of opinion that there is 7.2 billion hectares of land available globally for rain-fed production with potential for various degrees of suitability, such as 1.6 billion including land under irrigation currently used for crop production, 75 million ha of which is classified as non-suitable while of the remaining 5.7 billion, 2.8 billion ha is under forest or under non-agricultural uses, like human settlements, infrastructure etc., and 1.5 billion ha of the remaining 2.9 billion ha (5.7 billion –2.8 billion = 2.9 billion) is of poor quality for rain-fed crops—marginally to very marginally suitable, and the land at present used for crop production includes about 220 million ha of which only 47 million ha is under irrigation (Alexandratos & Bruinsma, 2012).

> "This leaves some 1.4 billion ha of prime land and good land (classes suitable and moderately suitable) that could be brought into cultivation if needed, albeit often at the expense of pastures and requiring considerable development investments, e.g. infrastructuring, fighting diseases etc."[8]

According to FAO (2017), about 100 million ha of additional land for agricultural use is needed by 2050,[9] which is not readily available, concentrated in only a few countries. Because of this 'increases in agricultural production to meet rising food demand' will have to be met 'mainly from improvements in productivity and resource use efficiency' (FAO, 2017). In other words, right steps need to be taken for realizing agricultural potential. As mentioned in Chapter 6, closing yield-gap may be one of the most effective measures in this respect, but to obtain larger output from existing land proves to be quite a challenging issue involving seed genetics, biotechnology, agronomic management techniques and other agricultural technology (Rachel Licker *et al.* , 2010). However, one of the very important reasons for very low yield rates is use of very small amount of nitrogen fertilizer such as less than five kilogram per hectare used in poor countries and, similarly, use of very low amount of other inputs in contrast to richest nations applying thirty times that amount (Tilman and Clark, 2015).[*] As mentioned earlier, in Chapter 6, use of improved techniques for narrowing the yield-gaps could increase food supplies 300-400 per cent using the existing cropland. Hence, closing the yield-gap should be given top priority all over the world. It has been pointed out by Tilman and Clark (2015), that shrinking yield-gap is going to implement revolutionary changes in crop production, capable of meeting 70 per cent or more of the food demand by 2050 from production on current cropland, besides saving global biodiversity by 'reducing the need for land clearing' and stopping the destruction of ecosystems. Besides, the most sustaining effect of this achievement will be in stabilizing the governments of the relevant countries and thus enhancing the scope of education and economic opportunities for their people in general.

In this regard, Tilman *et al.* (2011),[†] in making an analysis of

---

* David Tilman and Michael Clark, "Food, Agriculture and the Environment: Can We Feed the World and Save the Earth?" *Daedalus, The American Academy of Arts and Sciences,* Vol. 144, Issue 4, 2015.

† David Tilman, Christian Balzer, Jason Hill and Belinda L. Befort, Global Food Demand and the Sustainable Intensification of Agriculture, *PNAS (Proceedings of the National Academy of Sciences of the United States of America),* Vol. 108, No. 50, 2011.

the global relationship between per capita GDP and per capita demand for crop calories or protein found a close relationship in their dependence across all the seven economic groups—ranging from the highest Group A to the lowest Group G GDP. They found that

> "magnitude of this dependence is surprisingly large. In 2000, for example, per capita use of calories and protein by the richest nations (Group A) were 256 per cent and 430 per cent greater respectively, than used by the poorest nations (Groups F and G). These large differences in crop demand particularly result from greater dietary meat consumption at higher income (6, 7) and the low efficiency with which some types of livestock convert crop calories and protein into edible foods."[10]

Climate change takes a very important role in defining agricultural productivity, considered as 'hunger-risk multiplier' (FAO, 2017), putting an additional 120 million people at the risk of undernourishment by 2050, half of which will remain concentrated in Sub-Saharan Africa. The situation is made further complicated by climate change with dual effects, such as increasing plant growth under warmer temperatures in temperate zones in higher latitudes contrasted with adverse impacts at lower latitudes, which is predicted to intensity further after 2030 with significant losses of yields in most parts of the globe, intensified further by recurrent appearance of droughts and floods resulting from such catastrophic effects which could be reduced by tackling the emission of greenhouse gases, 25 per cent of these coming from agriculture alone. This can reasonably be reduced with cutting down on animal breeding which, on its own, is a great emitter, and dietary changes with rising income making a greater demand on animal breeding. Hence, we repeat the following observation made by Tilman and Clark (2015):

> "agricultural emissions are overwhelmingly from beef and lamb production, nitrogen fertilization and land clearance. Minimising beef and lamb consumption,

> eating moderate amounts of other meats and low-fat animal products, eating crops grown with moderate fertilization and minimizing food waste are effective ways for individuals to decrease their dietary greenhouse gas emissions."[11]

If agricultural practices are pursued in similar fashion as it is done now, the global greenhouse gas emission is predicted to increase by 50 per cent of its current level by 2050.

> "The major reason why a world with about 30 per cent more people in 2050 would demand about 100 per cent more production of agricultural crops is because of the feed necessary to meet increased demand for animal-based foods resulting from the rising incomes of billions of people in the developing world. Increased demand for empty calories directly consumed by people, often in the form of sugars, fats, oils and alcohols contributes to this demand, thought to a lesser extent."[12]

At the same time, it has already been demonstrated that efficient use of fertilizers, irrigation and pesticides can increase crop-yields effectively, relieving at the same time the environment of detrimental effects. On the contrary, shift in dietary patterns, as initiated and persisted by dietary transition increases environmental footprints in terms of greenhouse gas emissions while dietary patterns consisting of lower red meat consumption with low environmental impacts 'can also be consistent with good health' and help in limiting GHG emissions (FAO, 2017).

Incidentally, the vast rural population, representing almost 46 per cent of global population in 2015 and nearly 34 per cent in around 2050, steeped in dire poverty and suffering from chronic hunger and malnutrition ultimately take recourse to migration from their rural surroundings for better destinations, such as the urban areas. It generally involves the younger generation aged between 15 and 24, comprising about 1 billion in 2015 to 1.2 billion by 2050 (FAO, 2017), mostly coming from Sub-Saharan Africa and South Asia. This undoubtedly represents a great loss of human capital could be prevented through 'provision of quality basic social services', involving education and health as means of reducing poverty. Migration of the young population undoubtedly affects agricultural production system when up to 90 per cent of food consumed in the rural areas come from domestic sources (FAO, 2017).

Is the Present System Capable of Feeding the World?

Food is freedom, as considered by Sen (1989), and according to him,

> "if a person is not free from hunger and lacks the means and the practical opportunities to feed himself or herself adequately then that person's positive freedom must be seen as having been thoroughly compromised."[13]

In other words, food is the basic right of every human being, irrespective of his/her economic status and turns out to be the most important responsibility of the society to satisfy every individual's need in adequate measure.

In this context it becomes imperative to know if global agriculture is capable of producing enough food to feed the growing population. According to Tilman and Clark (2015).

> "global agriculture seems capable of feeding ten billion people by 2050, the resulting environmental impacts—if agriculture grew along established global trajectories—would be great.... There are, however, several major ways to reduce the environmental impacts of agriculture providing a fully populated Earth with healthy and nutritious diets. These include increasing crop yields, avoiding or reversing the shift to less healthy and more environmentally harmful diets, reducing crop and food waste, and using fertilizers and irrigation water more efficiently."[14]

Here, we may refer to narrowing yield-gaps using improved agronomic methods such as application of the right amount of fertilizers could act as the most effective measure for obtaining a much larger harvest from the same amount of cropland, contributing to the tune of 300 to 400 per cent on the one hand while, on the other, sparing clearing of land for agricultural expansion, save the environment from destruction of the habitat along with greenhouse gas emissions by land clearing. It is very encouraging to know that if closure of yield-gap by 95 per cent is properly achieved all over the world, along with using fertilizers at rates of 80 per cent of those in the richest nations, would decrease environmental harm and would increase global crop production by 70 per cent (Tilman and Clark, 2015) and 'no new land would be needed to meet 2050 global food demand'. Ultimately, closing the yield-gap and applying more fertilizers by poor nations together derive triple benefits which are very significant, such as (a) much larger harvest; (b) rescue habitat from damage with greater harm to biodiversity, and (c) reduction in land clearance amounting to nearly 500 million ha between now and 2050, as well as greenhouse gas emission to a considerable scale.

The second most important step to be taken is reduction in waste of agricultural production amounting to almost one-third of the total annual harvest (Tilman and Clark, 2015). Such losses take place at various stages: in field, in storage and at processing stages, which appear to be exceptionally high and unacceptable.

> "A recent five-year survey of grain losses in leading cereal-producing provinces found that about 15 per cent of grain crops are lost annually during harvesting, threshing, drying, storage, transport and processing."[15]

According to the same author, such losses may be as much as 40 per cent. In his opinion, in the case of fish, it may even be higher, 'with rates rising up to more than 50 per cent in some locales'. Further, as mentioned earlier, deterioration in the quality of crops undergoing chemical changes during storage, losing some amino acids, affects the quality of the crops. Besides, vitamins are the most vulnerable group of nutrients to be damaged during the processing. For example, Vitamins A, C, D and E are susceptible to 'inactivation' by oxidation; C and B-group of vitamins get degraded by heating as well as freezing (Smil, 2000).

Reduction in food waste is quite possible by adopting better crop harvesting methods and storage facilities with increased access to refrigeration. Further, reducing waste in retail stores and households, particularly in advanced economies, holds great possibilities.

In preparing food balance sheet we are reminded of the fact that while it is possible to make an assessment of the total amount of food required by the developed world on the basis of the per capita consumption of food consisting of high protein-fat and sugar content provided by relevant ingredients, it is rather difficult to make this estimate for people living in the developing countries since wildlife makes a very important component of food taken by them in the rural areas. Though wild birds make a great attraction for diet in the temperate regions as well, it is an extremely rare addition in contrast to sub-tropical and tropical diets which always contain 'nearly all available local species of a very wide range consisting of ants, snails, small birds, hedgehogs etc., making it difficult to quantify as they are often caught by hunting or collected, invariably providing a large share of local diet. For example,

> "during the rainy season wild foods, gathered mainly from paddy fields, made up about half of the total food consumed by farmers in Thailand's central north-east ... at least 160 tonnes of meat were for sale in a single market in Accra, Ghana, during a period of eighteen months ... in many areas of Africa and Latin America wild meat can provide at least 20 per cent of all animal protein. ... Besides Equatorial Africa, high rates of wild meat consumption also prevail in some parts of Latin America, South-east Asia and Siberia. ... In comparison with animal protein, collection of leaves, seeds, tubers, fruits and nuts may be generally of much lesser importance, but there are instances where such wild foods may, too, be the source of high-quality nutrients. An outstanding example of such a neglected contribution is the production of high-protein concentrate from the beans of *Parkia biglobosa,* a leguminous tree growing throughout Western Africa. After boiling, fermentation and drying this concentrate

> (*dawadawa*) has about 20-50 per cent of protein (with lysine content similar to that of egg), 30-40 per cent of lipids (three-fifths unsaturated fatty acids) as well as plenty of iron and calcium. ... Various African populations also use powdered leaves of baobab—extract butter from shea nuts ... In Tanzania four-fifths of all leafy green vegetables (excellent source of vitamins and minerals) eaten in rural areas are collected from wild plants which accompany almost half of all meals."[16]

It is estimated that greater consumption of such food available directly from nature supplemented, as required, by 'low feed-input animal-based food' such as eggs, milk and poultry meat coupled with the elimination of the food-based biofuels, as mentioned earlier, would allow current crop production to feed an extra one billion people without going into land clearance for agricultural expansion. This further stresses on narrowing yield-gaps as the most important measure for much larger harvest.

In assessing the actual requirement of food in the world, it has to be done on the basis of the level of per capita food consumption which obviously varies widely across the globe. As mentioned in Chapter 6, the amount of food, amounting to 2 billion tons of grain, available for feeding the world population varies widely on the basis of the level of consumption, which is 2 billion at American levels of consumption, 5.6 billion at Italian level and would support a population of 10 billion at Indian level of consumption (Brown, 2006).

In this regard, Tilman *et al.* (2011), making an analysis of the global relationship between 'per capita GDP and per capita demand for crop calories or protein' found a close relationship in their dependence across all the seven economic groups—ranging from the highest Group A to the lowest Group G GDP. They found that

> "the magnitude of this dependence is surprisingly large. In 2000, for example, per capita use of calories and protein by the richest nations (Group A) were 256 per cent and 430 per cent greater, respectively, than used by the poorest nations (Group F and G). These

large differences in crop demand partially result from greater dietary mean consumption at higher income and the low efficiency with which some types of livestock convert crop calories and protein into edible foods (Fig. 7.1)."[17]

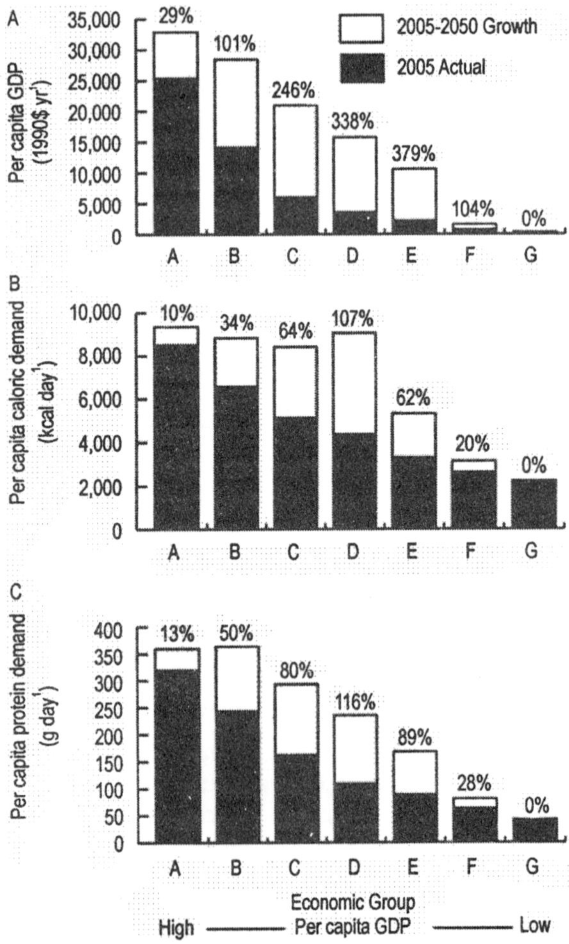

Fig. 7.1: Per Capita GDP, per capita demand for crop calories and crop protein per day in 2005 (shown in black) and mean projected 2050 increase (shown in white with % increase)

Source: Tilman *et al.*, 2011, Vol. 108.

According to these authors, the observed relationships between per capita crop use and per capita real GDP provide a basis for 'forecasting future crop demand'.

It is estimated that 'global demand for crop calories would increase by 100 per cent ±11 per cent and global demand for crop protein would increase by 110 per cent ± 7 per cent between 2005 and 2050 which, in other words, mean a double increase on both counts (Tilman *et al.*, 2011) but this is

> "lower than the 176 per cent (caloric) and 238 per cent (protein) increases in global crop use that would occur if per capita demands of all nations in 2050 reached the 2005 levels of Group A nations. ... Our forecast of a 100-110 per cent increase in global crop production by 2050 is larger than the 70 per cent increase that has been projected for this same period."[18]

The doubling of global crop production between 2005 and 2050 naturally would depend, as mentioned earlier, on the processes of 'extensification' or clearing of additional land for crop production obviously entailing associated problems of enhanced emission of greenhouse gas, destabilization of biodiversity etc., while adopting the process of intensification higher yields could be obtained through the application of 'increased inputs, improved agronomic practices, improved crop varieties and other innovations'. For example, soil fertility can be increased by legumes and cover crops. It is observed that the requirement of land cleared for crop production would effectively decrease with obtaining increased global yields through the application of improved technology and increasing use of Nitrogen fertilizer, ultimately contributing to the reduction of greenhouse gas emissions by about three times. This, carried on with transfer of technology to countries with poor yield rates, would ultimately lead to agricultural sustainability promising larger harvests and 'more equitable global food supplies' (Tilman *et al.*, 2011) rooting out hunger and malnutrition in developing countries.

In this context, although it may sound repetitive, one cannot avoid sounding cautions in order to escape the worsening situation that the shift in—

> "dietary patterns will have a larger environmental footprint in terms of greenhouse gas emissions and the use of natural resources. The shift to diets high in milk and meat, particularly from ruminants, is associated with increasing emissions of methane from enteric fermentation, carbon dioxide from deforestation for pasture and nitrous oxide from feed production. Higher consumption of processed foods requires additional use of water and energy, which has negative environmental impacts, if these resources are not sustainably managed. ... Evidence suggests that dietary patterns that have low environmental impacts can also be consistent with good health. For instance, national dietary guidelines that recommend lower red meat consumption, particularly among high-consuming groups, could limit GHG emissions,"[19]

and thereby save the environment for keeping production of healthy food in sufficient quantities to feed the global population.

Feeding the Global Population is far from a Simple Issue

Agriculture in its various forms feeding the global population faces today a critical situation with many challenges emerging from sudden price rise for food crops commensurate with rise in oil prices, the major source of energy for transport and many associated industries, coupled with climate change and the increasing use of bioenergy. All these factors joining together make one in seven people without access to food with sufficient protein and energy from their diets. In the backdrop of this crippling prospect of agriculture the growth of population along with dietary changes in the affluent part of the world worsening the situation further with rising income as a corollary of growing urbanization in the developing world makes it necessary for food production to double by 2050. The greater purchasing power of people leading to higher consumption with greater demand for processed food, meat, dairy and fish creates greater pressure on the overall food system.

In this context one, however, cannot ignore the most contrasting role of agriculture as a direct source of environmental degradation responsible for over a quarter of the total greenhouse gas emissions, as mentioned before, which is instrumental for climate change, biodiversity loss besides turning land and freshwater into scarce commodities through excess as well as wrong uses (Foley, J.A. *et al.*, 2011).*

As estimated by the FAO, croplands cover 1.53 billion hectares or nearly 12 per cent of the earth's land surface comprising best land suited for farming, and pastures making a larger coverage amounting to 3.38 billion ha, or almost 26 per cent, together making use of 38 per cent of the earth's land surface, the largest land use on earth. The coverage made by croplands and pasture has increased by 154 million ha—about 3 per cent—between 1985 and 2005 with major part of this expansion having taken place in the tropics. This resulted in an increase in the production of crops, consisting of cereals, oilseeds, fruits and vegetables by 47 per cent between 1985 and 2005, though all 174 crops taken together, actual increase was about 28 per cent during this period (UN, FAO).

Notably, only 62 per cent of the crops grown in the world are used directly as human food while 35 per cent is consumed as animal feed and 3 per cent for the production of biofuel, seed and other industrial purposes. Interestingly, the proportion of land used for production of crops for direct human consumption varies from a low of 40 per cent in North America (and Europe to the high of 80 per cent in Asia and Africa, coming down to the lowest of less than 25 per cent in Upper Midwestern US) and over 90 per cent in South Asia. (Foley, Johnathan, A. *et al.*, 2011).† However, as Foley *et al.* (2011)

---

* Jonathan A. Foley, Navin Ramankutty, Kate A. Brauman, Emily S. Cassidy, James S. Gerber, Mart Johnton, Nathaniel D. Mueller, Christine O'Connell, Deepak K. Ray, Paul C. West, Christian Balzer, Elena M. Bennett, Stephen R. Carpenter, Jason Hill, Chad Monfreda, Stephen Polasky, Johan Rockstrőm, John Sheehan, Stefan Siebert, David Tilman and David P.M. Zaks, (2011), Solutions For a Cultivated Planet, in *Nature*, Vol. 478, 20 October, 2011, Macmillan Publishers Limited.

† *Ibid.*

observe, the absurdity of the situation of giving greater preference to animal-based agriculture comes out when croplands devoted to animal-feed amounts to 350 million ha and, added to 3.38 billion ha of land used as pasture and grazing land, comes to a total of 3.73 billion ha devoted to animals, together representing 75 per cent of the world's agricultural land. However efficiently the land devoted to raise animals instead of crops is managed, it merits no justification considering it as a 'net drain on the world's potential food supply',[20] as the experts regard.

One cannot ignore the impact of agriculture on the environment when land cleared of vegetation cover/forests adds greatly to GHG emissions. As a matter of fact, the environment has already been severely impacted by agricultural expansion affecting habitats, biodiversity, carbon storage and soil conditions in the perspective of having

> "cleared or converted 70 per cent of grassland, 50 per cent of the savanna, 45 per cent of the temperate deciduous forests and 27 per cent of the tropical forest biome."[21]

Incidentally, reduction in the conversion of forests into agricultural land in the tropical forests will undoubtedly make a noticeable reduction in carbon emissions besides the loss of biodiversity and thus improve the status of ecosystems for their services beneficial to human society. Production of food without increasing the amount of land and reducing the environmental impacts may be achieved through sustainable intensification when sustainability implies "the use of resources at rates that do not exceed the capacity of the Earth to replace them",[22] and implementation of such projects over an area of 37 million ha involving 12.6 million mainly small landholders in developing countries claimed 79 per cent increase in yield, one-quarter of these projects achieving double yield for a very wide variety of crops.[23] According to experts, the demand for food increases by 70 per cent to 100 per cent by 2050 requires proper steps to be taken for tackling negative externalities affecting food production. The combined effect of negative externalities, as represented by environmental pollution arising from 'nutrient run-off, water shortage caused by over-extraction, soil degradation and the loss of biodiversity and habitat losses if tackled properly will play a deciding role in boosting production.

As mentioned earlier, closing yield-gaps plays a very important role in adding largely to the total production of food crops, though it is not a very easy process in different physical conditions. As pointed out by Godfrey *et al.* (2010),* best yields to be obtained from land directly depends on the farmers having access to 'seeds, water, nutrients, pest management, soils, biodiversity and proper knowledge'. In this connection the case of Southeast Asia may be cited where, with irrigation 'average maximum climate-adjusted rice-yields are 8.5 metric tons per hectare' but actually only 60 per cent of this is obtained. According to Godfray *et al.* (2010), per capita food production during the last 50 years has increased two-fold in Asia (almost 3.5 fold in China) while 1.6 fold was obtained in Latin America but in Africa it came down from mid-1970s, reaching the same level as in 1960. As a matter of great concern, low yields in general results from many deficiencies in the system of production, such as farmers often do not have proper access to the 'technical knowledge and skill necessary for increasing production', lack finances to invest for "irrigation, fertilizers, use of machinery where required, or animal energy as used by poor farmers in many parts of the developing countries, or take proper steps for crop protection when necessary, adopt soil conservation measures and enjoy transport facilities as well as crop preservation facilities like refrigeration/cold storage, and market. Besides, absence of subsidies or price support, as given to farmers in many of the developed countries, act as a great disincentive in getting proper access to the world market" (Godfrey *et al.*, 2010).

However, in spite of such limitations, closing yield gaps may

---

* H. Charles J. Godfray, John R. Beddington, Ian R. Crute, Lawrence Haddad, David Lawrence, James F. Muir, Jules Pretty, Sherman Robinson, Sandy M. Thomas and Camilla Toulmin, (2010), "Food Security: The Challenge of Feeding a Billion People", in *Science, New Series,* Vol. 327, No. 5967 (February 2, 2010): American Association for the Advancement of Science: p. 814.

be the most effective way of increasing global food supplies when

> "bring yields to within 95 per cent of their potential for 16 important food and feed crops could add 2.3 billion tons (5×10^{15} Kilocalories) of new production, a 58 per cent. Even if yields for these 16 crops were brought up to only 75 per cent of their potential, global production would increase by 1.1 billion tonnes (2.8×10^{15} Kilocalories), a 28 per cent increase."[24]

According to the same source, involving greater dependence on poultry, pork or pasture-fed beef than grain-fed beef, coupled with not using crops for biofuel production, will make a substantial increase in food crops available for human consumption with much less environmental cost. However, it does not improve the situation, as quite a significant portion of the food available for human consumption is lost in various ways, such as one-third of the food, according to FAO, is 'never consumed' while in the opinion of some other sources 'as much as half of all food grown is lost with some perishable commodities undergoing almost 100 per cent post-harvest losses. As mentioned earlier, post-harvest loss is more than 40 per cent of the total production in developing countries happening at different stages, like processing, storage, transport etc., while in developed countries this is more than 40 per cent particularly at 'retail or consumer level' (Foley *et al.*, 2011).

On the whole, however, with many possibilities available, it does not seem to be a desperate situation, but undoubtedly quite a difficult one to assure a larger supply of food available for direct human consumption, adequate to meet the requirements of a larger population in or around 2050. However, one of the major aspects to be considered in this perspective, to ensure a sizeable increase in the amount of food available for human consumption, is closing yield-gaps in different climatic and economic zones, which requires a very careful approach.

Second, change in agricultural practices including multiple cropping involving different crop-combinations with stress on no-till methods, reverting to gainful irrigation processes like drip irrigation, saving water as one of the most scarce resources, application of chemical fertilizers, particularly N-fertilization in terms of time and requirement, steps taken for soil conservation, use of technologically improved seeds without displacing the local ones used for generations adjusted with climatic factors, pest and diseases, with the provision of proper transport facilities, along with storage facilities are expected of a larger amount of food for human consumption.

Third, one of the most important ways of saving more vegetable food for direct human consumption involves dietary changes, having food less rich in animal protein and thus converting crops from animal feed to human food, a practice restorative of environmental loss and saving biodiversity besides abandoning use of crops for the production of bio-fuel.

Fourth, adoption of serious steps for reducing food losses at stages of preparation and preservation, including controlling rodents, insects, fungi and other organisms, and transport besides wastage of food on flimsy grounds like cosmetic values.

But what is more alarming in this respect is the deliberate wastage of food among the affluent class, which can easily be avoided by changing the wasteful habit of throwing away good food as excess which, as mentioned earlier, could feed millions of hungry people in the world. The sheer absurdity of the situation is very clearly brought out, as mentioned in Chapter 4, by the fact that almost 1.6 billion tonnes of good food, worth about $1trillion, is thus wasted globally, mostly in the rich countries, thrown away as 'excess' food or in barbecues which, if saved, could feed millions of hungry people in the world.

In this context it is very important to note that,

> "wasted food is not only a benefit lost. It is harm done when uneaten food ends up in landfill, where rot turns it into methane with 22 times more global warming effect than carbon dioxide—while methane can almost effortlessly be harvested from landfills as a clear-burning fuel akin to natural gas. Also in the Global North, perfectly good but undervalued foods and food by-products are wasted that could more easily provide positive functions and address global warming reduction targets ... (Quoting from Smil, 2000) Roberts states that nearly half of all cereals on the world market could be conserved if the rich world reduced its overall

> waste by 20 per cent. ... Nothing is wrong with these items from the standpoint of safety, nutrition or taste. They just don't look the way they do in the food magazines. The carrots are misshapen, the broccoli heads are a little small and the apples have a few scabs—they are all cosmetically challenged. About a third of the fruits and vegetables grown in North America don't get to store, and may never even be harvested ... Standard estimates for consumer wastage in the Global North are in the 25-40 per cent range."[25]

Perhaps most essential step to be taken over and above the steps mentioned above—First to Fourth—for enhancing agricultural prospects is to keep the farmers well-acquainted with technological progress through proper training so that they can apply their best in agricultural practices. In this connection we have an idea about the availability of major crops in the world may be useful. However, steps (First to Fourth) mentioned above, taken seriously and implemented with determination, are likely to contribute to increase global food supply by

> "100-180 per cent, meeting projected demands while lowering greenhouse gas emissions, biodiversity losses, water use and water pollution."[26]

Preference for organic food making it more vegetable-based than based on meat/egg etc. will prove to be an effective way of saving the environment, with reduction in greenhouse gas emissions. In furtherance to this view we may refer to Wayne Roberts (2013, New Ed.)* pointing out that the earth's atmosphere has already passed the milestone of 400 parts per million (ppm) of carbon and claims that "we CAN feed and nourish the world"[27] on the basis of astounding success achieved by 9 million small farmers working for ten years in 208 innovative farm projects spread in 28 countries increased the amount of land under 'earth friendly' practices by 28000 per cent, from 100,000 to 29,000,000 hectares achieving the

---

* Wayne Roberts, *The No-Nonsense Guide to World Food,* New Internationalist, 2013 (New Ed.).

> "greatest increase in farm productivity by paying attention to 'natural' and 'social' capital—with improvements to the environment and community, as is done when fish are raised in rice paddies ... there's a health, environmental and economic dividend. The fish eats insects that might otherwise spread malaria. The fish also enrich the soil with their excrement. Then they provide a protein-rich meal to the farmers."[28]

This idea of producing higher yields from small farmers who cannot afford expensive inputs like hybrid seeds, fertilizers and insecticides, pesticides etc., besides suffering from lack of access to the market, involves doing the needful on the basis of organic farming using animal manure being available at hand. This forms the strongest feature of organic agriculture. Roberts (2013 New Ed.) refers here to the findings of Dadia-Hage Scialabba, mentioned by FAO in 2007, who strongly supports organic agriculture, further claimed by Svette Perfecto of Michigan University the same year (2007) that organic agriculture can make a yield of "over 2,641 calories per person per day".[29] Perhaps no instance of higher production per hectare of land could match with what has been obtained by a small-holder farmer named Sumant Kumar in Bihar, 'India's poorest state', where he produced 22.4 tonnes of rice on one hectare of land, thus making a world record, following organic method without the use of 'genetically engineered seeds', any fertilizer or pesticides and any help from agricultural researchers. Similarly, another astounding world record was made by Sumant's friend, Nitish, in potato yields followed by another farmer from a nearby village for wheat. Each of them obviously used composted manure, while Sumant followed the technique of planting rice-seedlings 25 centimetres apart instead of transplanting, taking the example of the French Priest, Henri de Laulanié, who developed this working in Madagascar.

> "The beauty of the method is that it boosts yields while reducing water use and avoiding the methane produced when rice grows under water ... (which undoubtedly proves that) the key to advancing productivity does not lie in labs where scientists manipulate miracle genes but

in the soil, where farmers create fertility with natural materials."[30]

It may be observed that the growing popularity of organic food for its "pastoral purity, natural goodness and wholesome integrity"[31] is corroborated by its acceptance all over the world from 1990s onwards, since when all resistance was won over and demand for organic food grew fast, showing an important place in food consumed in different countries. For example, in 2011, organic food accounted for 4.2 per cent of US food sales while its production having increased to 37.2 million hectares worldwide in 2009, its sales increased to $1.3 billion in Australia, $8.4 billion in Germany and $4.7 billion in France in 2012 (Roberts, 2013 New Ed.). The importance of organic food may further be assumed from the fact that some of the respected corporate giants like General mills, Kellogg, Mars, Heinz, Con Agra, ADM, Dole, Danoe and Coke (Roberts, 2013 New Ed.) are already buying organic food as a part of their food supply, which is undoubtedly an extremely significant indication for gradually changing food habits of people with a sustaining choice for more healthy food and thus indirectly supporting improvement of the environment, with significant cut in GHG emissions.

One of the surprising issues to be taken up by us for serious consideration in regard to saving the world from environmental deterioration is sustaining the lives of the 27 billion-strong livestock as the major source of methane emissions, which points out the necessity of family planning measures in the way of, at least, the domestic ones. One of the most effective way of doing it is to neuter or castrate a major section of the domestic animals, particularly the ruminants which may, no doubt, affect the economy to a considerable extent but, taken up on a careful assessment, making animals of all categories including the stray ones—like dogs and cats—sterile may go a long way in fighting CO_2 emissions on the one hand and making a heavy cut on the supply of meat leading to the reduction in animal protein in human diet on the other. Truly, it will prove to be an extremely difficult task very likely to face strong opposition from meat-producing lobbies unless an understanding is reached between them and the respective governments, involving economists and scientists, as well as public opinion in its favour. An idea about the livestock production by the domestic livestock sector may give an idea about the enormity of the problem.

Taking all these factors into account, it may be heartening to note that the overall situation of meeting global need for food for a burgeoning population may not be an unassailable proposition provided agricultural production system all over the world makes a co-ordinated effort on following the principles of

> "precision agriculture, drip irrigation, organic soil remedies, buffer strips and wetland restoration, new crop varieties that reduce needs for water and fertilizer, perennial grains and tree-cropping systems, and paying farmers for environmental restoration ... (along with) reforming global trade policies, including eliminating price-distorting subsidies and tariffs will be vital to achieve our strategies."[32]

All these considerations, however, do not lead us away from the most basic truth that the burgeoning requirement for healthy food in adequate amount providing nutritious diets requires a secure food system which demands that all the goals of production in future should aim at investing in increasing yields primarily in developing countries (Tilman and Clark, 2015). In this context, the growing tendency in diet change with rising income in developing countries should not be side-stepped, rather should be tackled in such a manner that the love for animal-protein is slowly shifted to greater emphasis on low animal-protein, such as fish, poultry etc., making their availability in plenty compared to red meat. It should be a co-ordinated effort in making food with low animal protein and fat tastier since food happens to be one of the greatest pleasures of life to get best out of individual contributions to the welfare of the society as well as the world as a whole. Perhaps, such a goal getting over the existing hindrances to food security for the globe is not unachievable, as pointed by Alexandratos *et al.* (2012 Revision) that 'global resources are sufficient, but the devil is in the details."[33]

Very interestingly indeed, some scientists are working hard to produce *artificial* food intended to cover a wide range of natural products, particularly consisting of animal meat such as beef, chicken, duck, poultry, fish etc. According to a report in *The Guardian*, U.K., 21 September 2017, scientists in some 'tech firms' in San Francisco are already engaged in these pioneering efforts. Founded in 2006, biochemists, Mike Selden and Brian Wyrwas are on a "mission" to save the oceans and bring affordable, contaminant-free fish to masses.... One such company (U.S.) is growing fish flesh in their laboratory ... without needing to kill a single animal ... Finless Food is the first firm to enter the race to take cellular agriculture—meat grown outside of animals—to market with marine, as opposed to land, animals. In 2013 the godfather of what is also known as cultured or *in-vitro* meat, Professor Mark Post from Maastricht University, unveiled the first ever cultured beef burger—no livestock required.[34] Gradually, such attempts are spreading further, providing not only artificial beef meat balls but also fried chicken and duck. Undoubtedly, the future is yet to see how far it goes and to what extent it usurps the place of natural food and agree with satisfying human tastes unhabituated with its artificial texture as well as flavour. It may be a question of compromise, but how far?

Quite obviously, developing artificial food in the laboratory is more of a dream than reality, as far as taking up the challenge of meeting the colossal requirement of humanity's extreme diversity in their nature, combination and taste developed over millennia of cultural evolution than a simple meal served on a plate on order. Human food in its mind-boggling varieties suiting tastes of people in countless societies is nothing less than a cultural product with inestimable varieties to be produced in laboratories.

On seeking a real solution to feeding the burgeoning global population, nothing short of practical means makes any real sense and we can justify their actual role and assess the practicability of each in the existing circumstances or, putting differently, how far we are capable of making such efforts successful with our existing resources.

First and foremost would be to lay emphasis on universal education and health, with greater stress on females which makes the topmost priorities in the developing countries, leading to the creation of **human capital** as its most essential target. It may be a time-consuming job, no doubt, but nothing short of this can serve the purpose of making people with skills as tools for utilization of their labour in raising the economic level of these people, turning them from liability to assets for the society, equipping almost 2 billion such people acquiring greater purchasing power to access adequate, nutritious food for their family, better sanitation, healthcare and educational facilities acquire better skill-based occupations in the society, and enjoy the life of better human beings. The cumulative effects of such achievements would improve life-expectancy, reduce infant mortality and thus reduce the size of the family, with less mouths to feed and take care of, with other resultant features like reduction in maternal mortality combining together in releasing them from the age-long entrapment in poverty, hunger and malnutrition.

Improvement in 'human capital' will have a greater impact on agricultural production of these countries where many of these people equipped with better skill turn food production into a more productive and profitable activity. At the same time, giving topmost priority to raise the living standard of people still afflicted with hunger and malnutrition will make food available for all at all time at all places.

Feasibility of attaining this target will depend very largely on larger harvests attained through narrowing yield-gaps using technological help in fighting natural elements, as well as climate change, and with the handling of yield-gaps—to the tune of 75 per cent to 80 per cent—it is possible to increase the supply of food crops by '300-400 per cent', as mentioned earlier, without any further addition to cropland it will make a very large addition to total crop production worthwhile, apart from increasing cropland through the destruction of forestlands, in particular, it will reduce carbon emission to a great extent. Further, realising 95 per cent potential of yield-gap (still leaving 5 per cent) there will be no need of new land for meeting the 2050 global food demand (Tilman and Clark, 2015).

On the other hand, cutting down on the wastage of good food on various accounts forms a very important way of saving food to be fed to millions of hungry people around the world. The most striking example in this respect is the wasteful habit of people mentioned earlier throwing away good food as excess by the affluent class, amounting to 1.6 billion tonnes, valued at $1 trillion, along with the wastage of good food, particularly in the United States where 25 to 40 per cent of food grown in the field is rejected, never harvested for their cosmetic values. Added to this further is the wastage of food lost during different stages following harvest, amounting to as much as 40 per cent of the total harvest. All these thoughtless attitudes, some of which can easily be stopped outright, will alleviate the situation to a very large measure, adding quite substantially to increase food available for human consumption, far above 62 per cent as available now.

Two other major steps towards increasing food available for human consumption comprise stopping the production of ethanol outright with immediate effect and thus save a huge amount of crops, such as maize and others as human-feed, along with stall-feeding of livestock, using crop residues like rice stalks, wheat and corn stalks in place of grains to enhance its availability for human needs.

However, there is a negative side of the entire development system going to create problems to be taken care of, since the entire issue of making food available for mankind without any hindrance is going to be challenged by the changing situation. For example, the development of a highly resourceful healthcare system lengthening the life-span of people is going to change the population structure to a great extent by 2050, becoming composed of lots of centenarians 'consuming but not producing'. At the same time, the current world's economic growth, around '3-4 per cent per annum' doubles at this rate every 15-20 years and, assuming that consumption remains at about the same proportion of income, the world will be consuming twice by 2030 what it does now, making "four times the current level before 2050, and at least 16 times the current level by 2100."[35] At the same time, Helm (2015) points out that a too hot planet because of climate change needs agriculture going through its own revolution to feed 9 or 10 billion much richer people, particularly in the developing countries, with larger meat, fish and other nutritional food, and thus the consumption requiring doubling of their production by 2050. On the other hand, as mentioned above, increasing demand for crops for larger production of biofuel will become instrumental to the loss of biodiversity, making the situation extremely harmful when already

> "25 biodiversity hotspots, now comprising only 1.4 per cent of the land surface (previously it had been nearly 12 per cent), contain 44 per cent of all species and 35 per cent of all species in four main vertebrate groups. Much of this 1.4 per cent is threatened in the foreseeable future ... by the end of the twenty-first century perhaps half of all biodiversity may have been lost"[36]

making it one of the greatest extinction span of geological history, and to challenge the survival of mankind, pushing it to the verge of the greatest food-crisis.

REFERENCES

1. Daniels, Peter, Michael Bradshaw, Denis Shaw and James Sidaway (2005). *An Introduction to Human Geography: Issues for the 21st Century*, Prentice Hall, p. 89.
2. Tilman, David and Michael Clark (2015). "Food, Agriculture and the Environment: Can We Feed the World and Save the Earth?" in *Daedalus, Journal of The American Academy of Arts and Sciences,* Vol. 144, Issue 4, Fall, p. 9.
3. Kearney, John (2010). Food Consumption Trends and Drivers, in *Philosophical Transactions: Biological Sciences, Vol. 365, No. 1554, Feeding the World in 2050* (27 September 2010): p. 2795 (Table 2).
4. FAO, UN, *The Future of Food and Agriculture: Trend and Challenges, 2017*: p. 106.
5. *Ibid.*, pp. 110-111.
6. Smil, Vaclav (2000). *Feeding the World: A Challenge for the Twenty-First Century,* The MIT Press, Cambridge, Massachusetts, p. 11.
7. Alexandratos, Nikos and Jelle Bruinsma, (2012). "World Agriculture Towards 2030/2050, in *FAO ESA Working Paper* No. 12-03, June, p. 11.
8. *Ibid.*, p. 10.
9. FAO, UN, *The Future of Food and Agriculture: Trend and Challenges, 2017*: p. 136.
10. Tilman, David and Michael Clark (2015). "Food, Agriculture and the Environment: Can We Feed the World and Save the Earth?" in *Daedalus, Journal of The American Academy of Arts and Sciences,* Vol. 144, Issue 4, Fall, p. 13.
11. *Ibid.*, p. 10.

12. *Ibid.*
13. Sen, Amartya (1989). Food and Freedom in *World Development* 17, p. 91.
14. Tilman, David and Michael Clark (2015). "Food, Agriculture and the Environment: Can We Feed the World and Save the Earth?" in *Daedalus, Journal of The American Academy of Arts and Sciences*, Vol. 144, Issue 4, Fall, p. 14.
15. Smil, Vaclav (2000). *Feeding the World: A Challenge for the Twenty-First Century*, The MIT Press, Cambridge, Massachusetts, p. 185.
16. *Ibid.*, pp. 194-195.
17. Tilman, David, Christian Balzer, Jason Hill and Belinda L. Befort, (2011). "Global Food Demand and the Sustainable Intensification of Agriculture", in *Proceedings of the National Academy of Sciences of the Unites States of America*, Vol. 108, No. 50 (December 13, 2011): p. 20260.
18. *Ibid.*, pp. 20260-20261.
19. FAO, (2017), *The Future of Food and Agriculture: Trends and Challenges*: p. 139.
20. Foley, Jonathan A., Navin Ramankutty, Kate A. Brauman, Emily S. Cassidy, James S. Gerber, Mart Johnson, Nathaniel D. Mueller, Christine O'Connel, Deepak K. Ray, Paul C. West, Christian Balzer, Elena M. Bennett, Stephen R. Carpenter, Jason Hill, Chad Monfreda, Stephen Polasky, Johan Rockstrőm, John Sheehan, Stefan Siebert, David Tilman and David P. M. Zaks, (2011). "Solutions For a Cultivated Planet Analysis", in *Nature*, Vol. 478, 20 October 2011, Macmillan Publishers Limited: p. 338.
21. *Op. cit.*
22. Godfrey, H. Charles J., John R. Beddington, Ian R. Crute, Lawrence Haddad, David Lawrence, James F. Muir, Jules Pretty, Sherman Robinson, Sandy M. Thomas and Camilla Toulmin, (2010). "Food Security: The Challenge of Feeding a Billion People", in *Science, New Series*, Vol. 327, No. 5967 (February 2, 2010): American Association For the Advancement of Science: p. 814.
23. *Op. cit.*
24. Foley, Jonathan A., Navin Ramankutty, Kate A. Brauman, Emily S. Cassidy, James S. Gerber, Mart Johnson, Nathaniel D. Mueller, Christine O'Connel, Deepak K. Ray, Paul C. West, Christian Balzer, Elena M. Bennett, Stephen R. Carpenter, Jason Hill, Chad Monfreda, Stephen Polasky, Johan Rockstrőm, John Sheehan, Stefan Siebert, David Tilman and David P. M. Zaks, (2011), Solutions For a Cultivated Planet Analysis, in *Nature*, Vol. 478, 20 October, 2011, Macmillan Publishers Limited: p. 339.
25. Roberts, Wayne, (2013). (New Edition), *The No-Nonsense Guide to World Food*, New Internationalist: pp. 72, 73 and 74.

26. Foley, Jonathan A., Navin Ramankutty, Kate A. Brauman, Emily S. Cassidy, James S. Gerber, Mart Johnson, Nathaniel D. Mueller, Christine O'Connel, Deepak K. Ray, Paul C. West, Christian Balzer, Elena M. Bennett, Stephen R. Carpenter, Jason Hill, Chad Monfreda, Stephen Polasky, Johan Rockstrőm, John Sheehan, Stefan Siebert, David Tilman and David P. M. Zaks, (2011), Solutions For a Cultivated Planet Analysis, in *Nature*, Vol. 478, 20 October, 2011, Macmillan Publishers Limited: p. 341.
27. Roberts, Wayne (2013). (New Edition), *The No-Nonsense Guide to World Food*, New Internationalist: p. 142.
28. *Op. cit.*
29. *Ibid.*, p. 143.
30. *op. cit.*
31. *Ibid.*, p. 153.
32. Foley, Jonathan A., Navin Ramankutty, Kate A. Brauman, Emily S. Cassidy, James S. Gerber, Mart Johnson, Nathaniel D. Mueller, Christine O'Connel, Deepak K. Ray, Paul C. West, Christian Balzer, Elena M. Bennett, Stephen R. Carpenter, Jason Hill, Chad Monfreda, Stephen Polasky, Johan Rockstrőm, John Sheehan, Stefan Siebert, David Tilman and David P. M. Zaks, (2011), "Solutions For a Cultivated Planet Analysis", in *Nature*, Vol. 478, 20 October 2011, Macmillan Publishers Limited: p. 341.
33. Alexandratos, Nikos and Jelle Bruinsma, (2012), "World Agriculture Towards 2030/2050", in *FAO ESA Working Paper* No. 12-03, June 2012: p. 17.
34. *The Guardian*, UK Ed., 21 September 2017, Is 'Frankenfish' the Start of a Food Revolution? p. 4.
35. Helm, Dieter (2015), *Natural Capital: Valuing the Planet*, Yale University Press, Newhaven and London, p. 25.
36. *Ibid.*, p. 28.

Bibliography

Agarwal, Anil and Smita Narain (1999). (First Reprint), *Dying Wisdom: Rise, Fall and Potential of India's Traditional Harvesting Systems,* Centre for Science and Development, New Delhi.

Alexandratos, Nikos and Jelle Bruinsma (2012). *World Agriculture Towards 2030/2050,* ESA Working Paper No. 12-03, FAO.

Altieri, Miguel A. (2010). "Agroecology, Small Farms and Food Sovereignty" in *Agriculture and Food in Crisis: Conflicts, Resistance, and Renewal,* Ed. by Fred Magdoff and Brian Tokar, Monthly Review Press.

Balmford, Andrew, Aaron Bruner, Philip Cooper, Robert Constanza, Stephen Farbes, Rhys E. Green, Martin Jenkins, Paul Jefferies, Valma Jessamy, Joan Madden, Kat Munro, Norman Myres, Shahid Naeem, J. Pavola, Matthew Rayment, Sergio Resendo, Joan Roughgarden, Kate Trumper and R. Kerry Turner, (2002). *Economic Reasons For Conserving Wild Nature,* in *Science Magazine,* American Association for the Advancement of Science.

Bello, Walden and Mara Baviera (2010), "Food Wars", In: *Agriculture and Food in Crisis: Conflicts, Resistance and Renewal,* Ed. by Fred Magdoff and Brian Tokar, New York: Monthly Review Press.

Bhattacharya, Bimalendu (2006). (Revised Edition), *Urban Development in India: Since Pre-Historic Times,* Concept Publishing Company Pvt. Ltd., New Delhi.

——, (2014). *Geography of Deprivation: An Unfair World,* New Delhi: Concept Publishing Company Pvt. Ltd., New Delhi.

Brown, Lester, R. (2004) (Reprint). *Eco-Economy: Building an Economy for the Earth,* Orient Longman.

—— (2006). *Plan B 2.0: Rescuing a Planet Under Stress and Civilization in Trouble,* Earth Policy Institute, New York and London: W. Norton and Company.

—— (2012). *Full Planet, Empty Plates: The New Geopolitics of Food Security,*

Earth Policy Institute, New York, London: W.W. Norton and Company.

Brown, Paul (2007). "Global Warming: The Last Chance for Change" in *Readers' Digest,* Readers' Digest Association Inc., New York: Pleasant Hill.

Collier, Paul (2008). (Paperback), *The Bottom Billion: Why the Poorest Countries are Failing and What Can Be Done About It?* Oxford University Press.

Collins, Daryl, Jonathan Murduch, Stuart Rutherford and Orlanda Ruthven (2009). *Portfolios of the Poor: How the World's Poor Live on $2 a Day,* Permanent Black.

Daniels, Peter, Michael Bradshaw, Denis Shaw and James Sidaway (2005). (2nd Edition), *An Introduction to Human Geography: Issues For the 21st Century,* Pearson/Prentice Hall.

Davis, Mike (2014) (Reprint). *Late Victorian Holocausts: El Niño Famines and Making the Third World,* London, New York: Verso.

Drewnowski, Adam (1997). "The nutrition transition: New Trends" in the global diet, In: *Nutrition Reviews,* 55(2).

Dreze, Jean (Ed.), (2017). Reprint, *Social Policy,* Orient Black Swan.

Dyson, Tim (1996). *Population and Food: Global Trends and Future Prospects,* Routledge.

Ehrlich, Paul R., Anne H. Ehrlich and Gretchen C. Daily (1993). "Food security, population and environment", In: *Population and Development Review,* 19(1) (March 1993).

FAO, *The State of Food Insecurity in the World 2008: Undernourishment Around the World: High Food Prices, Another 75 Million Hungry.*

FAO (2017). *The Future of Food and Agriculture; Trends and Challenges,* Rome.

Foley, Jonathan A., Narin Ramankutty, Kate A. Brauman, Emily S. Cassidy, James S. Gerber, Matt Johnston, Nathaniel D. Mueller, Christine O'Connell, Deepak K. Ray, Paul C. West, Christian Balzer, Elena M. Bennett, Stephen R. Carpenter, Jason Hill, Chad Monfreda, Stephen Polasky, Johan Rockstrőm, John Sheehan, Stefan Siebert, David Tilman and David P.U. Zaks (2011). "Solutions for a cultivated planet", In: *Nature,* Vol. 478, 20 October, 2011, Macmillan Publishers Limited.

Ghosh, Amitav, (2016). *The Great Derangement: Climate Change and the Unthinkable,* The University Press of Chicago, Chicago and London.

Godfrey, H. Charles J., John R. Beddington, Ian R. Crute, Lawrence Haddad, David Lawrence, James F. Muir, Jules Pretty, Sherman Robinson, Sandy M. Thomas and Camilla Toulmin (2010). "Food security: The challenge of feeding 9 billion people", In: *Science, New Series, 327(5967) (February 2, 2010),* American Association for the Advancement of Science.

Goldring, Mark (2016). "We are Sleepwalking into Catastrophe Unless We Tackle Runaway Inequality", in *Resurgence and Ecologist,* September-October.

Haggag, Wafaa M., Hoballa Essam and Lashin, S. (2015). "Microbial biotechnology: Role in sustainable agriculture and environmental management", In: *Biotechnology, Agro-Ecology and Environment,* Ed. by Avnish Chauhan, Pawan Kumar Bharti, New Delhi: Discovery Publishing House Pvt. Ltd.

Helm, Dieter (2015). *Natural Capital: Valuing the Planet,* New Haven and London: Yale University Press.

Holt-Giménez, Eric (2010). "From food crisis to food sovereignty: The challenge of social movements, in agriculture and food", In: *Agriculture and Food in Crisis: Conflict, Resistance, and Renewal,* Ed. by Fred Magdoff and Brian Tokar, Monthly Review Press, New York.

IPCC Fifth Assessment Synthesis Report: *Climate Change 2014 Synthesis Report.*

Kearney, John (2010). "Food consumption trends and drivers", In: *Philosophical Transactions: Biological Sciences,* 365(1554).

Kerbs, John (2013). *Food: A Very Short Introduction,* UK: Oxford University Press.

Licker, Rachel, Matt Johnston, Jonathan A. Foley, Carol Barford Christopher J. Kucharik, Chad Monfreda and Navin Ramankutty (2010). "Mind the gap: How do climate and agricultural management explain the 'yield-gap' of croplands around the world?" In: *Global Ecology and Biogeography,* 9(6).

Magdoff, Fred and Brian Tokar (2010). "Agriculture and Food in Crisis: An overview", In: *Agriculture and Food in Crisis: Conflict, Resistance, and Renewal,* Ed. by Fred Magdoff and Brian Tokar, New York: Monthly Review Press.

Magnuson, Joel (2013). *The Approaching Great Transformation: Towards a Liveable Post-Carbon Economy,* Policy Press at the University of Bristol.

Mazhar, Farhand, Daniel Buckles, P.V. Satheesh and Farida Akhter, (2007). "Food Sovereignty and Unchallenged Biodiversity", In: *South Asia: Essays on the poverty of Food Policy and the Wealth of the Social Landscape,* International Development Research Centre, Academic Foundation.

McCully, Patrick (1998). (Indian Edition), *Silenced Rivers: The Ecology and Politics of Large Dams,* Orient Longman.

McMichael, Philip (2010). "Food sovereignty in movement: Addressing the triple crisis", In: *Food Sovereignty: Reconnecting Food, Nature and Community,* Ed. by Hannah Wittman, Annette A. Desmarais and Nettie Wiebe, Pambazuka Press.

Meadows, Donella (2002). *Resurgence and Ecologist,* September-October 2016.

Michael, Philip (2010). "The World Food Crisis in Historical Perspective", In: *Agriculture and Food in Crisis: Conflict, Resistance, and Renewal,* Ed. by Fred Magdoff and Brian Tokar, New York: Monthly Press Review.

Natarajan, P.M., (2016), "Ex-Member of presently defunct Planning Commission, Government of India", in *The Statesman,* Kolkata Issue, India, 20 May 2016.

Patnaik, Utsa (2010). "Origins of the food crisis in India and developing countries", In: *Agriculture and Food in Crisis: Conflict, Resistance, and Renewal,* Ed. by Fred Magdoff and Brian Tokar, New York: Monthly Press Review.

——, 2014 (Fourth Printing), *The Republic of Hunger and Other Essays,* The Three Essays Collective.

Planning Commission, Government of India, *Eleventh Five Year Plan, 2007-2012, Vol. III,* 2008, Oxford University Press.

Popkin, Barry M., (2017). "Relationship between Shifts in Food System Dynamics and Acceleration of the Global Nutrition in Transition," In: *Nutrition Reviews,* Vol. 75(2).

Postel, Sandra and Brian Richter, (2003). *Rivers for Life, Managing Water for People and Nature,* Island Press, Washington, Cavelo, London.

Rhoads, Robert E., (1991). "The world's food supply at risk", In: *National Geographic, Washington, Vol. 179, No. 4.*

Roberts, Wayne, 2013 (New Edition), *The No-Nonsense Guide to World Food,* New Internationalist Press.

Rosset, Peter, (2010). "Fixing our global food system: Food sovereignty and redistributive land reforms", In: *Agriculture and Food in Crisis: Conflict, Resistance, and Renewal,* Ed. by Fred Magdoff and Brian Tokar, Monthly Press Review, New York.

Sachs, Jeffrey D. (2005). *The End of Poverty: How We Can Make it Happen in Our Life Time,* Penguin Books.

Schiavani, Christina and William Camacaro, (2010). "The Venezuelan effort to a new food and agriculture system", In: *Agriculture and Food in Crisis: Conflict, Resistance, and Renewal,* Ed. by Fred Magdoff and Brian Tokar, New York: Monthly Press Review.

Sen, Amartya, (1981). *Poverty and Famines* (12th Impression), Oxford University Press.

——, (1989). "Food and freedom", In: *World Development 17, 1989.*

——, (2006). *The Argumentative Indian: Writings on Indian Culture, History and Identity,* Penguin Books.

Smil, Vaclav, (1994). "How Many People Can the Earth Feed?", In: *Population and Development* Vol. 20, No. 2 (June 1994)

——, 2002 (Paperback Edition), *Feeding the World: A Challenge for the*

Twenty-First Century, The MIT Press, Cambridge, Massachusetts, London, England.

The World Bank, The World Development Report (2008). *Agriculture for Development*.

The Encyclopaedia Americana International Edition, (1973). Americana Corporation, New York.

Tilman, David, Christian Balzer, Jason Hill and Belinda L. Befort, (2011). "Global food demand and the sustainable intensification of agriculture", In: *PNAS (Proceedings of the National Academy of Sciences of the United States of America), Vol. 108, No. 50.*

Tilman, David and Michael Clark, (2015). "Food, agriculture and the environment: Can we feed the world and save the Earth?" In: *Daedalus, Journal of The American Academy of Arts and Sciences, Vol. 144, Issue 4, Fall 2015.*

The Guardian, UK, 13 December 2014

——, 20 December 2016, Milman Oliver: For Native Hunters, Choice will be to Move or Starve.

——, 21 December 2016, Harvey Fiona, Arctic Special: Cutting Soot Fastest Way to Slow Global Warming, Say Experts.

——, 14 July 2016, Suzanne Goldenberg.

——, 4 August, 2016.

——, 12 August, 2016, Rupert Neate, Wealth Correspondent

——, 18 July, 2017.

——, 20 July, 2017.

——, 1 August, 2017.

——, 5 August, 2017.

——, 25 August, 2017.

——, 12 September, 2017.

The Statesman, Kolkata Issue, 21 September, 2017: "Is Frankenfish' the start of a Food Revolution?"

——, 4 March 2016.

——, 16 April, 2016: India Dying Out. News Service.

——, 5 June, 2016, Bharat Dogra: Farming in the Days of Climate Change

——, 13 April, 2017.

——, 14 October, 2017.

——, 21 October, 2017.

——, 1 November, 2017.

——, 15 November, 2017.

——, 16 November, 2017.

——, 17 November, 2017.

——, 2 January, 2018.

United Nations, World Water Development Report: *World Water Assessment Programme, Water for People, Water for Life,* 2003, 8UNESCO Publishing, Berghahn Books.

— —, World Resources 2000-2001, *People and Ecosystems: The Fraying Web of Life.*

UNDP, *Human Development Report 2007/2008: Fighting Climate Change: Human Solidarity in a Divided World.*

Wittman, Hannah, Annette Desmarais and Nettie Wiebe, (2010). *The Origins and Potential of Food Sovereignty,* In: *Food Sovereignty: Reconnecting Food, Nature and Community,* Ed. by Hannah Wittman, Annette Desmarais & Nettie Wiebe, (2010). Pambazuka Press, Books for Change: International Publication House.

Index